St. Louis Community College

Library

5801 Wilson Avenue
St. Louis, Missouri 63110

ALSO BY WILLIAM K. EVERSON

The American Movie
The Art of W. C. Fields
The Bad Guys
A Pictorial History of the Western Film
The Detective in Film

Classics of the Horror Film

BY WILLIAM K. EVERSON

THE CITADEL PRESS   Secaucus, N. J.

ACKNOWLEDGEMENTS

Grateful thanks are extended to Alex Gordon of 20th Century-Fox, James Card of George Eastman House, Ken Wlaschin of the British Film Institute, and Jacques Ledoux of the Royal Film Archive, Belgium, for their extremely generous help in providing screening facilities and stills; sincere thanks are due to Joseph Goldberg for the supplying of several stills, to Jonas Mekas for permission to reprint excerpts from an article of mine that appeared in the first issue of *Film Culture,* and to Alan Barbour for permission to use notes that I wrote for his *Screen Facts* publication.

WKE

First edition
Copyright © 1974 by William K. Everson
All rights reserved
Published by Citadel Press
A division of Lyle Stuart, Inc.
120 Enterprise Ave., Secaucus, N. J. 07094
In Canada: George J. McLeod Limited
73 Bathurst St., Toronto, Ont.
Manufactured in the United States of America by
Halliday Lithograph Corp., West Hanover, Mass.
Designed by A. Christopher Simon
Library of Congress catalog card number: 74-80828
ISBN 0-8065-0437-4

Contents

Classics of
the Horror Film

1 Introduction

Frankenstein (1931): Stately Gothic horror

Recently, reading an article about director Ernst Lubitsch, I was surprised to learn that in the mid-20s he knocked off—quickly, casually and consecutively—five masterpieces. Now a masterpiece used to be something that was the crowning glory of an artist's work, and perhaps if he were exceptional and worked in more than one field, as in the case of Michelangelo, there might conceivably be more than one. But masterpieces were never produced casually, en masse, in any art form, and least of all in the movies, where the minor matter of commercial viability had also to be considered. This preamble is by way of admitting (and deploring) the fact that superlatives are tossed around far too freely these days, so much so that they have often lost real meaning, and perhaps the title of this book is likewise guilty to a degree. So before examining any individual horror films, it is essential that we establish the criteria by which our "classics" have been selected.

The horror film *genre* (almost as difficult to define as "classic") is a branch of filmmaking that has produced some magnificent films, but should have produced far more. More than any other kind of film, it depends for its ultimate effect on the scaring of the audience by manipulating their emotions. Dealing as he often is with Monsters and the supernatural and bizarre sets, the director doesn't have to concern himself too much with logic or realism. He may choose to underplay sensation and aim at a queasy uneasiness—or he may elect to bludgeon his audience with shocks. Either way, he has at his command the full reserves of a filmic arsenal of techniques, grammar and devices: color, sound, dialogue, editing, music, trick effects. Where a comedy director may decide not to use a particularly funny scene or effect only because it destroys the balance or the logic of his whole film, a director of horror films need not feel so strictured. Some of the most chilling moments in horror films have actually been extraneous ones, unnecessary to the plot and often devoid of logical explanation. There are several such moments in James Whale's *The Old Dark House*. And it is significant that the directors of the best horror films have used this great reservoir of tricks and techniques with imagination and taste.

The subtlest and most terrifying moments in Robert Wise's *The Body Snatcher* are achieved through suggestion and sensitive editing rather than an undisciplined charge through a series of shock close-ups and brutalities. An excellent example of how the audience can be "manipulated" and made to contribute to the success of a horror scene is pro-

vided by *Isle of the Dead,* one of the later Val Lewton films for RKO. It is rather heavily and pretentiously directed by Mark Robson, a former editor, and not surprisingly, its very best moment comes from knowing how to edit sound and picture to best advantage. The story concerns a group of travelers stranded on a war torn, plague wracked island near Greece. One of the sub-plots involves Katherine Emery, a middle-aged woman subject to cataleptic trances, and obsessed by the fear of being buried alive while in such a trance. The audience, of course, is aware that such a situation is bound to arise eventually, and their tensions are increased by the woman's constant fears and her pleadings that certain simple tests be made before she is buried. Towards the end of the film, she does apparently die, the tests are performed—negatively—and she is buried.

The audience is conditioned to the fact that she is not dead, and awaits the harrowing scene of her revival within the tomb. When it comes, it is done with simplicity and understatement—coupled with an almost sadistic absorption of the collective audience mind—that is quite incredible. It is night, and the camera tracks slowly up the slight incline to the tomb where the coffin rests. The music builds to a crescendo; the audience, tensed, waits for the inevitable scream, or perhaps the sound of coffin wood being torn asunder. There is silence then, except for the sound of dripping water, a sound that itself calls for concentration on the part of the audience before it can be identified. The camera stands still for a moment: this obviously is going to be it. Perhaps the woman has already broken out from her coffin, and in a moment the tomb doors will be pushed open. Will she have been driven mad by her experience? There is just enough time to entertain such conjectures, and then the camera starts to pull back again. Nothing is going to happen after all; the shock, whatever it is, is being delayed for a later sequence.

The audience relaxes and then—as if having timed their changing mood with a stop watch—it happens. We hear a scream from within the vault and the sound of finger nails scratching at the coffin lid. But the camera maintains its stately retreat without further comment, and the scene fades out. Not only has it caught the audience with its guard down, but having re-stimulated its tensions, the film doesn't relieve them by telling us what has happened. All we know is that the woman is still alive—which we knew anyway. Yet one simple shot, showing nothing, telling nothing new, a shot without menace and without a single person shown on the screen, has become one of the single most chilling moments in the history of the screen!

Forgetting for a moment the "fun" element of horror films—the Monsters and the crackling electrical laboratories—assuming that the measure of a horror film's success is its ability to scare its audience, then the best horror films have always been those that relied more on suggestion than on outright statement. No director could ever come up with a scene to equal what the individual human mind can conceive. All he can do is to plant the suggestion—and rely on the individual viewer to create what to him, personally, is the most horrifying visualization of that suggestion. Fritz Lang understood that fully when he kept the child murders off-screen in *M*: he knew that no matter what he shot, he was bound to come up with scenes that might be offensive, tasteless, possibly censorable, but above all, far short of the horrific impact that he would achieve if he showed nothing at all, leaving it to the adult viewers to fill in their own details. Obviously concerned parents would create far grimmer images than youths, viewing the film primarily as a thriller, but in all cases the human mind could take over from and amplify the single locked in image that Lang would have been able to create, had he decided to stage an on-screen murder.

This is probably, at least partially, why the silent film was unable to create any really memorable horror films. While the horror film doesn't have to be logical or realistic, it does have to be *convincing* in order to be effective. And it is the more convincing by showing less, and—as in the case of *M* and *Isle of the Dead*—suggesting more. While the silent cinema achieved tremendous subtlety, and in certain films (especially with emotional subjects) was often superior to talkie equivalents, using the silence and lack of dialogue as an asset rather than a liability, conversely, there were other films that needed the total reality of dialogue and sound effects. This is why there are no silent equivalents of such frenetic talkies as *20th Century* and *The Front Page*. In creating horror, the silent film could not implant suspicion, uneasiness, and terror by those realistic little touches which often involved sound, or build audience tensions by making them strain to hear noises in the night. (The virtually continuous application of a musical score to silent films also worked against the subtler uses of silence.) One of the biggest audience jolts in *The Body Snatcher* is caused by the unexpected appearance

Fritz Lang, director of *M*.

Peter Lorre as the psychopathic killer of *M*.

of a horse's nose and nostrils at the extreme left of the screen, and its accompanying snort—a logical act, since the scene is set in a stable, but a scene needing the *sudden* introduction of sound. It could never have worked in a silent film. Denied such subtleties, the silent horror film often had to work in tableau form. It was handsome to look at—the sets, art direction, and lighting were often superb— but they left nothing unsaid. Audiences sat back and enjoyed them, but they were never involved in them, much less manipulated by them.

It is, however, interesting that the early Danish cinema—certainly more sophisticated than the American cinema up until 1913—was aware of the possibilities of suggested screen horror, while not always able to develop them to their fullest potential. Their early one- and two-reel melodramas had a surprising and recurring motif: that of the premature burial. The Great Northern Company, in their publicity, stressed that the effectiveness of these thrillers was guaranteed because everyone in the audience was automatically afraid of death, afraid of the dark. *The Necklace of the Dead* (1910) seems to have been filmed much in the mood of *Isle of the Dead,* with a plot involving the burial of an apparently dead girl with her fiancé's betrothal gift, a necklace, about her throat. A thief breaks in to steal the necklace, only to find the girl stirring back to life. He rushes to find the fiancé, and together they return to the tomb to find that the girl is, in fact, very much alive. The film is no longer available for study, but it would appear from a fairly detailed synopsis that the bulk of the film takes place outside the tomb, and carefully builds up tension as to what may be happening in the blackness within. The critic for *The Moving Picture World,* an American film trade publication, rather astutely (for that early period in film reviewing) points out that very little is actually shown, and that it is what is suggested that counts. The same company's *Ghosts of the Vault,* of the following year, was a similar kind of film.

The extreme importance of sound in the effectiveness of the horror film can be gauged by the reaction of young children to them. Silent horror films, such as *The Phantom of the Opera,* rarely frighten children today (children of the 20s, less inured to horror and fright, may well have been a different matter), who just do not believe them and regard them only as a form of pantomime. But with the talkie horror film, belief and conviction are there and children react quite differently. Girls tend to be easily frightened by the nightmare im-

Images of terror from Alfred Hitchcock's *Psycho* (1960)

age: they bury their heads in their hands, looking away from the screen even before a grim scene gets under way. They listen to the sound track, using it as a guide to when it is safe to look back at the screen again.

Boys, on the other hand, look on the horror film as a kind of test of courage. This was particularly true in Britain, in the late 30s, where horror films obtained an "H" censor's certificate, and attendance was forbidden to children under sixteen, a regulation that was strictly enforced, and when violated was subject to heavy fines. Thus, the horror film provided the British male youth with a double test of manhood. First of all, if he was a mature looking thirteen-year-old, it was something of a coup to brazenly buy a ticket and walk in. (It was also something of a social disgrace if one was refused admission because obviously under age.) Secondly, it was a greater test, once in the theatre, to stick it out through the entire feature and not beat a cowardly retreat. Of course, horror films in the 30s were not that terrifying—but still, one's first encounter with that forbidden "H" certificate on screen, the self-doubts caused by the eerie credit music—had one after all made a mistake, was one yet ready for such an onslaught?—the determination to steel oneself for whatever was in store, all these added up to a form of ritual which was surprisingly satisfying once successfully undergone.

Now, doubtless, there are other more enterprising ways by which British youth enters manhood. Much younger boys, however, still regard horror films as a kind of "test"; they have the same kind of fears as girls, but perhaps a greater curiosity. Whereas the the girl will use the sound track as an informative guide, the boy will dispense with the sound track when scared. He will continue to watch the film, but clasping his hands over his ears, will block out sound, and thus the reality, restoring the film to its silent-style pantomime. He uses the picture as a guide, removing his hands from his ears and returning to sight and sound reality only when the image on screen tells him that the horrors have been modified or sidetracked.

Determining, and passing judgment on what is or is not a "classic" is a problem that has perplexed critics of art for centuries; small wonder that there is often such a vast divergence of opinion in the less than a century-old art of movies. Even in that short space of time we have already seen that films once acclaimed as masterpieces have survived only as milestones; conversely, films that thirty years ago were thought to be of passing interest only because they reflected their time so exactly (or perhaps for other reasons) have quite unexpectedly acquired a permanent validity.

Can we toss that word "permanent" around quite so freely? Who is to tell what movies will have permanent value, historically or artistically, five hundred years from now? However, judged by the standards of today, there are a few—a very few—horror films that can be considered classic motion pictures, and not just classic horror films. Carl Dreyer's *Vampyr* certainly is a film that transcends its own category, to become a great film by any standards. Others can be considered only comparative classics within their own *genre*. So many cheap, shoddy, cliché-ridden "B" horror movies were made in the 40s that, in comparison with films like *Voodoo Man* and *Return of the Apeman,* fairly standard but at least stylish films like *The Wolf Man* and *Son of Dracula* seem outstanding, while the gulf between the cheapies and such first-rate films as *The Body Snatcher* and *Curse of the Demon* is so enormous that categorizing them as classics seems not at all unreasonable.

Source has a great deal to do with it as well: the effort and initiative that went into getting a film like *Strangler of the Swamp,* made at the economy-conscious PRC studios, make it in many ways a more remarkable film than an admittedly better film like *The Monster and the Lady,* made as a deluxe special at Republic. More than thirty years after it was made, acknowledgement of *Strangler of the Swamp* can obviously do nothing to encourage its director (now dead) or its studio (now defunct), but it is certainly not too late to give it its neglected due.

Time of production is an important consideration. In terms of content, the stylish Gothic horror films of the early 30s may seem mild indeed by today's standards, but they were simpler times. The horror film was new, talkies were new. Censorship (official and parental) was stricter, and children certainly had less easy access to horror films. Films, designed and sold then for adult consumption, are now standard fare on the kiddie matinees and on television. Audiences in the 30s were generally tense and more vulnerable to movie shocks—the depression, after all, affected almost everybody—but we were far less inured to horror in our daily lives. Today, any child can switch channels on television and see not only the great horror films of the past and the increasingly gory and brutal horror films of more recent years, but also the real undiluted newsreel horror of warfare and mob violence. In

Phantom of the Opera: Claude Rains prepares to cut the chandelier in the 1943 remake

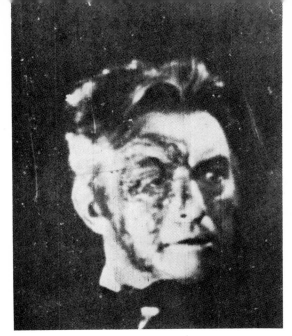

The Phantom unmasked: Claude Rains' make-up decidedly tame in comparison with Chaney's.

Strangler of the Swamp (1945): Rosemary LaPlanche and Charles Middleton in an enterprising and imaginative poverty-row horror quickie.

Day of the Triffids (1963): Increasing mingling of horror and science-fiction genres; Janette Scott menaced by deadly plant life.

theatres, where movies have become ever more competitive, the horror film has been diverted to one of two tangents. First, it is lampooned and ridiculed; secondly, it attempts to outdo its predecessors in the only way it knows, by adding grisly shock upon repugnant sensation. It is no trick to revolt and nauseate an audience via blood, decapitation, detailed killings, closeups of floating hearts and eyeballs. It is the easiest, laziest trick in the world. And it proves over and over again, that the most effective screen horror is still the least detailed screen horror.

The best moment in 1973's *Theatre of Blood* is a killing that one hears only over a walkie-talkie set. Not only is it the funniest moment in a film often too bloody to realize its full comic potential, but it is also one of the most chilling, since it leaves the details of a violent death entirely to the audience. While nobody pretends that the new crop of horror films is great art, and while obviously, there is a commercial market for them, their constant deployment of grisly detail and physical shock has made such ingredients commonplace. The only reason that such a physical shock (a bloody disembodied hand emerging from a wall picture) really works and genuinely jolts an audience in 1973's *And Now the Screaming Starts* is that it is employed so early in the film, before there has even been time to establish place and atmosphere. It certainly does wake the audience up at the very beginning of the film, but it also blunts the monotonous parade of similar shocks throughout the rest of the film. Contemporary audiences, hardened by bloodletting, increasingly laced by graphic sex, must find it hard to believe that the slow, stately, underplayed, and often theatrical chillers of the early 30s really scared audiences. Yet they did, and were so effective at it that there was no need to sell the films via sensational ad campaigns. The simple catchline "It's alive!" was all that was necessary to stimulate advance interest in Karloff's *The Mummy*.

Critics were genuine in their concern for audiences when they warned that these films were strong meat and that the nervous should stay home. In the light of the world we now live in, these films are no longer frightening—real life has overtaken them—but as stylish essays in Gothic romanticist melodrama, they survive rather well. Since it is we, the audiences, rather than the films that have changed, is it fair to rob a film like *Frankenstein* of its classic categorizing merely because it no longer produces the shudders it once did? Many

Dr. Terror's House of Horrors (1965): Bloody disembodied hand menaces Christopher Lee in typical latter-day (and far from classic) horror film, an omnibus of short stories with a concentration on blood and the physically repellent.

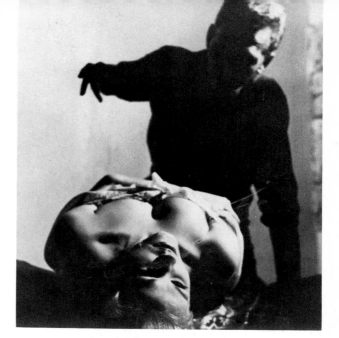

Caltiki, the Immortal Monster (1960): Violence and sex substitute for style in typical assembly-line chiller of the 60's.

The Mummy (1932): Boris Karloff and Zita Johan

films (in all *genres*) are often far more important for what they achieved at the time in terms of innovation and influence on other filmmakers than for their sometimes short-lived merits as individual works of art. Chaplin's *A Woman of Paris,* Murnau's *The Last Laugh,* and D'Arrast's *Laughter* are all films that have been superseded by later, better works: but those later works might not have existed at all had it not been for the innovations and guidelines laid down by the originals. This is particularly true in the case of the horror film.

All of this preamble is by way of emphasizing the impossibility of deciding just what a "classic" is, or of being too dogmatic about what a horror film is. Films like Jack Clayton's *The Innocents* and Albert Lewin's *The Picture of Dorian Gray* contain far more genuine and sophisticated horror than Edward Dmytryk's *The Devil Commands.* Alfred Hitchcock's *Psycho* is another case in point. When it first came out, it was almost universally disliked. It was a "sick" thriller, before that brand of film became fashionable. Critics as a whole were

against it. There was never any official change of stance towards it. Yet within a couple of years, when "black" comedies and thrillers had become more commonplace, and Hitchcock had made a couple of disappointing films, critics were able to attack them by pointing out how inferior they were to the "classic" stature of *Psycho.*

Standards for inclusion in this book are, therefore, very arbitrary. For the most part, although there are exceptions, I have limited myself to films which aim purely and simply at being horror films, eliminating thereby virtually all of the later science fiction films, *The War of the Worlds, Them,* and such psychological thrillers as the first *Love from a Stranger* or the British *They Drive By Night,* all of them films that certainly had horrific content. Films such as Hitchcock's *Psycho* and *The Birds,* or Polanski's *Rosemary's Baby,* have been so thoroughly reviewed, analyzed, interpreted, and dissected that any further comment would not only be superfluous and a waste of time, but would probably detract from one's continued enjoyment of the film. By now, *Psycho* must certainly have overtaken *The Birth of a Nation, Potemkin* and *Citizen Kane* as the most written about film of all time, while its shower-bath-murder scene undoubtedly holds the world record as the one sequence used most consistently by film students in their term papers. Better by far to let *Psycho* and a few others rest on their blood-clotted laurels, and instead, stir up a little excitement about some of the admittedly lesser members of the same family.

As a guide, one can only turn to the mad doctors and wise old philosophers who infest so many of our beloved horror films. With a profound nod of his wizened head, Professor Edward Van Sloan will tell us, "Ah my friends, there are some things it is better not to know!" And perhaps by that stricture, such films as *Strangler of the Swamp* and *Man Made Monster* might be better buried and forgotten. But the rather colorless philosophers usually tended to be spoil-sports, moralizing neatly for the fadeout without really having earned the right to do so. The inspired scientists, even though they came to a bad end and their little worlds collapsed around them in the last reel, were far more positive in their desire to create "eternal life" and to "preserve beauty for all time." It is with that somewhat immodest aim that *The Ghoul* and *The Magician* appear as pretenders to the title, rubbing shoulders with *The Old Dark House* and *The Bride of Frankenstein,* genuine "Classics of the Horror Film."

The Picture of Dorian Gray (1945): Only marginally a horror film, this adaptation of Oscar Wilde was still a much scarier film than the traditional horror films of its period. Hurd Hatfield as Dorian Gray, with the horrendous portrait that changes and ages and permits him to stay eternally young.

The Picture of Dorian Gray:
George Sanders, Hurd Hatfield

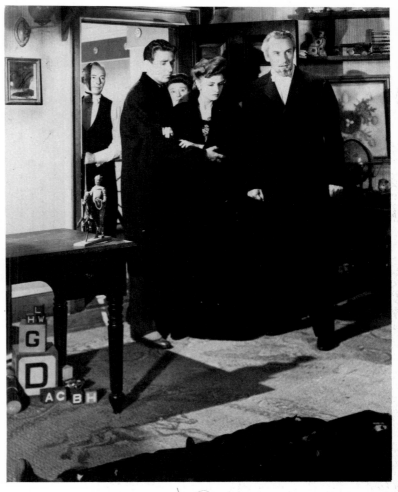

The Picture of Dorian Gray: The
final revelation of Dorian's awful
secret: Peter Lawford, Donna Reed,
George Sanders

10

11

2 The Silents

Influence of *The Magician* a decade later: from *Dante's Inferno* (1935), in which these visions of Hell were clearly patterned after the earlier film. (Director Harry Lachman worked on both films.)

THE PHANTOM OF THE OPERA

(Universal, 1925) Directed by Rupert Julian. Additional scenes directed by Edward Sedgwick. Adapted from the novel of Gaston Leroux by Raymond Shrock and Elliott J. Clawson. Camera, Virgil Miller, Charles Van Enger, Milton Bridenbecker. Art Director, Charles D. Hall.

With Lon Chaney, Mary Philbin, Norman Kerry, Gibson Gowland, Snitz Edwards, John St. Polis, Arthur Edmund Carewe, Virginia Pearson, Edith Yorke, Anton Vaverka, Bernard Siegel, Cesare Gravina, John Miljan, Ward Crane, Chester Conklin.

Even though it invariably disappoints when seen today, *The Phantom of the Opera* rates a "classic" definition, if for no other reason than that it is the finest showcase for Lon Chaney's unique pantomimic art. Universal went all out to ensure that the film would surpass—in artistry, showmanship, and box office allure—their earlier Chaney film, *The Hunchback of Notre Dame.* Admittedly, it was not a difficult ambition; *The Hunchback* owed most of its huge success to the astonishing performance by Chaney. As a film it was turgid and even a little oldfashioned, and as a spectacle it was a decidedly economical one.

The Phantom of the Opera, bigger, less downbeat and depressing, full of color and rich melodrama, was from the outset destined to be a box office smash. And Universal, regarding it as their most important film, and certainly the most expensive since von Stroheim's *Foolish Wives,* were taking no chances on its being anything but a sure-fire hit. Technicolor sequences were inserted for their artistic and novelty values. When the film was completed, it seemed to have rough edges, to be lacking certain elements of popular appeal. So Universal, to whom post-production tampering was virtually unknown, emulated MGM by testing their product at sneak previews, revising, re-cutting, re-shooting. Comedy footage and love scenes were added to provide relief from the grotesque horror. Much of the additional footage was subsequently scrapped, but the final version still had the choppy look of too many cooks having been involved.

It's doubtful that the revising really helped the film, for its basic attributes were handsome, rich sets, and the eloquent pantomime of Chaney—qualities that had been there from the very beginning. Nevertheless, if all the fussing didn't really help

the film, it didn't hurt it either; the delays and publicity created enormous advance interest in the film, which turned out to be one of the box office smashes of the year—a year, incidentally, that needed all the financial success it could get, since radio had just been introduced to American audiences, and its free entertainment had brought about the same dent in box office profits that television would in the 1950s.

With its roots in French melodrama, and with continuity and situations deriving from old serials, *The Phantom of the Opera* is a series of shocks and thrills—more melodrama than horror. In 1925, before horror was a familiar screen commodity, Chaney's fearsome makeup gave the film a sustained note of horror. His initial appearances were fleeting and the first half of the film devoted itself to building up suspense and speculation concerning the Phantom's motives. His face, hidden beneath a mask, cunningly revealed just enough of his mouth to suggest that there was something hideous and unearthly about the rest of his features.

Early in the film, the Phantom kidnaps Christine, the rising young opera star (Mary Philbin), and takes her to his chambers below the Opera House. She has reason to be grateful to him (for his tutoring, whispered secretly through the walls of her dressing room); yet, understandably, she fears him, too. His own actions are a curious combination of motives: revenge, paternal love, lust. The inevitable unmasking scene is built up steadily and cunningly: when it arrives, it is full of hesitations and arrested movements. The Phantom, playing, stops for a moment to speak; Christine's hands, stretched out to tear off his mask, advance slowly, hover poised in mid-air, then pull back as the Phantom turns. The unmasking itself is a beautifully conceived episode, providing the audience with a double shock. Both Christine and the Phantom are facing the camera and the audience; when she finally tears the mask from his face, she is behind him and does not see the hideous exposed face. For the audience it was—and still is—a genuinely jolting scene. Then, the Phantom turns, and we now see the Phantom subjectively, from Christine's viewpoint. He presents a totally different image now—distorted, and out of focus—as he advances on the terrified girl.

Whatever the shortcomings of the rest of the film, this one scene must surely rank as one of the screen's peak moments of terror. It is not merely a good "shock" scene either, for a certain amount of audience sympathy for the Phantom has been

Lon Chaney as Erik, the Phantom

Lon Chaney threatens to destroy the opera house unless
Christine (Mary Philbin) does his bidding.

14

created by this time: audiences are thrilled, but divided in their emotions, torn between identification with the heroine in a precarious situation and pity for the Phantom. No other shock introduction or a sudden unmasking of a Movie Monster —not even the carefully built introduction of King Kong, or the famous unmasking near the end of *The Mystery of the Wax Museum*—has ever quite duplicated the skill and excitement of this memorable scene.

In the Technicolor remake in the 40s, the unmasking scene was held to the very end as the major thrill of the production. And a sad anti-climax it was to a production which was consistently good to look at, but more generous to opera than Phantom in its allocation of footage. In the Chaney film, the unmasking was a mid-film high spot. Wisely, they never tried to surpass it in terms of horror.

Chaney's face remained unmasked for the bulk of the rest of the film. The pace quickened considerably, the mood changing from suspense and mystery to a series of thrills and rescues, climaxed by a chase. All of this action and excitement exploited the elaborate sets to the full, and was stylishly photographed. Only occasionally were there images that were imaginative in themselves: the Phantom stalking a victim under water, breathing through a tube, his hand shooting upwards from the canal to drag a victim to death; the searchers in the catacombs, advancing steathily, with arms upraised to ward off the Phantom's rope noose.

For the most part, the director, Rupert Julian, was content to let the richness of the production, the melodramatic plot, and the Chaney artistry do most of the work for him. And he may even have been right: a better director could certainly have made a stronger picture (especially, one suspects, Alan Crosland, a master of rich melodrama), but perhaps in this case more style and artistry might have robbed the film of its serial-like simplicity and excitement. Chaney, behind such startling and grotesque makeup, could have been forgiven for relaxing with the role and relying on his death's head makeup for the bulk of his characterization, but he does not. With subtlety of facial pantomime denied him by the restrictions of his makeup, he uses his body gracefully and eloquently, most notably his hand movements.

James Whale and Claude Rains studied his performance carefully, since many of Rains's gestures in *The Invisible Man* (1933) are obviously copied from Chaney's head and hand movements in this film. The grace and animation of the Chaney performance is made all the more apparent by the stiffness of Norman Kerry's hero. Like so many horror film heroes (particularly David Manners in the Universal chillers of the 30s), Kerry is virtually useless in a crisis, once even fainting dead away when his aid is most sorely needed. Manners, a sensitive, non-muscular hero, could be forgiven for this kind of inefficiency, but Kerry, uniformed, dashing, handsome, in the Errol Flynn tradition, could not. With such an unreliable hero, one warmed to the resourceful Phantom even more, and felt that his energy and devotion to the heroine deserved some kind of reward. With moral values being turned so topsy turvy in contemporary cinema, we may yet get a fourth version of *The Phantom of the Opera*, in which the ubiquitous Phantom kidnaps his Christine and lives happily ever after with her in the Opera House catacombs.

A postscript comment on the "choppiness" of the film. Many of the prints currently in circulation are actually silent prints of a sound reissue of 1930. On that occasion, the film was edited still further, and additional singing/operatic sequences inserted, together with odd lines of dialogue and a prologue speech by a mysterious wanderer in the catacombs. Music and effects glossed over some of the clumsiness of this additional editing, but in the extant prints of this version—*minus* the added sound—the editing is decidedly ragged. With all of its post-production tamperings, it never seemed quite that crude originally, and whatever editorial ineptness it did possess was doubtless minimized by the pleasure of seeing a pristine 35mm print with all the richness of tinting and toning and the occasional Technicolor insert.

THE MAGICIAN

(Metro Goldwyn, 1926) Produced and directed by Rex Ingram. Adapted by Ingram from the 1908 story by Somerset Maugham. Camera, John F. Seitz. Production Manager, Harry Lachman. Sets by Henri Menessier. Editor, Grant Whytock. Assistant to Director Michael Powell.

With Alice Terry, Paul Wegener, Ivan Petrovich, Firmin Gemier, Gladys Hamer, Henry Wilson, Stowitz, Michael Powell.

Although both author Somerset Maugham and prestige director Rex Ingram might resent the honor, *The Magician* is one of the few authentic silent examples of the "Mad Doctor" *genre* of horror thrillers. Its story is of the mad *Doctor Haddo,* who, mad or not, is a genuine sorcerer who has discovered through ancient documents the method of creating artificial life. Unfortunately, a key ingredient in the experiment is a supply of "the heart's blood of a maiden." The documents are surprisingly specific about the other requirements of the maiden, even to the color of her eyes, and they tally almost exactly with the physical characteristics of Alice Terry. Miss Terry, serene and undeniably beautiful, was perhaps a trifle too mature to suggest the youth and sexual innocence that the part called for, but inasmuch as she was married to producer-director Ingram, one can forgive this minor shortcoming.

Having discovered Miss Terry and determined to use her in his experiment, the Doctor takes a page out of Svengali's notebook, and from that point on the scenario very much resembles that of *Trilby,* until the wild and woolly finish of the spectacular laboratory experiment, the hero's timely arrival, a fight to the death, and the traditional holocaust of the laboratory/castle going up in flames.

Rex Ingram films—the legendary ones like *Mare Nostrum,* the few big box offices successes, *Scaramouche, The Four Horsemen of the Apocalypse,* and the less famous films such as *The Conquering Power* and *The Garden of Allah*—all invariably and automatically disappoint when viewed today. (Not that it is easy to see them outside of film archives, and even here there are big gaps in the Ingram chronology.) The reason is probably that Ingram approached his films essentially as a painter. As a dramatist he was weak, being neither a very cinematic adaptor of the other writers' works, nor an imaginative translator of the written word to the silent image. One has only to place his French revolution film, *Scaramouche,* side by side with D. W. Griffith's *Orphans of the Storm* (made a year or so *earlier)* to realize Ingram's deficiencies. Griffith's film is vibrant and exciting, full of fast cutting and detail shots that give it life and authenticity. Ingram's film is merely a stagy tableau, done mainly in medium and long shots, stiff in its duel scene, and not even coming to real life in its spectacular mob scenes. But he understood composition and lighting; if one is lucky enough to see an Ingram film in an original 35mm print, with all its richness, clarity and subtlety of color tinting, it becomes an entirely different and superior entity.

Since dramatic structure takes such a definite second place to pictorial beauty, it is virtually unfair (and sometimes impossible) to judge Ingram's work accurately unless one has access to an original print. Unfortunately, the majority of his films are available (if at all) only in black and white prints, and usually *dupe* prints at that. They are turned out gracelessly and insensitively by labs, more concerned with mass production for television, on the theory that as long as you can see it, it's enough. One is thus left with pale shadows of the originals, which may not have been works of dramatic art but may have been masterpieces of *pictorial* art.

Ingram was, not surprisingly, a disciple of the greatest of all pictorialist directors, Maurice Tourneur, and many of his films—*The Magician* among them—contained compositions included almost as a direct homage to Tourneur's technique. *The Magician,* alas, is a film that needs the pictorial sensitivity that it undoubtedly had in its original release prints: the beautifully used Paris and Nice locations are an interesting blend of warm romanticism and documentary skill, while the dream sequences of a baroque bacchanal in Hades, and the grim terror of the castle laboratory, with its roaring furnace below the floor—an apt suggestion of Hell—are strikingly different in their lighting and design. Obviously, there were subtle differences in photographic approach as Ingram shifted from sequence to sequence, and his cameraman, John Seitz, one of the best in the business, was fully capable of achieving those pictorial nuances. Yet the only prints that have survived—the *preservation prints* that were made in the early 70s—are all bland, flat, lifeless, the same pale and washed-out look applied to the whole seven reels. Still, it is all that we have, and it is better than nothing; it does a disservice to Ingram, but at the same time it fills in a major gap in our knowledge of the silent horror film.

The Magician is suggested by the "career" of the much maligned, if far from admirable, Aleister Crowley, who also inspired two of the most interesting sound horror films, *The Black Cat* (with Karloff in the pseudo-Crowley role) and *Curse of the Demon,* with Niall McGinnis doing the honors. In the 20s, horror films had not yet become a *genre* unto themselves (Chaney excepted), and critics generally looked on them with disfavor as being "unnecessary" and harmful for children. *The Magician* was referred to by critics as being tasteless, horrible, and "un-entertaining," despite its restraint. Somerset Maugham himself did not endorse or approve of Ingram's adaptation, which was sometimes so deliberately vague in its details as to make recourse to the original story almost a necessity.

16

Ivan Petrovich and fiancée Alice Terry encounter self-styled sorcerer Paul Wegener.

The Magician reads the magical formula from which he hopes to create artificial life.

In the sorcerer's laboratory, Wegener and Petrovich engage in a battle to the death.

At one point in the story, the doctor places his potential victim in a trance, and creates an erotic vision of Hell—or does he, in fact, transport her soul there? Curiously, after the event he tells her (in a terse subtitle, without subsequent followup) that she now cannot marry her fiancé. Odder still, the film was made in Europe with a largely European cast, and German Paul Wegener would have had difficulty speaking English, even phonetically, had it been necessary. However, one can see Wegener's lips carefully speaking the word "rape" in the post-bacchanal scenes, and Alice Terry's reaction is in keeping with a belief in his statement. Whether the rape was an actual or mental one is never really ascertained, but either way, it apparently does not diminish Wegener's enthusiasm for the "maiden's heart's blood" in his upcoming experiment. Incidentally, it is worth nothing the presence of Harry Lachman as production manager for the film; Lachman's own later *Dante's Inferno* (1935) seems to have been much influenced by the Hell sequences in this film. (Other embryo talents involved in *The Magician* were Michael Powell, who acted as Wegener's assistant and also played a bowler-hatted comedy Englishman in the fairground sequences and, in a supporting role as Alice Terry's friend, Gladys Hamer, the mother of Robert Hamer, director of the chilling mirror sequence in *Dead of Night*, as well as many notable British films.)

19

With its interweaving of Svengali and Mad Doctor themes, *The Magician* is a fascinating, if far from wholly successful work. Its climatic reel, with its laboratory experiment in a castle tower, and its wild juxtaposition of all-out horror with bizarre humor (including a dwarf lab assistant as token comedy relief), provides such a strong blueprint for Universal's first two *Frankenstein* films that one feels that James Whale must have seen it, been impressed by it, and drawn from it, just as he drew from Wegener's earlier *The Golem*. Even the miniature of the castle tower, used for establishing scenes and for final destruction in an explosion, is a dead ringer for the miniature used in *The Bride of Frankenstein*. Like James Whale's films, too, it is at its best when it takes a tongue-in-cheek approach. For the most part, it is too serious, but there are moments when its florid nature seems about to get out of hand, and Ingram wisely checks it by poking fun at a situation which might cause the audience to laugh anyway. "He looks like something out of a stage melodrama," comments Alice Terry, after an early meeting with the bizarre Dr. Haddo. Overhearing, Paul Wegener stiffens, draws himself up, throws his cloak around his shoulder, glowers, and strides off in a perfect stage exit!

Like Rex Ingram's other four final films for MGM (including *Mare Nostrum* and *The Garden of Allah*), *The Magician* was filmed at Ingram's Riviera studios and on location in France. Like all of them, perhaps due partially to leisurely shooting methods and lack of studio discipline, it was a commercial failure, as opposed to his Hollywood-produced MGM films which were big money makers.

SPARROWS

(1926) Mary Pickford Corporation-United Artists. Directed by William Beaudine. Scenario by C. Gardner Sullivan from a story by Winifred Dunn. Camera, Charles Rosher, Karl Struss, Hal Mohr. Art Director, Harry Oliver. Titles, George Marion, Jr.
With Mary Pickford, Gustav von Seyffertitz, Roy Stewart, Mary Louise Miller, Charlotte Mineau, Spec O'Donnell, Lloyd Whitlock, A. L. Schaeffler, Monty O'Grady.

Sparrows opens with a marvelously atmospheric long shot (actually a miniature, but so well done and so expertly matched up later with full scale

Handsome enough to be a star himself, Rex Ingram, director of *The Magician*

20

sets that it is never apparent) of a desolate swamp, trees growing up out of the soggy ground, branches bending down to return to it, a ramshackle farmhouse in the middle of it all. An opening title tells us:

"The Devil's share in the world's creation was a certain Southern swampland—a masterpiece of horror. And the Lord, appreciating a good job, let it stand."

Then, as a dark, gaunt, shadowy figure glides beneath the trees, a second title follows through:

"Then the Devil went himself one better and had Mr. Grimes live in the swamp."

Mr. Grimes is played by the satanic-visaged Gustav von Seyffertitz, and in one quick shot—as he scratches the stubble on his chin and muses over thoughts that produce glinting eyes and an evil grin—there is no questioning the implication, only seconds into the movie, that here is the villain of the piece. At a showing of the film in New York, early in 1973, one little tot, doubtless taken to the film by her mother on the fairly safe premise that it would be good wholesome fare, began to squirm uneasily. Mr. von Seyffertitz runs a form of baby farm, to which mothers who are too ill, poor, or hard working to support their own children send them for tender care, along with whatever money they can afford. Mr. Grimes pockets the money that has just been delivered, along with a crude doll and a loving note. He contemplates the doll for a moment, then crushes its face in his hand, a grimy thumb all but gouging out the painted eye. (The watching child was by now visibly and vocally upset, although her mother assured her that the man wasn't really bad and was "just pretending.") As if to throw the lie in her face, and superbly on cue, Gustav hurled the now misshapen doll into the quicksand where it proceeded to sink slowly to its doom, first, painted cheeks, and then an upstretched porcelain hand disappearing beneath the slime. (With a howl of terror, the child bolted for the movie theatre's closest exit, her mother close to heel. Neither came back.)

If *Sparrows* can have that effect in the 70s, when we are, after all, inured to screen horror, one wonders what the reaction must have been in 1926. By that time, Mary Pickford was making only one film a year. It was a big budget special, a treat very

much to be looked forward to and savored. And while admittedly, her films were made with adults in mind, it was also with the knowledge that youngsters always formed a large part of her audiences. For, despite concessions here and there, *Sparrows* is a genuine horror film to which those opening scenes are merely mild, appetizing teasers. As Mr. Grimes, Seyffertitz not only wrings dollars out of unfortunate mothers, but also sells off his charges to neighboring farmers as field laborers and, in the basic plot line of the film, accepts custody of a millionaire's kidnapped toddler. As his obnoxious son, Spec O'Donnell aids him by taunting and bullying the children, informing on them, and looks forward to the time when he can help his pa get rid of them by chucking them in the swamp—an event which, the titles imply, had already happened more than once. Mary Pickford, the oldest of the children (all of whom look a trifle too chubby on the sparse diet of raw potatoes rationed out none too frequently), is their unofficial mother and protector, the only one big enough and strong enough to ultimately take a stand against Mr. Grimes, whose lameness (as opposed to their youthful agility) gives them the only slight advantage that they have.

Photographed by three of the best cameramen in Hollywood (two of them, Rosher and Struss, also photographed that loveliest of all silent films, *Sunrise*), *Sparrows* is a showcase for their superbly atmospheric camerawork and their lighting of equally expert and well designed sets. The blackness of the whole film, the stress on mud, squalor, storms, lightning, produces a Dickensian kind of horror throughout. Apart from the physical menace itself, there are poverty, hunger, and the fact that both God and man seem to have turned their backs on these innocents. Perhaps recognizing the extremes to which she has gone, Mary Pickford does try to lighten the mood where possible, by seeing (in the manner of Disney with the later *Bambi*) that there are frequent cutaways to scenes of comedy and sentiment, and that the sequences of the adults plotting their villainies are interrupted (often to the point of weakening their dramatic tension) to keep us abreast of what the children are up to at the same moment. However, even the comedy has its macabre side—Spec O'Donnell, trying to throw the baby into the quicksand, himself falls in, and is rescued (and almost lynched into the bargain) by looping a rope around his neck and being dragged out by a horse. Since, in the process, he also ruins his pa's turnip patch, there

Spec O'Donnell threatens to throw Mary Pickford's infant charge into the swamp.

is further punishment rather than consolation at the end of his wild ride.

The attempt to escape from the farm consumes the better part of the last half of the film, and every means of wringing suspense is exploited to the full. With Grimes and his hound on their trail, Mary and her charges—some of them so small that they cannot walk, and have to hang on to the necks of others—escape by throwing boxes and piles of hay into the quicksand, and make their way across the shivering "bridge" which has sunk out of sight beneath the mud before they finish their crossing. Taking to the trees, they swing across mud on old vines, and clamber across a rotting tree bough which—in a brilliantly executed trick shot—constantly breaks and slips further down to swamp level, where scores of ravenous crocodiles are waiting for them.

Mary Pickford was a deeply religious woman, and frequently inserted motifs of religious faith into her movies. It is not inappropriate to the theme of *Sparrows*, but at times it becomes rather tastelessly (though probably not intentionally) condescending. Mary's heroines seemed to possess a kind

of private "hot line" to the Deity, and on at least one occasion in *Sparrows*, after Divine intervention, Mary looks heavenwards, considers, and then nods her approval! However, the scenes of sentiment and pathos are so superbly handled in *Sparrows*—both pictorially and emotionally—that one can readily forgive Mary these lapses in taste. Less forgiveable, however, is the piling of so-called showmanship on top of superb artistry. The film comes to a perfectly logical and satisfying climax with the rescue of the children from the swamp, and Grimes's inevitable death in the quicksand. But conscious of the fact that the film is a "special" and her only offering of the year, Mary seems unable to let it go at that. The children take refuge in a motor launch, which is then involved in a hectic chase through the bayous, as the kidnappers try to elude the pursuing police.

Not only is the chase unnecessary for an already sated audience, but it is badly anti-climactic. It is so artificially contrived that its rather obvious model shots negate the conviction so carefully achieved by the earlier reels. And this chase concluded, Mary spends too much time packing a pro-

Gustav von Seyffertitz as Mr. Grimes—a stock name for a really dastardly villain that probably originated with the chimneysweep villain of *The Water Babies*.

longed closing reel with enough wrap-up comedy to compensate for the grimness hitherto. This is one film where one feels sorely tempted to wield editorial scissors for the overall good of the movie. Nevertheless, it's still a chilling piece of screen horror, a welcome reminder not only of the tremendous variety that could be found within the Pickford films, but also of what a powerful director William Beaudine (never taken seriously in the sound period because of his virtual exiling to "B" pictures and programmers) was in the 20s.

THE WIZARD

(Fox, 1927) Directed by Richard Rosson. Scenario by Harry O. Hoyt and Andrew Bennison with titles by Malcolm Stuart Boylan from the story "Balaoo" by Gaston Leroux. Camera, Frank Good.

With Edmund Lowe, Leila Hyams, Gustav von Seyffertitz, E. H. Calvert, Barry Norton, Oscar Smith, Perle Marshall, Norman Trevor, George Kotsonaros, Maude Turner Gordon.

With the recent re-discovery, after a quarter of a century, of the apparently lost *Mystery of the Wax Museum, The Wizard* now assumes pride of place as the most fascinating, elusive, and sought after of all "lost" horror films. Unfortunately, the most obvious sources have all been scoured without success; Fox, who produced the film, have nothing left, and if it is to turn up at all, it will probably be from an unlikely European source where it may

be lying dormant under a misleading changed title. *The Wizard* is thus the only film discussed in this book without the benefit of either re-appraisal or memories of a long ago screening. It is a film that belongs in such a survey, yet it is difficult to assess its possible values, since what is known about the film tends to be somewhat contradictory.

It is based on a 1912 story by Gaston Leroux, author of *Phantom of the Opera* and other excursions into Gallic *Grand Guignol*. His original story was in a serious, if florid vein. Fox's film worked around a legitimate enough blood and thunder thread—the mad Doctor Coriolos, played by Gustav von Seyffertitz, uses an Ape creature (played by George Kotsonaros, whose face and build caused him to be so cast on more than one occasion) to exact revenge on those whom he considers responsible for his son's execution for murder. It veers to the "Old House" comedy-thriller pattern, so popular at that time. Indeed, another stage adaptation of a like nature, *The Gorilla*, preceded *The Wizard* into release by a week, and it, too, was concerned as much with laughs as with thrills. But at least *The Gorilla* was designed as a partial comedy from inception; *The Wizard* was a matter of taking a straight thriller play and grafting on to it comedy elements with the inevitable dumb detectives, to cash in on a currently fashionable market. Reviews indicate that the comedy interpolations were too frequent and too obvious, and

Edmund Lowe menaced by the ape-man

23

Dr. Renault's Secret, the much-changed sound remake, with George Zucco as the scientist, J. Carroll Naish as the ape-man

Ape-man George Kotsonaros still on amicable terms with sinister mentor Gustav von Seyffertitz

Dr. Renault's Secret:
J. Carroll Naish

Dr. Renault's Secret: George Zucco

the decision to shift the balance of the film in this direction may have been taken during actual production. The original script of the film, which still exists, would seem to contain less comedy than the final film. It also suggests that they were aiming at a certain Chaney-like pathos in the character of the Ape, an element not substantiated by any of the reviews.

Points, potentially very much in its favor, are its brevity (a short six reels), the fact that it was directed by Richard Rosson, an excellent action director who always kept his films on the move, and most of all, the fact that it was photographed by Frank Good. Reviews were unanimous in praising the excellence and eeriness of the photographic effects. Good was an excellent cameraman who contributed superb, crystal clear, well composed photography to many "B" films of the 30s. With its moving camera shots through the "Old House," its cobwebs, clutching hands, and standard accoutrements, it would probably have been a grade "A" showcase for Good's virtually unrecognized talents today. Regardless of the fun it must have been on its own, and the pleasure that surely accrued from seeing Gustav von Seyffertitz let loose with a meaty

role, it is perhaps most sorely missed as a major gap in our knowledge of Good's camerawork in the silent period.

While the original film is probably gone beyond recall, a less ambitious but still interesting "B" remake, done by Fox in 1942, is more readily available. Titled *Dr. Renault's Secret,* it simplified the plot to the more standardized scientific-experiment formula, but it did return its locale to its original France, and it restored the sympathetic, Chaney-like concept to the Apeman, played now by J. Carroll Naish. Gustav von Seyffertitz was replaced by George Zucco, a less Satanic, but by no means unworthy descendant. Under the direction of the always interesting Harry Lachman, well photographed by Virgil Miller, and with really handsome sets and art direction by Richard Day and Nathan Juran, it was a good film to look at, a 58-minute "B" that gave the impression of being far more expensive than it was.

THE MAN WHO LAUGHS

(Universal, 1928) Directed by Paul Leni. Production Supervisor, Paul Kohner. Story Supervisor, Dr. Bela Sekely. Scenario by J. Grubb Alexander, assisted by Charles Whittaker, Marion Ward and May MacLean, from the novel by Victor Hugo. Camera, Gilbert Warrenton. Art Director, Charles D. Hall. Costumes, David Cox and Vera West. Editors, Maurice Pivar and Edward Cahn. Assistant Directors, Louis Friedlander (Lew Landers), Jay Marchant and John Voshell.

With Conrad Veidt, Mary Philbin, Olga Baclanova, Josephine Crowell, George Siegmann, Brandon Hurst, Sam de Grasse, Cesare Gravina, Stuart Holmes, Nick de Ruiz, Edgar Norton. Torben Meyer, Julius Molnar, Jr., Charles Puffy, Frank Puglia, Jack Goodrich, Carmen Costello, Lon Poff, Zimbo the Dog.

Made between Paul Leni's *The Cat and the Canary* (1927) and *The Last Warning* (1928), *The Man Who Laughs* was a product of Hollywood's, and especially Universal's, European and predominantly German-influenced period. Paul Fejos was another imported prestige director working on the same lot; his *The Last Performance,* also starring Veidt and Mary Philbin, was an interesting if less spectacular example of filmed Gothique from the same period. Even some of Universal's "B"

Westerns of these years had a Germanic look to them.

Although not strictly speaking a horror film, either in intent or outcome, the Veidt character was sufficiently close to a Monster character for closeups of his fearsome looking face to be one of the key selling angles at the time. It was also one of the principal reasons why the film has been remembered. The film is based on the Victor Hugo story about an outlawed band whose surgeons carved huge, distorted, permanent grins on the features of young children, who grow up to become, sideshow and circus freaks. In the prologue, Gwynplaine, a small boy, has this operation performed on him as an additional revenge against his father (additional, that is, to death in the Iron Lady), a political enemy of the King.

The prologue: Nobleman Conrad Veidt about to be tortured and executed by an evil King (Sam de Grasse) and his jester (Brandon Hurst).

Gwynplaine, abandoned, recues a blind girl from freezing during a blizzard, and the two of them are taken in by a circus troupe. Years later, Gwynplaine becomes a beloved clown, in love with the girl he rescued. She is still blind and can see only the beauty of his soul and not the ugliness of his face. Various complications and intrigues cause his noble ancestry to be revealed. He takes his place in court, where his hideous grin is at first seen as an insulting rebuke to the Queen. Ultimately, after separation and arrest, he is able to rejoin his Dea just as her ship sets sail for the New World.

The film was an obvious attempt to duplicate the success of Universal's earlier Victor Hugo adaptation, *The Hunchback of Notre Dame,* and as a film was far superior to it—more elaborately produced, more imaginatively designed, and certainly better directed. But it lacked popular appeal, as well as the showmanship and magnetism of Lon Chaney. (Veidt's performance was a subtle but stylized one, and had neither the warmth nor the menace of Chaney's Quasimodo.)

Actually, while it might not have been a better picture, *The Man Who Laughs,* directed by Tod Browning and starring Chaney, could have been a magnificent collaborative venture for that star-director team. Its morbidity and cruelty were a logical and necessary part of a much larger canvas, and were not the entire *raison-d'être* for the whole film, as they so arbitrarily were in the Browning films. In an attempt to popularize the rather heavy and downbeat Hugo story, Universal injected several deviations from the original, including a happy ending (which worked well and seemed quite justified) and a reel of Dumas-inspired chase and swashbuckling action leading up to it.

In a scene deleted from the final film, the young Gwynplaine, deserted, tries to find refuge with a family whose children have, like him, had their mouths carved into grotesque permanent smiles.

Supporting characters were often deliberately photographed in bizarre angles, or with low-key lighting to add suspense and elements of horror to their fairly passive characters. At the beginning of the film, as King James (Sam de Grasse) and his evil jester, Barkilphedro (Brandon Hurst, the film's basic villain, as he had been in *The Hunchback of Notre Dame*), go to witness torture and execution, they are shown in prancing, mincing steps in a long sweeping tracking shot that picks them up from below, and transforms them into inhuman demons—a forerunner of many similar shots of Karloff and Lugosi in later horror films like *The Black Cat* and *The Raven*. A Movietone (sound on film) score was also added to help along its box office chances. Sometimes the music works well, sometimes it is lazy (a constant use of *British*

Grenadiers to try to reinforce the illusion that the wholly Germanic sets represents England of the 17th century), sometimes derivative (wholesale uses of the themes from Murnau's *Sunrise* in the same context, the musical motif for the drunken pig in that film re-emerging here to back up the drunken antics of Stuart Holmes) and once, *disastrous*. One can accept reluctantly the idea of a vocal, as a last-reel wrap-up, and doubtless in such late silents as *Seventh Heaven* and *Four Sons* it had emotional impact (at the time). But the intrusion of Erno Rapee's very modern *When Love Comes Stealing* into a fragile love scene is a deplorable lapse in taste. Sound effects and crowd noises are sometimes out of proportion, too.

Though long and slow, it is, however, an incredibly good film to look at. The marvelous pro-

Another scene deleted from the released version: Gwynplaine (Conrad Veidt) restored to his noble station, drinks to the health of the blind girl who loves him (Mary Philbin).

A production shot of a courtroom scene. In the finished scene, glass shot trickery provided a roof to the chamber, balconies, spectators, and luxurious chandeliers!

logue, with its grim torture chamber scenes, the blizzard, with bodies swinging from gibbets and the abandoning of the young child as the boat pulls away from the dock, sets a high-powered standard of visual eloquence. Throughout the film, both in structure, in editing, and in individual compositions, there are signs of intelligent borrowings from Griffith and from the German cinema; a figure emerging from the tomb-like shadows of an English prison is a virtual re-staging of Dracula's first appearance from his castle in the German *Nosferatu*.

The sub-plot of Duchess Josianna (Olga Baclanova) and her attempted seduction of Gwynplaine —stripping away his mask and kissing his deformed mouth in a manner combining lust and loathing at the same time—results in some of the most remarkable scenes of sensuality and animal passion ever seen in the screen. It proves once again that true eroticism doesn't require nudity and the blan-

ket freedom of an "X" certificate. Incidentally, in the late 60s, a big elaborate remake was planned by Kirk Douglas—ironically, an actor whose fixed widescreen grin had become one of his less attractive trademarks. The project was called off when he was finally able to track down and screen a copy of this Universal original. Presumably, he found it morbid and less of a star vehicle than he had anticipated. It is probably those qualities that have always worked against its being remade, though its basic idea probably inspired Ray Russell's short horror story, *Mr. Sardonicus,* which did find its way into film form. Dumas has been remade constantly; even Hugo's grimmer and more serious *The Hunchback of Notre Dame* and *Les Miserables* have been afforded multiple remakes all over the world. But Universal's *The Man Who Laughs* of 1928 is still Hollywood's only foray into his most macabre story.

DR. MABUSE

(Decla-Bioscop, Germany, 1922) Directed by Fritz Lang. Scenario by Thea von Harbou, from the story by Norbert Jacques. Camera, Carl Hoffman. Sets and Design, Otto Hunte and Stahl-Urach. Released by UFA in two parts of ten reels each.

With Rudolph Klein-Rogge, Bernard Goetzke, Aud Egede Nissen, Alfred Abel, Paul Richter, Gertrude Welcker.

THE TESTAMENT OF DR. MABUSE

(Nerofilm, 1932) Directed by Fritz Lang. Produced by Seymour Sebenzal. Script by Thea von Harbou. Camera, Fritz Arno Wagner. Art Direction, Karl Vollbrecht, Emil Hassler. Music by Hans Erdman.

With Rudolph Klein-Rogge, Otto Wernicke, Gustav Diessl, Oscar Beregi, Vera Liessem, Camilla Spira, E. A. Licho, Karl Meixner, Theodore Loos, Theo Lingen.

THE THOUSAND EYES OF DR. MABUSE

(CCC Films, Germany, 1960) Directed by Fritz Lang. Scenario by Fritz Lang, Heinz Oskar Wuttig and Jan Fethke. Camera, Karl Lob.

With Wolfgang Preiss, Dawn Adams, Peter van Eyck, Gert Frobe, Werner Peters, Lupo Prezzo.

THE RETURN OF DR. MABUSE

(CCC Films Berlin, in collaboration with SPA Cinematografica Films of Rome and Criterion Films, 1961) Directed by Harald Reinl. Screenplay by Ladislas Fodor and Marc Behm. Produced by Arthur Brauner. Music by Peter Sandloff.

With Gert Frobe, Lex Barker, Daliah Lavi, Rudolf Forster, Wolfgang Preiss, Fausto Tozzi, Werner Peters, Rudolf Fernau, Joachim Moch, Laura Solari.

Although Dr. Mabuse originated in (and was limited to) only one literary work, Fritz Lang and the movies elevated him to a position equal to those other arch-fiends, Dr. Fu Manchu and Professor Moriarty. Like them, he employed a world-wide organization run with matchless efficiency, and like them, too, he was more concerned with power and the manipulation of people than with the mere acquisition of wealth. Mabuse was also a hypnotist in the grand manner of a Cagliostro. Although all of the *Mabuse* films are technically crime melodramas, all of them contain elements of the supernatural, having highlights of sheer horror which more than justify their inclusion in this survey.

The original *Dr. Mabuse* was long thought to be lost in its complete 20-reel form, and for many years we had to content ourselves with the drastically edited 8-reel version, as released in Britain and the United States. Then, in 1966, the full original edition became available again. Many rediscovered primitives (and despite its 1922 date, *Dr. Mabuse* is primitive in its relation to other Lang works) turn out to have amazing vitality and beauty; such has certainly proven to be the case with *The Vampires*, and other early Feuillade serials from France. *Dr. Mabuse*, on the other hand, disappoints a little if one takes the attitude that it is only four years prior to the very polished *Metropolis*. However, this is rather like being disappointed in Griffith's *Judith of Bethulia* because it is only two years before *The Birth of a Nation*. The emphasis surely is wrong; rather, one should be astounded at the mastery achieved in the later films over such a short period.

On its own merits, *Dr. Mabuse* is a fascinating work, not only because of its clear ties to the detailed novel of mystery and detection, and for roots which obviously derive from the early serial films, but also because here one can see at the source so many of the themes, characters, incidents and individual shots that were to permeate Lang's later films, most specifically *Metropolis*, *Spies*, and his two *Mabuse* sequels. Lang's criminal world was always a dark and nightmarish one, but here he hasn't quite reached that plateau. The world is grey rather than black, and it is dreamlike rather than nightmarish. All of the characters—good and bad—seem to glide through its vast, cheerless rooms, as in a somnambulistic trance.

What is most surprising of all is Lang's comparative playing down of melodramatic content. His later films had considerable pace and zip, and here his sequences of action and chase are interspersed methodically, dropped in where they'll do the most good, but never sustained for too long. This rather too deliberate pacing reminds one of the first *The Indian Tomb* (which Lang scripted for Joe May's direction) and Lang's own remake of the film in the 50s. Possibly Lang, not yet too sure of himself, was carefully following a formula which he knew was acceptable. His too frequent use of the iris device further slows the film. Lang liked the long film as a matter of policy (especially in the sound era), not just because he enjoyed that kind of framework but also because, as he remarked in all seriousness in 1963, ". . . if my films were long they couldn't put anything else on the bill, and I got all the money!"

But if the influence of Joe May and the detective novel tend to dilute some of Lang's vigor, there are still ample signs of the glories that were to come. The sets, with their bizarre and nightmarish design, intermingling functional and surrealistic decor, are often superb. The whole opening sequence in the Stock Exchange (Mabuse has documents of a trade deal stolen, is on hand at the market to buy cheap when the news is released and panic hits; and remains to corner the market and re-sell when the documents are found and the market stabilized!) gets the film off to a magnificent start. Lang's talent for suddenly turning the everyday into an unreal world of terror is beautifully displayed in the card game sequence, where the hideous face of Mabuse suddenly surges forward out of a totally black background, like some evil spider on an invisible web. (Mabuse, the hypnotist-psychiatrist, effects a disguise, contrives to play with wealthy and influential men, hypnotizes them into cheating, and after they are caught and disgraced, uses them and their wealth as pawns in his operation when they come to him—as Mabuse—for treatment or solace.)

There are welcome moments of humor, but somehow they always manage to stay outside the main plot stream, so that—as opposed to Alfred Hitchcock's deliberately lighthearted approach to similar material—one is never encouraged to regard any of it with anything but the utmost seriousness. And when Lang does swing into his action and chases, he builds them by simple, yet unexpected devices, in which movement is perpetuated on two planes. As Detective Wenk pursues Mabuse's car in one sequence, for example, Mabuse's auto goes under a railroad bridge and to the *right*. Almost simultaneously (and this is an optical effect, confirming that Lang did it deliberately), the wheels of a train are seen crossing the bridge in the opposite direction. This is the kind of movement within the frame that Lang was to use more and more. Here, of course, it is not done by editing, but in *Metropolis*, the same pace-building effect is created by a direct cut—from Klein-Rogge falling

outward to the right of the frame (from a cathedral roof), to the crowd below surging forward to the left of the frame.

Lang himself claimed that his major interest in making *Dr. Mabuse* was that it enabled him at the same time to attack the shocking conditions of crime and perversion that were rampant in postwar Germany. It is true that none of Mabuse's victims are very sympathetic. Most of them are society parasites, living empty, useless lives. Mabuse feeds on them like a wolf on a dying carcass, not from necessity, but because playing with human destinies is the only exciting game left in a jaded and decadent world. For the most part, the socialites look and behave like debauched sleepwalkers, and even the virile Hull (played by Paul Richter), ostensibly the hero in part one, stirs so little sympathy in Lang that he allows him to be killed off so casually, in a long shot, that his death has to be confirmed by a later subtitle. A sign of the times, perhaps, is that Mabuse is contemptuous of expressionism and modern art, and considers it merely a time-killer for the rich; later Lang villains were often presented as being decadent, partially because *they* had now become collectors of modern art!

But the sociological content of *Dr. Mabuse* plays second fiddle to the melodrama. Lang claims that he wasn't "allowed" to make the film the way he wanted, but one wonders. In all of the films where he has a message, actual or alleged—*Metropolis, Fury, You Only Live Once*—one has the feeling that he doesn't really give a fig for social content, and that he's much happier playing around with his lights and cameras in bizarre scenes of suspense and thrill. For all of the implied degeneracy in *Dr. Mabuse* (the very first title refers to drug addiction, and there is a delightful all-purpose cabaret where different code words can produce a variety of vices!), the impression is not so much of a debauched Germany in the 20s as of a vintage Robert Louis Stevenson or Bram Stoker novel, somehow brought up to date with automobiles and nightclubs, much as the Sherlock Holmes stories were updated by Universal into a World War II milieu. Sometimes one forgets entirely that this is a modern story, and it is quite a shock to see an automobile emerging from the Caligari shadows. It must have seemed even less contemporary in 1922, when the real thing surrounded it on all sides.

More so than in *Spies*, and the later *Mabuse* films, Mabuse is here really the "hero," in the sense that Fu Manchu was the hero of the Sax Rohmer novels. Rudolph Klein-Rogge, Lang's favorite vil-

Rudolph Klein-Rogge as Dr. Mabuse

Rudolph Klein-Rogge in one of his many disguises .

lain, was Chaney, Karloff, and Lugosi all rolled into one. He was also the first husband of scenarist Thea von Harbou, who later became Mrs. Lang! His marvelous face, handsome and sinister at the same time, is here used to excellent effect in some first rate disguises, which convince and work so well that the audience doesn't always realize right away that it is he beneath it all. (Mabuse spends so much time donning disguises and being in the right place at precisely the right time, that one wonders where he ever found the spare time to run the rest of his huge organization!) Because of the influence of the original story—a solid selling number in German bookstores right through the 50s, long after Mabuse had apparently faded from the film scene—far more emphasis is placed this time on the personal and titanic struggle between Mabuse and the humorless but dogged policeman, Wenk.

The hero of *Spies* was a carefree James Bond blueprint; Inspector Lohmann from *M* and *The Testament of Dr. Mabuse* a more human but not very active opponent. Wenk here assumes the

Sherlock Holmes or Nayland Smith role, and is far more involved and more dedicated personally in the proceedings. Mabuse, too, like Moriarty, leaves less to his organization and takes up the fight in person. His aims are less ambitious than in later years, but his motivations are more clearly spelled out, and he emerges as a more human (and slightly less menacing) opponent because of it. Sometimes he is even human enough to give way to rage and frustration, something that the later master criminals were always too self-assured to permit. Mabuse has his vast organization, his band of blind counterfeiters, his autos fixed up with gas chambers, and a laboratory full of snakes, but it is clearly his own dynamic personality that really holds his empire together. After his total triumph in part one, it is rather sad to see him brought to heel in part two—even though we now know that he'd be back with a vengeance, in the 30s, and again—via a whole series of films—in the 60s.

Curiously, though part two has more basic action than part one—the detective, driving to his death at a quarry under the hypnotic influence of Mabuse,

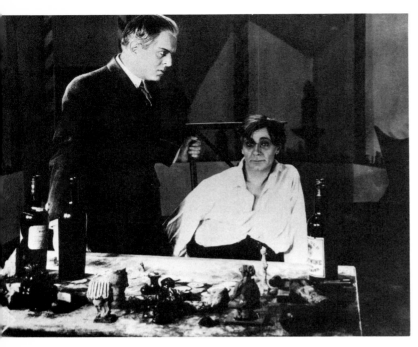

Dr. Mabuse and victim: Alfred Abel (right)

Example of the spacious, cheerless rooms and expressionistic decor that characterize *Dr. Mabuse* sets

the gun battle and gang roundup, and Mabuse's impressionistic descent into madness, the spirits of his victims surrounding him, the machines of his counterfeiting plant transforming themselves into robot monsters, it is slower paced and a little less exciting than part one. It is as though Lang had spent the first half in establishing Mabuse and had used all the serial-like gimmicks and twists to that end; whereas, in part two, he seems more concerned with telling, and concluding, his story in a wholly serious vein. With Lang, the seemingly extraneous and unrelated incident has often been a dynamic high point—as witness *Metropolis*, with the visions of Moloch and the coming-to-life of the statues of the *Seven Deadly Sins*—and it is a pity to see him bear down on the "fun" aspect of the second half.

In a way, it is easy to see why both American and British distributors decided on a single condensed version, rather than a two-part release. (This is a fairly frequent decision when applied to non-European releases of two-part features; Lang's remake of *The Indian Tomb* was likewise edited down to a single feature under the title *Journey to the Lost City* for its U.S. release.) But part two disappoints only in relation to part one. In terms of its horror content, it is perhaps more interesting. In any case, it was never Lang's intention that both 10-reel films be shown on the same bill; seen with a span of days or weeks between them, the differences in style and pacing are less apparent and also less crucial.

Lang's second *Mabuse* film—a talkie, made exactly ten years after the first—is in many ways one of his best works, and certainly contains some of his finest sequences of eerie horror. *The Testament of Dr. Mabuse* (again with Rudolph Klein-Rogge as Mabuse, now somewhat drawn, and much older looking than the mere ten-year gap would have suggested) became something of a *cause-célèbre* when it was banned by Dr. Goebbels. It was promptly smuggled out of Germany, with Lang making his escape at the same time. The reasons for this (outlined quite fully in Siegfried Kracauer's book *From Caligari to Hitler*) were its anti-Nazi sentiments, and its placing of Hitler and Nazi slogans into the mouths of a mad Mabuse and his associates. However, just as it is unlikely that German moviegoers would have recognized that Professor Baum (the operator of the insane asylum, whose mind and body are taken over by Mabuse's spirit) was an extension of Dr. Caligari, it is even more unlikely that they would have recognized the film as a piece of propaganda against the "New Order."

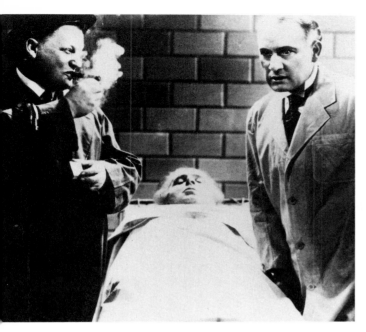

The Testament of Dr. Mabuse: Inspector Lohmann (Otto Wernicke), the dead Mabuse (Rudolph Klein-Rogge) and Professor Baum (Oscar Beregi)

All that Dr. Goebbels really did was to deprive Germany of a wonderfully exciting and eerie piece of melodrama. Its claims to anti-Nazi content have, in any case, been exaggerated. In wartime, Lang, with the original no longer available to dispute him, indulged in a combination of hindsight and showmanship to describe his propagandist "message" in terms which suggested a far more outspoken anti-Nazi undercurrent. Then, in the early 1950s, a dubbed English-language version of the film was released, and its producer-editor based much of his new dialogue on what Lang had *claimed* was there. (There were other strange manipulations of language too; in the original, the detective hero is constantly being frustrated in his efforts to leave the office at night and go to the opera; perhaps thinking that American audiences wouldn't buy a detective of such cultural leanings, opera was changed to "the fights"!)

Just as Lang used the car chase from his first *Mabuse* film as an amplified climax to the second, so does he use the murder in the car in this film in the third *Mabuse*. In fact, it is the method of murder that suggests to an old-timer on the force that Mabuse is behind it. And there is a link with *M* in that it is the same stolid and methodical detective, Inspector Lohmann (played by Otto Wernicke), who tracks down both child murderer

and Mabuse. Lang also anticipates the popular melodrama cliché of the 40s and 50s in having his mad master criminal a devotee of grotesque modern art! (Hitchcock's *Saboteur* also makes reference to a killer's being caught at the Museum of Modern Art.) Like the first *Dr. Mabuse* film, this sequel draws its roots from the old serials, but it is no series of cheap thrills. It builds steadily and methodically, almost to the same pattern as a Laurel and Hardy film, heightening its suspense to fever pitch in the last third, alternating horror sequences with more conventional crime episodes, so that the mood is constantly changing, and finally, literally exploding into the nightmare climax of sabotage, fire, chase—and, as in the original, a retreat into insanity.

Just as *Metropolis* can be considered Lang's definitive contribution to the science fiction *genre*, so is this *Mabuse*—despite its crime framework—Lang's one real horror film. Its action and its melodrama thrill the viewer—particularly a protracted escape from a locked room, which the hero is flooding with water in the hope of deadening the effects of a coming explosion—but it is the casual eeriness of the supernatural elements that leaves the most lingering impression. Mabuse's wraith, appearing after his death to take over the body of his subordinate, the expressionistic use of glass and distorted angles to give a subjective view through the eyes of a madman, and above all, the final car chase, are scenes of genuine nightmare proportions.

This chase, with its occasional switch to a negative image, to indicate the now total madness of Mabuse's victim, the car headlights picking out the white, undulating shapes of phantom trees, left a lasting impression, not only on audiences but on filmmakers too. Jacques Tourneur was quite obviously influenced by this sequence in his opening episode of *Curse of the Demon*, some 25 years later!

Lang's uncanny ability to translate the world around us into a totally black world of shadows and menace is perfectly exemplified by one scene, very late in the film. As the police are gradually closing in on Mabuse's gang, one of the crooks looks out of the window to see what is going on. For the first time in the film we see sunlight and a normal thoroughfare, with street cars, pedestrians, people going about their everyday business. It comes as somewhat of a shock to realize how totally we have accepted Lang's nightmarish, studio-created world until that point. Lang doesn't even let us off the hook at the end: as Baum/Mabuse lapses into insanity, we do not stay with the detectives, but instead remain shut up with Mabuse. The last shot in the film is of the cell door clanging shut, its two observation peepholes staring at us like inhuman, spying eyes. It is a perfect metaphor of life under a tyrannical dictatorship, yet oddly, it is one that Lang has never referred to in his attempts to bolster the film's anti-Nazi claims.

American audiences saw Lang's French version of the film in the 40s, and the cut and dubbed version in the 50s. The full original German version was not made available until the very end of 1973 (when the *New York Times* waxed enthusiastic over its unveiling), but those of us who had seen the film in the 30s found it strangely lethargic today. Even when new, it had had its over-long and padded sections; now, conditioned by the cut version, it seemed excessively long. In terms of melodrama, the edited and dubbed version did the film a real service: it cut away all the padding, and trimmed the film to its melodramatic bone. Not only did it move faster, but its terror was concentrated; in the original, the long stretches of normalcy (and particularly the overly detailed boy-meets-girl sub-plot) dissipate that tension. For once —looked at dispassionately from the point of view of the end result, if not from that of the creator's intent and integrity—an original work has possibly been enhanced rather than mutilated. There is a five-reel difference between the original and the cut lengths—yet those five reels consist largely of extensions of scenes that were retained. No plot elements, characters, or incidents were eliminated. True, a good deal of subtlety was lost; Lang had time to build up more satisfying motivations in his full version. His brilliant opening—a man, desperately afraid, crouches, hiding from unexplained enemies in a room that thunders and vibrates, likewise without explanation (only later do we find that it is Mabuse's counterfeiting plant)—was lessened in the edited version by being shortened, and having a narrator tell us right away that this is a counterfeiting plant. But apart from that one lapse, the treatment was intelligent and respectful.

Lang claims that he had not wanted to make this second Mabuse film originally, but found justification for it in its anti-Nazi undercurrent. He had wanted even less to make a third Mabuse film in 1960, feeling that the Nazis had organized super-crime to such a degree that a Mabuse now would be an anachronism. However, he was persuaded to make *The Thousand Eyes of Dr. Mabuse*, and again found a justification in having his criminal (actually not Dr. Mabuse, but a disciple, basing his methods and ambitions on those of the dead Doctor) use super-modern technology and equipment, much of which had been perfected by the Nazis' espionage network during World War II.

The Thousand Eyes of Dr. Mabuse need not concern us too much here; it is a surprisingly slick and stylistic thriller for a film made in 1960 by a man is his 70s, but it is essentially a *thriller,* with repetitions from the previous *Mabuses,* and with a typically explosive action and car chase climax. But there were no elements of horror or the supernatural this time. It provided a very apt farewell to the screen for Lang: back in his native Germany, and back on his old filmic ground, too. The success of the film prompted its makers to launch a whole new series of Mabuse films, and Lang was asked to continue making them—but he had no interest in such a standardized product, and wisely declined. The group of films that followed, however, were varied and interesting. The original Dr. Mabuse was brought back—in vigorous middle age—to organize his crime empire on a bigger scale than ever. Lang's *The Testament of Dr. Mabuse* was remade, virtually verbatim, and Gert Frobe was an excellent successor to Otto Wernicke as Lohmann, though, with a view to the non-German market, Lex Barker was brought into them too, as an American agent.

Most of the post-Lang *Mabuses* were carefully made but lacking in style, using the Mabuse character only as a framework and an excuse for gimmickry and action more properly belonging to the James Bond school. Thus, one film had a subplot involving invisibility, while another had its villains engaged in underwater crime as frogmen. But one film was an exception: *The Return of Dr. Mabuse* emerged as a kind of homage to Lang, and a *Mabuse* mosaic, although its trite title suggests that its producers were unaware of what a good film they had. Many of its characters and incidents are directly derived from specific Lang films: the opening sequence on a train is borrowed from both the original *Dr. Mabuse* and the later *Spies.* For the rest, it creates a typically Lang world, in which a church and an insane asylum are equally suspect as fronts for the crime empire, and in which originality and imagination on the part of the criminals (as well as a reinstatement of Mabuse's genius for disguise) supplant the fancy gadgets of Bond's spy world.

The film is written by a veteran scenarist and

playwright, whose own roots are in the "Golden Age" of late silent and early sound cinema. It has a pleasingly oldfashioned look to it, even down to some of the elaborate methods of murder, and gets under way a little faster than Lang would have liked. He preferred to start slowly and build, methodically and steadily. The newer approach is to arrive at a high plateau of excitement early and then sustain it. Lang's method is more oldfashioned but also more satisfying. However, he had maestros like Klein-Rogge to carry out his schemes, and he didn't have to worry about audiences conditioned to instant sensation from the TV teaser-technique of grabbing audience attention immediately, before it can wander to another channel.

Despite its slavish copy of Lang's incident, milieu, and people, it misses on a few essentials. It is rather too graphic in its depiction of the various murders (one victim is incinerated by a flame-thrower, another dissolved in a vat of acid!) and it employs goons to take on the hero in fistic mayhem. When the menace is spelled out, and much of it is on a physical level, there is little room left for the mind to conjure up its own fears and horrors. Too, much of the film takes place in broad daylight: again, when you can see what is going on, when the hero is in a position to either escape or summon aid, the quality of nightmare vanishes. But still, it's Lang's world, or a remarkable facsimile of it, and he wouldn't have been ashamed of it.

A cheap and obscure minor horror film, one of many which suggested that its star *might* be Lon Chaney by using an actor who *looked* like him!

3 Frankenstein== and Successors

The Bride of Frankenstein: The Monster, discovered alive, is carried off by the villagers.

FRANKENSTEIN

(Universal, 1931) Directed by James Whale. Screen-play by John L. Balderston, Garret Fort and Francis Edwards Faragoh, from the novel by Mary W. Shelley and the play by Peggy Webling. Camera, Arthur Edeson. Settings by Herman Rosse.

With Colin Clive, Boris Karloff, Mae Clarke, John Boles, Edward van Sloan, Dwight Frye, Frederick Kerr, Lionel Belmore.

Although blazing a trail for horror films, and indeed made before the descriptive phrase "horror film" came into usage, *Frankenstein* was carefully thought out as a morality play, designed to provide food for thought as well as enjoyable shudders. The hard to read, but even more bizarre original novel merely provided a point of departure for the film. Moreover, the filmed concept was itself changed by James Whale from a reputedly equally original treatment, conceived by another notable director, Robert Florey. Never dreaming that it would spawn a whole *genre* of much stronger chillers, reviewers were generally impressed by its artistry and the way it almost ripped a kind of raw poetry out of a charnel house of horrors, but wondered whether viewers were ready for such nightmarish stuff, and indeed, whether the screen had a moral responsibility to avoid such frightening material.

Its leisurely developed story of Dr. Frankenstein's creation of a Monster from the bodies and tissues of the dead—quite literally, and with no pun intended—now seems like the bare bones of the many imitations and sequels that followed. In some ways, its relative crudities, including the total lack of a musical score and the obvious use of studio "exteriors," give it a kind of rough hewn realism, which the later, slicker ones lacked. And the word "relative" crudities should be stressed; for its day, it was an extremely well done and stylish film. Only its lack of music dated it, in a technical sense, and it held up so well (both artistically and commercially) in endless reissues that it is surprising that Universal did not see fit to modernize it by the addition of a score.

Colin Clive, fresh from his Stanhope in James Whale's earlier *Journey's End* (still a powerful if theatrical film, and by no means a lesser Whale, despite being his first), made a perfect dedicated, frenzied, tortured Frankenstein. In key, supporting roles, Edward Van Sloan and Dwight Frye were towers of strength in the kind of roles they were to specialize in throughout their careers. But it was the dynamic presence of Karloff, launched into his first major role after more than a decade of bits, extras, villains, and only very occasional worthwhile parts, that of course commanded—and rightly so—the major attention.

Two key cuts have plagued *Frankenstein* ever since its release. One is the removal of Clive's line —"Now I know what it feels like to be God"— after the Monster has been successfully brought to life, the removal of the line and the accompanying footage resulting in an awkward jump cut that weakens Clive's near hysteria. The other is the more notorious scene: Karloff's happy dalliance with the child by the lake, and how he unwittingly throws her into the lake, expecting her to float like the daisies that she has thrown in. Initially, audiences were either shocked by its apparent callousness, or amused by its incongruity; the result, in either case, was laughter—and destruction of the mood. The scene was cut, although the sudden appearance of the father, holding his child's mud-caked body, unfortunately suggests a crime of bestiality rather than one of lack of comprehension.

Frankenstein not only shows that Whale had studied the silent and specifically, the German cinema well—there are obvious echoes from *The Cabinet of Dr. Caligari* and *The Golem*—but it also stresses the theatricality that was always to be a cornerstone of Whale's work.

Mordant humor was equally present, although in this initial film, more serious in concept than most of its successors, it is largely absent, and the jovial Baron Frankenstein—inexplicably stage English, despite his name and ancestry, complete with monocle and stereotyped "aristocratic" accent—is used as an antidote to the generally downbeat atmosphere. The theatricality could hardly be more pronounced than in the scene of the Monster's creation, which Dr. Frankenstein literally stages for his guests, by seating them in chairs while he performs his experiment. When the Monster is unveiled to the audience, the confontation is first delayed, and then developed slowly. The Monster is seen in several varied closeups, the action freezing until we have had a good look at him, much as a noted actor will pause on stage for his initial appearance, accept the applause, and then go into his performance. This gradual revelation of his principal menace is a device that Whale repeated

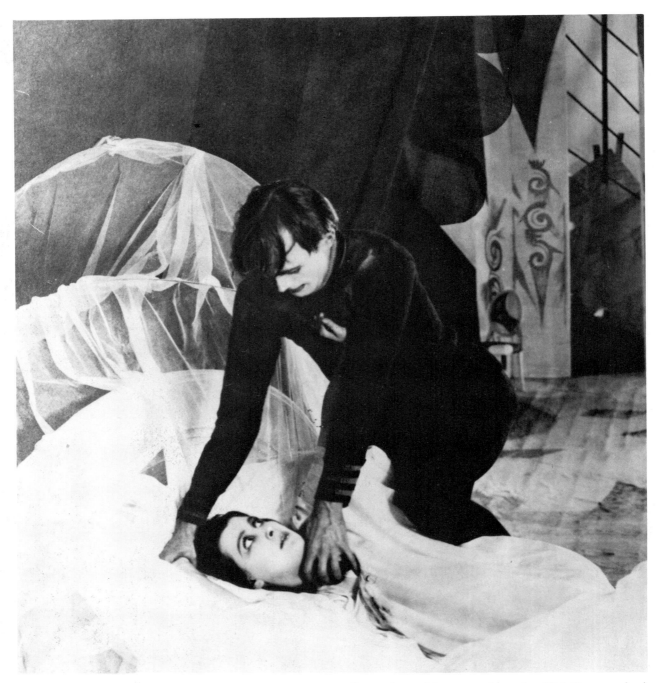

Conrad Veidt, Lil Dagover

Comparison with a scene from the 1919 German classic *The Cabinet of Dr. Caligari* stresses the close relationship between James Whale's 1931 film and the silent German films of the macabre.

Frankenstein (1931): Boris Karloff, Mae Clarke

Superb examples of the high sets utilized in *The Bride of Frankenstein* (1935). Left, Dwight Frye; right, Ernest Thesiger, Colin Clive.

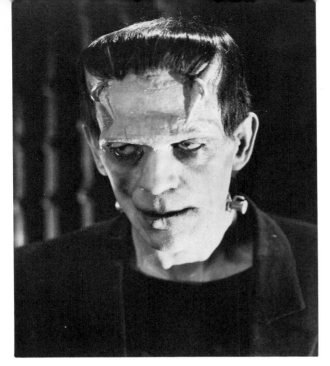

Boris Karloff in an early test makeup for the Frankenstein monster; it was later modified.

profitably in other films: *The Old Dark House*, in particular, and twice in *The Bride of Frankenstein*.

Bravura exits and entrances punctuated all of Whale's films, as did his use of huge windows as a backdrop to form a logical, if not totally realistic proscenium arch. Frequently too, Whale would track his always mobile cameras *through* the walls of multi-roomed sets, as if to remind us that none of this was real, but an exercise in theatrical style. Perhaps most of all, he knew exactly how to pinpoint editing (long shot cutting to closeup), camera movement, and lighting, to get the most out of a given line of dialogue. Interviewed in the New York *Post* in August of 1973, actress Susan Clark commented on the necessity of having "in depth" roles and writing for an actor to make an impression. She asked: "How can anyone make a dramatic impact on audiences with the line, 'Please pass the potato salad'?" Obviously, she had never

Frankenstein: The Monster tries to kill his creator. Karloff, Colin Clive

James Whale clowns for the publicity photographer on the set of *Frankenstein*.

seen James Whale direct Ernest Thesiger in a classic reading of an even simpler line—"Have a potato"—one of the thespian joys and highlights of *The Old Dark House*!

THE BRIDE OF FRANKENSTEIN

(Universal, 1935) Directed by James Whale. Produced by Carl Laemmle Jr. Camera, John Mescall. Screenplay by John L. Balderston and William Hurlbut. Music by Franz Waxman. Special effects by John Fulton.

With Boris Karloff, Colin Clive, Valerie Hobson, Elsa Lanchester, Ernest Thesiger, O. P. Heggie, *Dwight Frye, E. E. Clive, Una O'Connor, Anne Darling, Douglas Walton, Gavin Gordon, Neil Fitzgerald, John Carradine, Reginald Barlow, Mary Gordon, Tempe Piggott, Lucien Prival, Ted Billings, Grace Cunard, Rollo Lloyd, Walter Brennan, Harry Northrup, Joseph North, D'Arcy Corrigan, Jack Curtis, Helen Gibson, Frank Terry.*

Beginning with a crackling thunderstorm, in the midst of which Mary Shelley, in a spacious chamber and accompanied by a charming minuet, tells of the further adventures of Dr. Frankenstein and his Monster, we are immediately taken back to the burning ruins of the old mill which saw the climax of the first film. Cheating a little, the sequel implies Frankenstein's death at the hands of the Monster, and has him regain his senses only after being brought home in a stately funeral procession. By far the best of Universal's eight *Frankenstein* films, *The Bride of Frankenstein* is probably also the best of the entire man-made-monster *genre* from any period. If one judges a horror film only by the genuine fright that it inspires, then *Bride* might perhaps have to take a secondary position, but in terms of style, visual design, literate scripting, performance, music, and just about every other individual ingredient, it is virtually unsurpassed. As an essay in Gothic *Grand Guignol*, it overtakes its predecessor and yet, despite its care and lavish budget, it still manages to retain much of the rough-edged quality of the original, which the later ones failed to achieve or, more probably, deliberately avoided.

There are admitted flaws. It tries a little too hard to become the absolute peak of its *genre,* and while it succeeded (so well, that it was not only the peak but also the climax of its particular cycle), its constant succession of shocks and sensations from the first sequence on, work against, rather than for it. One is never again as afraid of the Monster as in his first scene in the charred mill; with less shock and a subtler handling of the character, Murnau's Nosferatu, and Mamoulian's Mr. Hyde became *more* horrendous as their films progressed. Too, the occasional mixture of sex and religions is sometimes close to being offensive, rescued only by James Whale's innate good taste, or the genuine poignancy that Karloff generates. Few other actors could carry off the scenes in which Karloff, trussed up by the mob on a form of crucifix, is photographed almost as a Christ figure; or the delicate and oddly moving scene (it has a Frank Borzage-

The Bride of Frankenstein:
Free again, The Monster seeks refuge in a cemetery.

like sensitivity to it) in which Karloff accidentally stumbles across the cobweb-covered body of the girl who is to be turned into his mate, and hums happily to himself as he strokes her face. (Removal of this scene by British censors lessened the impact of the later scene in which the mate is shown to have emerged as a monstrosity in his own likeness.)

Just as the original *Frankenstein* drew much inspiration from the silent German film, so does *The Bride of Frankenstein*, originally made and publicized as *The Return of Frankenstein*, draw on it too. The movements of Elsa Lanchester's head, the framing of her closeups, are quite clearly patterned on those of Brigitte Helm, as the robot in Fritz Lang's *Metropolis*. Indeed, Brigitte Helm, as well as Louise Brooks, was among the players that Whale had in mind at one time for the role of the Monster's mate. Originally, and briefly roadshown at a 90-minutes-plus length, the film shows signs of having been reshaped, with sequences transposed after completion, and one cut (after the Monster has kidnapped Frankenstein's bride), rendering inexplicable one of Ernest Thesiger's lines. Continuity is a bit vague. It seems as though the redoubtable Dr. Frankenstein has been living in sin, since he and his beloved are sharing the same quarters before their marriage. The period is somewhat in doubt, too, with Thesiger beating Alexander Graham Bell to the invention of the telephone (herein called just "an electrical device"), yet using a great deal of post-Bell equipment in his laboratory work. The post-Production Code moralities of the 30s come through quite plainly, however, in the Burgomaster's admonition that "it is high time every man and *wife* was home in bed."

But it seems churlish to quibble over such a lavish and enjoyable fairy tale, which has genuine pathos to offer along with all its thrills. Karloff's performance remains one of his best, although not surprisingly, Ernest Thesiger steals the whole show with a marvelously written and played bravura performance as the mad Dr. Praetorius, who enjoys a light snack of bread and cheese, toasting a skull atop a pile of bones, before getting down to his graveyard endeavors. Dwight Frye, too, gets some of the best and juiciest lines of his career in this film.

Entirely studio made (unlike *Frankenstein*, which did use one or two actual exteriors and deliberately contrasted the serenity of the real world with the nightmare world of laboratories, gibbets, and graveyards), *The Bride* is never at too many

Dr. Praetorius and aides discover the cadaver they need in the creation of a mate for the Monster.

Dr. Frankenstein is joined in his work by the insane Dr. Praetorius, played by Ernest Thesiger.

Dwight Frye, the scientists' assistant; medically valueless, but adept at procuring "fresh hearts."

Befriended by a hermit, the Monster is introduced to the pleasure of smoking . . .

. . . and drinking. In this curious episode, the scene fades out to spotlight the crucifix at left.

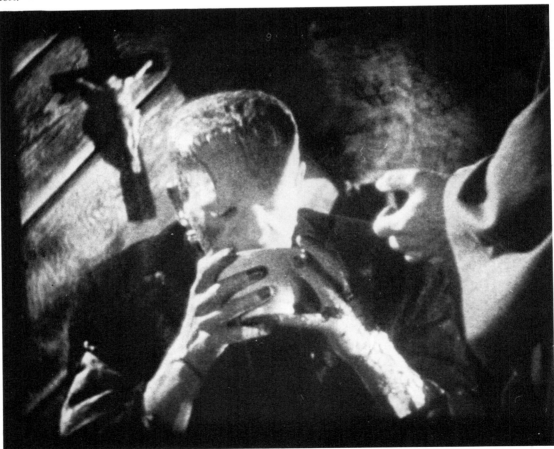

46

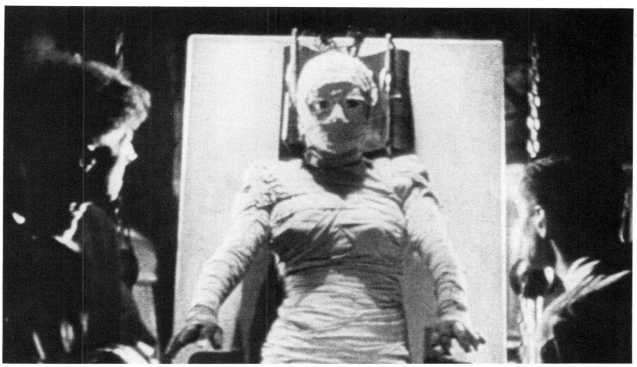

The creation of a new monster. The end result: Elsa Lanchester.

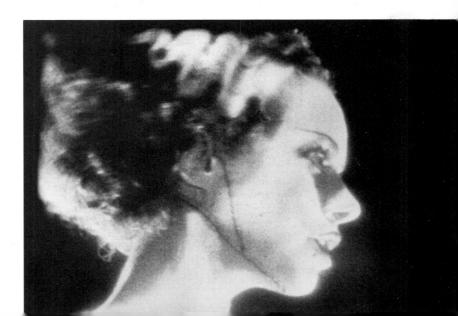

Ernest Thesiger standing below the convenient lever that causes the last-reel destruction of Monster, Mate and himself.

pains to make its sets convincing, but since they are consistent, with a grey twilight predominating, they work. The trick work—especially involving Thesiger's miniature people in bottles, an episode played largely for comedy—is always ingenious, and the long laboratory scenes are the best and most elaborate ever created for this kind of film. (The laboratory set itself, with its stress on height, accented by tilted camerawork, is a beauty.) Franz Waxman's score, ranging from the march theme, as the dimwitted villagers take to their torches yet again, to the peals of church bells when the bride is presented, is likewise superb. The interior sets, making good use of painted shadows and also of such standing sets as the crypt, used earlier in *Dracula*, and later in *The Mystery of Edwin Drood*, are all beautifully designed—though one does wonder what kind of oversized delinquents ran wild through the countryside with such regularity as to justify the presence of that huge stone throne with chains and neck-clamps, all conveniently exactly the Monster's size.

48

The plot humanized the Monster somewhat this time, bringing him in contact with a blind hermit, introducing him to the pleasures of drink and music, and allowing him to learn a little English—a sequence suggested by, though hardly copied from, a like episode in the original novel. His new found wisdom persuades him to return Dr. Frankenstein and his bride to freedom and life in the last sequence, while (presumably) killing himself, his mate, and the colorful Dr. Praetorius (who, after all, had been a genuine friend to him) with one of those convenient all-purpose levers that exist in most horror-movie laboratories as a handy last-reel tidy-upper. "Don't touch that lever—you'll blow us all to atoms!" cautions Dr. Praetorius. No more explanation is offered for its existence than is vouchsafed for why the Monster survives the ensuing holocaust (in the sequel), but his mate does not.

SON OF FRANKENSTEIN

(Universal, 1939) Produced and directed by Rowland V. Lee. Screenplay by Willis Cooper. Camera, George Robinson. Art Direction, Jack Otterson and Richard Riedel. Music, Frank Skinner.

With Basil Rathbone, Boris Karloff, Bela Lugosi, Lionel Atwill, Josephine Hutchinson, Emma Dunn, Donnie Dunagan, Edgar Norton, Gustav von Seyffertitz, Lionel Belmore, Tom Ricketts, Ward Bond, Clarence Wilson, Lawrence Grant, Perry Ivins, Michael Park, Caroline Cooke, Lorimer Johnson.

Although James Whale was still at Universal, and in 1939 made *Green Hell*, Rowland V. Lee was getting the bigger plums now, and was handed *Son of Frankenstein*, *Tower of London*, and *The Sun Never Sets*, all of them films far better suited to Whale's talents. Lee had nowhere near Whale's taste, and veered toward the unpleasant far more than Whale had ever done. However, Lee was expert at imitating the style of others, and the best of *Son of Frankenstein* is the best of Whale. Lee's own style was plodding and Germanic, and *Son of Frankenstein* at 10 reels is much too long to sustain feelings of terror or genuine excitement. Since an obnoxious brat of a child obviously has no fear of the Monster, we, the audience, have little reason to be scared either. Moreover, in its attempts at "class," the film downplays physical action: the

Monster's first appearance comes very late in the day, and episodes of violence—murders, nocturnal prowlings, the laboratory scenes—are cursory.

Nevertheless, it's a fascinating film, and if only on the level of its art direction, sets, lighting, and overall visual elegance, must certainly rank as the second best film in the series. Via constant rain, thunder, and gloomy darkness, it creates its own nightmare world: we never see the sun or sense the fresh air, and the only trees we see are all dead. The little town is as unreal as Douglas Fairbanks' Bagdad, but is as convincing, since Lee never shows it to us in juxtaposition to things that *are* real. Everything—from the rain to the door knocker and the distorted stairway—is magnified to giant, dreamlike proportions. It is one of the most exciting, and certainly one of the most Germanic visual moods to be created by any Hollywood film, especially notable in that rather prosaic period.

The Monster's voice is discarded, but his humanity retained in his love for his friend, Ygor (an ex-shepherd who somehow survived the gallows), and his fascination for books of nursery rhymes. However, on being brought back to full strength, he rampages through the countryside, killing off the jurymen responsible for Ygor's "execution," and is eventually disposed of by being knocked into a volcanic sulphur pit. The villagers retain their fickle reliability: unreasonably hostile at the beginning of the film, they are all smiles and devotion at the end as they bid Baron Frankenstein farewell at the railway station . . . blissfully unaware that Sir Cedric Hardwicke, another son, is within commuting distance a couple of stops down the line!

The melodrama is a little more logical in *Son of Frankenstein* than in its predecessor. The performances are restrained, Lugosi being especially good and touching as Ygor (one of his best and most underrated performances), Atwill lends dignity and his excellent diction to a strong role, but Rathbone, sad to say, hams it up rather badly, even allowing for the hysterical note on which his role is written. The dialogue is a joy, though the best lines are those underplayed ones that become funny only in context, as opposed to the rich and fruity dialogue of *The Bride of Frankenstein.*

"Strange country . . ." muses Rathbone, looking at the forest of dead trees and dry-ice mist. Examining the Monster, he also diagnoses that "no human heart could beat like that," quite forgetting that it is the "very fresh" heart that the enterpris-

Son of Frankenstein (1939): A new friend for the monster: Ygor, played by Bela Lugosi.

ing Dwight Frye acquired by somewhat direct methods in the previous film. The maid's solemn little verse—"When the house is filled with dread, place the beds at head to head"—is a piece of Transylvaniana worth remembering, as is Lugosi's ambiguous "He does things for me!" referring to his chumminess with the Monster. Atwill has one marvelous lapse in tact when he is describing a victim's mutilations ("The cart passed over his chest . . . his heart burst!") and raises the blanket just in time to give the corpse's grief-stricken widow a good eyeful. But perhaps the best line comes when poor Edgar Norton, the doctor's assistant, as also in *Dr. Jekyll and Mr. Hyde,* has vanished. A helpful servant offers the information: "We sent him up to the nursery for the baby's supper tray, and we haven't seen him since." Lines like this seem to fit in the surrealist nightmare framework of the whole, in which a man-eating tot would seem not at all out of place.

An example of the fine sets of *Son of Frankenstein,* which look even better (with more height and richer lighting) in the film itself. Edgar Norton, Basil Rathbone, Josephine Hutchinson, Donnie Dunnagan, Emma Dunn.

Son of Frankenstein: Basil Rathbone, Lionel Atwill

50

THE GHOST OF FRANKENSTEIN

(Universal, 1942) Director, Erle C. Kenton. Produced by George Waggner. Screenplay by Scott Darling, from a story by Eric Taylor. Camera, Milton Krasner, Woody Bredell. Art Director, Jack Otterson. Music Director, Charles Previn.

With Lon Chaney, Jr., Evelyn Ankers, Sir Cedric Hardwicke, Ralph Bellamy, Bela Lugosi, Lionel Atwill, Doris Lloyd, Olaf Hytten, Leyland Hodgson, Janet Ann Gallow, Otto Hoffman, Dwight Frye, Barton Yarborough, Holmes Herbert, Lawrence Grant, Brandon Hurst, Julius Tannen, Harry Cording, Dick Alexander, Ernie Stanton, George Eldredge, Jimmy Phillips, Teddy Infuhr, Michael Mark, Lionel Belmore.

The Ghost of Frankenstein (1942): Lon Chaney, Jr. assumes the role of the Monster.

Apparently not hurt by the sulphur pit, though slowed up a little, the Monster is brought back to renewed, but not total vigor, by a direct hit from a bolt of lightning, and is taken in hand by the faithful Ygor, likewise unaffected by the bellyful of bullets from Basil Rathbone's gun. "We go to new country—better place than this!" remarks Ygor, an unarguable statement in view of the set of desolation and dead trees in which the decision is made. So off they trot to the home town of a second Frankenstein son, who is to be victimized into repeating his father's experiment. Once again, the intent is to place a normal brain in the Monster's head; and once again, with Atwill and Lugosi on hand, the intent is doomed to failure.

The last good and reasonably serious entry in Universal's *Frankenstein* series, and the last one to be able to produce a genuine Frankenstein as the scientist, *The Ghost of Frankenstein* is probably the least appreciated of the entire series. Too often dismissed, because it isn't as good as the first three (and there's no denying that it isn't), and because it heralds the reduction of the series to programmer status, it is still vastly superior to the three penny-dreadfuls that followed (each one sinking a little lower than its predecessor), until Universal killed the series off with an Abbott and Costello lampoon. In its own way though, it is a model of its kind, and almost matches that other 68-minute gem, *The Most Dangerous Game,* in the story values, incident, cast, production values, and pacing crammed into its fast moving six reels.

If it has less style and more stress on action and sensation, it is partly because the expert and versatile Erle C. Kenton (no stranger to horror films) was still no James Whale, and because Lon Chaney, Jr., taking over from Karloff, played the Monster purely as a beast (backed up by distorted from-the-ground-up angles to emphasize his height) with none of the innate sympathy that Karloff brought to the role. Some of the physical detail in the film— the brain being wheeled into the lab on a trolley and into a closeup, almost like a tray of desserts in a restaurant, and the Monster's face blistering in the climactic fire scene—seemed very strong stuff in 1942, but they have less impact today when horror films have inured audiences to physically repellent sights.

As usual in this series, there are some glaring inconsistencies from picture to picture, and *The Ghost of Frankenstein* has its full quota. The villagers, so radiantly happy at the end of *Son of Frankenstein,* are full of gloom and despair again at the beginning of this one. "My child is hungry

The Ghost of Frankenstein: Evelyn Ankers, Sir Cedric Hardwicke, Janet Ann Gallow and Lon Chaney Jr.

. . . there is no bread!" complains one whining mother, as though the poor Monster was to blame for that, too. At least two of the town council, killed off in *Son,* are still in office here. The Monster learned to talk in *Bride,* and he was mute again in *Son;* here he talks again with Lugosi's brain in his skull. But in the sequel, where Lugosi himself plays the Monster, he loses his voice yet again! The dialogue has some curious anachronisms: "There'll be a new Mayor after the Fall election!" is a threat that seems far too American to apply to middle-Europe.

But the cast is in grand form: Dwight Frye rushes forward to urge the destruction of Frankenstein's castle, and Atwill underplays, with superb aplomb, as he talks about the "slight miscalculation" that had him drummed out of the medical profession. And dear old Sir Cedric Hardwicke, rather tactlessly reminding Atwill of the incident, winds up with a lame and condescending "But you blazed the trail!" while Atwill glares daggers at him. Hardwicke is a logical blood relation to Colin Clive and Basil Rathbone, appearing quite effectively as the ghost of his father in one brief sequence. As always, at Universal, the special effects—lab scenes, fire, exploding castles—are flawlessly done, the miniatures well nigh perfect.

The Ghost of Frankenstein is in many ways the last of the vintage horror films. Val Lewton, *The Uninvited* and *Dead of Night* were about to bring a new sophistication and literacy to the *genre*. If *The Ghost* is already an assembly line job, it's a good, thoroughly professional, and highly entertaining one, an honorable close to a solid decade of first rate chillers.

FRANKENSTEIN: A wrap-up

Universal's final four *Frankenstein* films, while spiraling steadily downhill, and hardly classics even by comparative standards, at least deserve a nod of appreciation in passing. The first four *Frankensteins,* having so thoroughly milked and repeated the basic situations, there was literally nowhere left to go, Universal came up with the new gimmick (itself doomed to early standardization) of co-starring their Monsters. First, came 1943's *Frankenstein Meets the Wolf Man,* by far the weakest of the series. It was a slick, workmanlike job, done with the speed and streamlined efficiency that director Roy William Neill was, over the same period, expending on Universal's modernized Sherlock Holmes thrillers. To its credit was one of Universal's best and most atmospheric graveyard sequences, a suspenseful and well designed episode that got the film off to a lively start. Essentially, the film was a sequel to *The Wolf Man,* and the Monster was a relative guest star.

For some reason, Universal had a great many second thoughts about the production (rare for their bigger productions, most uncommon for a programmer), and changes were made during and after production. One of the basic decisions was to follow through directly from *The Ghost of Frankenstein* and to leave the Monster blind. Lugosi played the role that way, and effectively. Later, the idea was scrapped—but not to the extent of re-shooting all of the existing footage, so that Lugosi's movements and actions sometimes become inexplicable for one who was not now supposed to be blind. Greater time and care was lavished on Chaney's Wolf Man characterization, including more elaborate makeup changeovers from man to beast. In the original, the transformations had been effected by concentrating on his feet, with a facial transformation reserved only for the final sequence. Here, the transformations, smoothly done, were executed via facial closeups. The only member of the Frankenstein family represented was Ilona Massey—playing the same character as Evelyn Ankers in *The Ghost of Frankenstein,* although inexplicably shed of husband Ralph Bellamy.

Chaney, as the Wolf Man who has made an unexplained return from the dead, finds that his father (earlier played by Claude Rains) has died of grief, and now desires a permanent death himself. Discovering the still alive body of the Monster frozen in ice, he hits upon the idea of having scientist Patric Knowles transmit his energy to the

Frankenstein Meets the Wolf Man (1943): The film starts promisingly with a graveyard sequence in which Lon Chaney Jr., a werewolf, returns to life when his grave is despoiled . . .

. . . and resumes his werewolfery.

Equal size of Lon Chaney Jr. and Bela Lugosi (left) as Monster reduced menace of the latter.

Frankenstein's old laboratory and notebooks were brought into play. The opening sequence in a prison cell showed mad scientist Dr. Niemann (Boris Karloff) telling a psychopathic hunchback (J. Carrol Naish) what Frankenstein had achieved by placing the brain of a dog in the head of a man—something the worthy doctor had certainly never attempted. Escaping, they encounter (and subsequently murder) Professor Lampini (George Zucco), whose traveling chamber of horrors features the bodies of the Monster (Glenn Strange), the Wolf Man (Chaney), and Count Dracula (claimed to have been stolen from the Count's castle in Transylvania, despite the fact that that was the one spot where he had *never* died!). Needless to say, it is but a matter of moments before Karloff has the boys restored to life, all dressed up and ready to go to work settling his own personal scores.

Dracula, played this time—and very well—by John Carradine, murders the burgomaster and then reverts back to skeleton form when he cannot retrieve his coffin before sunrise. The Wolf Man falls in love with the girl beloved of the Hunchback. When the moon rises, he kills her—but not before she has fired into his heart the fatal silver

Monster, thereby killing himself. With the operation in progress, however, Knowles is obsessed with the notion of seeing the Monster at its full powers. As the moon rises, Chaney becomes a Wolf Man again, and he and the Monster battle it out to the death, during which time a disgruntled villager dynamites a dam. Both Monsters are (presumably) drowned in the flood, and the last of the Frankensteins—Miss Massey—disappears from the screen into matrimonial bliss. Incidentally, the Monster's scanty education received another setback, and for the second time in his career he forgot that he could talk!

Frankenstein Meets the Wolf Man had less atmosphere than any of the previous films; its photography and lighting were brighter and more cheerful; and a lengthy village festival allowed some song and dance to creep in for light relief. However, there was some atmospheric compensation—the title and cast credits are formed from wisps of smoke emerging from test tubes. The film having presumably paid off, Universal went it one better in 1945 with *The House of Frankenstein*, originally announced under the more original title of *The Devil's Brood*. No member of the illustrious medical family appeared in this opus, although

Lon Chaney Jr., Bela Lugosi, Maria Ouspenskaya.

In *House of Frankenstein* (1944) Boris Karloff returned to the fold as a mad doctor.

bullet he had given her for such emergencies. Methodically, the Monster then kills the Hunchback, and he and mad doctor Karloff literally force their way into the ooze of a quicksand. They are pursued by the inevitable howling mob of villagers who, after twenty-four years of this sort of behavior, should have been sufficiently familiar with the pattern of things to stay at home and let nature take its course. With nobody else left alive for the camera to pan around to, *The House of Frankenstein* climaxes with a closeup of Karloff's head disappearing beneath the mud, with the "End" title superimposed. Despite its all star cast, and the return of Karloff to the fold, the film was the silliest and dullest of the entire series. In its nonstop and methodical rushing through stock horror sequences, it approached the standardization of

House of Dracula (1944): Onslow Stevens, Glenn Strange

the "B" Western, and even lacked the kind of bravura dialogue that at least can provide a pseudo-Gothic veneer.

While at this stage Universal were still reasonably careful about observing all the standard laws of mythology, they threw them recklessly overboard later that same year in *The House of Dracula* which, like its immediate predecessor, was directed by Erle C. Kenton. Incredibly, with years of mayhem behind him, Chaney's Wolf Man suddenly became the hero! Carefully seeing to it that he had no occasion to murder anyone this time, and hoping that the memories of the Production Code administrators were faulty (or perhaps assuming that his previous three deaths compensated for his previous murders), the writers contrived to have Chaney come to mad scientist, Onslow Stevens, seeking death. Stevens, however, assures him that he can be cured—and cured he is, to settle down happily with the heroine for the fadeout. Dracula, again in the person of John Carradine, had little to do, although he did manage to contaminate the blood of otherwise quite sympathetic scientist, Stevens, and drive him to madness and death. The Monster (Glen Strange again) was never even off the operating table until the final reel, and by now

he had degenerated into being a useful henchman, no longer a creature even of menace, let alone horror. The film contained an interesting nightmare montage composed of stock footage from earlier films. But while it was an obvious attempt to repeat the formula of *The House of Frankenstein,* and was the shortest (67 minutes) and cheapest film in the once great series, it was at least a trifle better than its immediate forerunner. Despite budget shortcomings, it was a fairly taut and sober little film, and there was a welcome attempt at some kind of Gothic style. Clearly, the series was at an end, but it was not altogether an ignoble one.

However, anyone who thought that Universal's Monsters were finished was vastly mistaken. Back they were at work in 1948 in *Abbott and Costello Meet Frankenstein,* which restored Lugosi to his Dracula characterization, while Glenn Strange continued as the Monster. Poor old Chaney wasn't allowed to enjoy his new-found domestic happiness; with no mention of his "cure," he was up to his old Werewolfery again, albeit with good intentions in that he was trying to thwart the activities in America of Dracula and the Monster. To Universal's credit, they staged the horror sequences with all the care of old. The visuals were extremely

House of Dracula (1944): Jane Adams, Lon Chaney Jr., Onslow Stevens as the scientist, and Glenn Strange as the Monster.

Abbott and Costello Meet Frankenstein (1948): In Universal's farewell to a long-running series, Bela Lugosi returned as Dracula. (Lou Costello, right.)

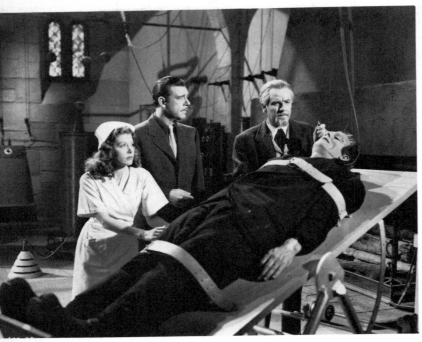

Peter Cushing, the new Dr. Frankenstein in the 1960's
and Christopher Lee, the new Monster.

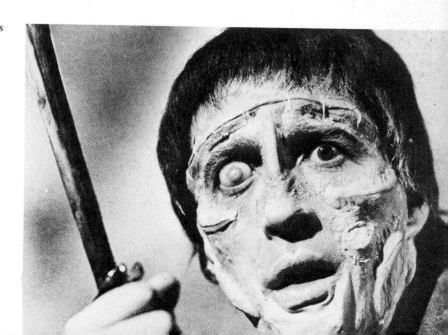

Typical latter-day monsters, attempting to revive the Frankenstein tradition: *The Creature from the Black Lagoon* (1954).

Tarantula (1955): Leo G. Carroll as the scientist who made a slight miscalculation in his experiments with spiders.

handsome, some glass shots of Dracula's castle, and some vampiric bat-into-human transformations being as good as anything Universal's horror, special effects technicians had done in their heyday. At 92 minutes, the film was the longest of all the Frankenstein films (apart from *Son of Frankenstein* which was a few minutes longer), and was also the longest and best of the recent Abbott and Costello comedies. (Their work and popularity had been slipping, too. The success of the film gave them a much needed boost, which Universal cashed in on rather typically by following through with cheap imitations—encounters with the Invisible Man, the Mummy, et al.—until their restored reputations were all but demolished again.)

In *Abbott and Costello Meet Frankenstein*, directed by Charles Barton (who proved surprisingly adaptable to unfamiliar *Grand Guignol* material), Universal did satirize horror traditions, often to amusing effect, but they never ridiculed them. The stars were allowed to play their roles straight. But, alas, all of the age old laws of the supernatural were ignored: Dracula's reflection shows in a mirror, Vampire and Werewolf both die by drowning, and the Monster, burning to death for the fifth time, was understandably somewhat *blasé* about it all. Overlooked, too, were the several minor characters who had been bitten by either Lugosi or Chaney, and thus were candidates for monstrosities themselves.

Although a co-starring appearance with Abbott and Costello seemed the final and most inglorious of exits for the *Frankenstein* Monster, it was merely the end of one existence, with reincarnation waiting just around the corner. The public domain status of the Frankenstein Monster and Dracula threw them on the none-too-tender mercies of other producers, and from the mid-1950s on, they—and others of their brethren—returned with a vengeance, in both elaborate color remakes and cheap quickies. They appeared in sexploitation nudie movies, and as the villains in Westerns. In addition, they were merchandized and expoited to the hilt via comics, makeup kits, horror masks, and sundry other devices. But Universal's own copyrights at least protected the physical likenesses of their creations, and no subsequent embodiments of the Frankenstein Monster have ever quite compared with their original.

In 1973, television also took up the *Frankenstein* legend. Its elaborate versions (one ran for four one-hour instalments) claimed to be the first adaptation which really respected both the intent and content of the original novel. (There was some justification for the claim, but no cause for jubilation over the results.)

The Mole People (1956)

The Horror of Party Beach (1964): An obviously not very frightening sea mutant

Monster on the Campus (1958): Arthur Franz, soon to be infected and transformed by a virus transmitted from a prehistoric fish.

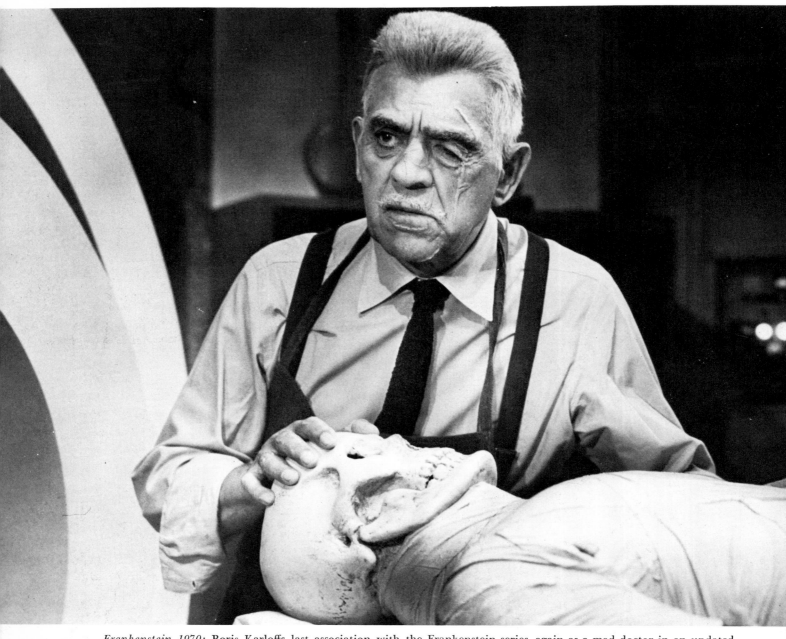

Frankenstein 1970: Boris Karloffs last association with the Frankenstein series, again as a mad doctor in an updated and silly modern story.

Almost a blueprint for the scene in *Bride of Franken-stein* in which scientist Ernest Thesiger creates and displays miniature humans in bottles, in this pre-1910 episode from one of the trick films of Georges Melies.

One of the many direct offshoots of the Frankenstein monster: the French (1937) version of *The Golem*.

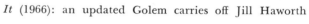

It (1966): an updated Golem carries off Jill Haworth

4 Vampyr

The vampire (Henriette Gerard) looks into the coffin
at her new victim.

(German/French, 1931) Produced and Directed by Carl Theodor Dreyer. Script by Dreyer and Christen Jul, suggested by Sheridan le Fanu's Carmilla. Camera, Rudolf Maté. Music, Wolfgang Zeller. also known as The Strange Adventure of David Gray.

With Julian West, Sybille Schmitz, Henriette Gerard, Jan Hieronimko, Maurice Schutz, Rena Mandel, Albert Bras, N. Babanini.

If one is to judge the effectiveness of the horror film solely by the degree to which it convinces the audience—and thereby frightens it—then *Vampyr* must surely be the greatest horror film of all. Certainly it is the one undisputed masterpiece of the *genre*. Yet it has none of the standard accoutrements of the species: it is devoid of shock, sensation, spooky atmospherics, even of physical action; it leaves far more to the imagination (and mental participation) of the audience than any other horror film. In addition, it has always been so painstakingly slow-paced as to be markedly non-commercial, in direct comparison with the great Gothic horror films of Hollywood's early sound cycle, of which it was an accidental contemporary. For the United States release, and to cash in on that horror market, it was cut down drastically, re-shaped, fitted out with a lurid voice-over narration, and retitled *Castle of Doom*. But you can only shorten a Dreyer film, you cannot speed it up. Even in its one-hour, re-edited form, it was still a slow-moving film, received sparse distribution, and was seen by few people.

Although the film is officially based on, or at least suggested by, Sheridan le Fanu's *Carmilla,* the only real connection between the two is that the Vampire is a woman. Even there the connection is slight, for Dreyer's Vampire is an old woman, entirely lacking Carmilla's sensuous quality, which suggested evil and power, yet at the same time invited a kind of pity, too. Despite her supernatural powers, she depends on the aid of her human aides and slaves; sometimes even on their physical help, since she appears frail and infirm, and the doctor, who is under her spell, helps her to walk, guiding her through doors with all the tenderness of a doctor ministering to a normal aged patient.

Nothing of a sensational nature occurs—or at least, is *shown*—in the entire film. Dreyer did shoot a sequence in which the Vampire summons the wolves of the forest to her aid, but then decided to cut it—ostensibly, because he feared that it might be considered a plagiarism from Bram Stoker's novel *Dracula*. However, it is equally possible that this sequence was removed because it was entirely too literal and physical an illustration of the Vampire's supernatural powers. While making the film, Dreyer outlined his approach to the story:

> Imagine that we are sitting in an ordinary room. Suddenly, we are told that there is a corpse behind the door. In an instant, the room we are sitting in is completely altered; everything in it has taken on another look; the light, the atmosphere have changed, though they are physically the same. This is because *we* have changed, and the objects are as we conceive them. That is the effect I want to get in my film.

That is the effect that he *does* achieve: it is almost as though the whole film takes place in that moment of suspended time, following the shock of being told about the corpse in the next room. The story is told through the eyes of a holiday-maker who stumbles, quite by accident, into the midst of a series of Vampire killings, and who is forced to *believe,* but never quite understands. (The role was played by the film's financial backer, Julian West—better known in non-filmic circles as Baron Nicholas de Gunzburg. He was no actor, but he had the right face and physical presence for the role, wandering through it all as in a somnambulistic trance. Later, he transferred his business activities to New York, where he became the editor of a fashionable sporting magazine, and could frequently be seen walking the streets of New York, his wide-eyed expression suggesting that he was still haunted and pursued by phantoms!)

Few of the physical details in the film are ever explained: a policeman sits down on a bench, and after a moment or two, his shadow arises by itself and walks off—presumably in response to the bidding of the Vampire. Later, it returns, and re-establishes itself in relation to its "owner." Then the policeman arises and walks off, quite properly accompanied by the shadow. Since we see it happen, casually and unsensationally, we have no option but to believe it, even if we cannot understand it. The most convincing evocation of the Vampire's terrible power comes, not from a transformation

The spirit of the policeman leaves his body to answer
the vampire's bidding.

The vampire summons the wolves: a sequence deleted
from the final version.

scene or an ascent from the grave, but from a scene almost illustrative of petty feminine pique.

It is evening, and the local inhabitants have gathered at the inn to relax. As a gay (yet somehow eerie) tune is struck up by the fiddlers, the camera tracks along the outside of the inn, picking up the silhouettes of the dancing and drinking villagers. (In this stylized and distorted form, even the innocent peasantry seem almost like phantoms!) The camera moves past the windows, along the outside walls, and then—as Wolfgang Zeller's grim and powerful score rises to a crescendo—looks down into a cellar where the Vampire stands alone, the empty space around her emphasizing her power. In anger at the pleasures she cannot be a part of, she raises her arms, and in one single subdued shriek, demands that there be quiet. Instantly, the music stops; even a wheel, suspended from the ceiling and turning idly, stops its gyrations in response to her command. There is no cutaway to the inn to show that the dancing has indeed stopped, yet we accept blindly that it has. The extremely subtle juxtaposition of sound with camera movement aids in this concealment of rational explanation; we hear sounds, and only gradually does the camera pan slowly to the source, which often does not satisfy us. The very sparse dialogue likewise frustrates more than it enlightens. At one point, the hero asks about the barking dogs (wolves?) and crying children (victims of the Vampire?) that he (and we) have heard, only to be told brusquely that "There are no dogs or children here," and the matter is dropped. A ledger about his research on Vampirism, left by one of the victims to be read after his death, actually tells us nothing more about Vampires than is generally known in mythology. A religious mural, illuminated by a flickering candle, somehow seems unholy and evil; a villager, scythe across his back, and the sharply angular figure of a woman (a witch?) that forms the inn's sign and rocks gently in the night-time breeze—innocent objects that seem to take on an evil life of their own in this naturalistic, yet unreal world.

The unreality is further stressed by Dreyer and his cameraman, Maté, who shot the entire film at dawn and dusk; thus everything is blurred into an existence that is neither night nor day—life nor death. It is impossible to see anything really clearly, impossible to decide where fact leaves off and imagination begins. Only the deaths, and the bloodless corpses, provide real evidence of the Vampire's existence. More than any other film, *Vampyr* suc-

cessfully re-creates that odd dreamlike sensation of both participating and being a spectator. This is magnificently visualized in one single shot where the hero is investigating a deserted barn; as he climbs a ladder and peers through a trap door, the camera becomes *his* eyes and subjectively examines the room. Then it completes its circular movement to pick up the figure of the hero, already some distance away, giving the audience the genuinely chilling sensation of being two entities at one and the same time.

This theme is later explored in-depth on a *tour de-force* sequence, where the hero, weak from loss of blood (a transfusion given to one of the Vampire's victims) dreams that he discovers his own body in a coffin, and becomes witness to and participant in his own burial. Done almost entirely in subjective camera shots, a corpse-eye view (through the glass window of the coffin) of the journey to the cemetery, this sequence draws much of its power, not only from the audience's innate fear of death, but also from its distaste for the *ritual* of death. Its great shot—the Vampire looking coldly and unemotionally through the glass—manages to cap its already claustrophobic horror by suggesting that death is not necessarily the end, and that unholy possession after death is much worse. Incidentally, this sequence illustrates the unique quality of Dreyer, and the futility of trying to copy him. Few directors have ever tried; not even his old camerman, Rudolph Maté, who later became a noted director himself. However, the French director Georges Rouquier did in his 1947 classic, *Farrebique,* attempt to copy the subjective, photographic style of *Vampyr's* burial sequence. It was the only mistake in that otherwise classic film; not only was the borrowing from Dreyer obvious and jarring, but such a stylized sequence in an otherwise warm and naturalistic film was totally out of place and disruptive of the film's own natural rhythm.

The dreamlike quality of *Vampyr* is sustained, not just by the dawn-dusk shooting, but also by the white, mist-like quality of the photography. Initially, Dreyer had intended to have his human villain, the doctor, killed off by being dragged down into quicksand. But by accident, he discovered an old flour mill. The white dust in the air, coating the walls, caused him to adapt the visual style of the film to that motif. Not only did the use of white—symbol of innocence and purity—add to the deliberate ambiguity of the film (and enable the villain to be suffocated in cascading

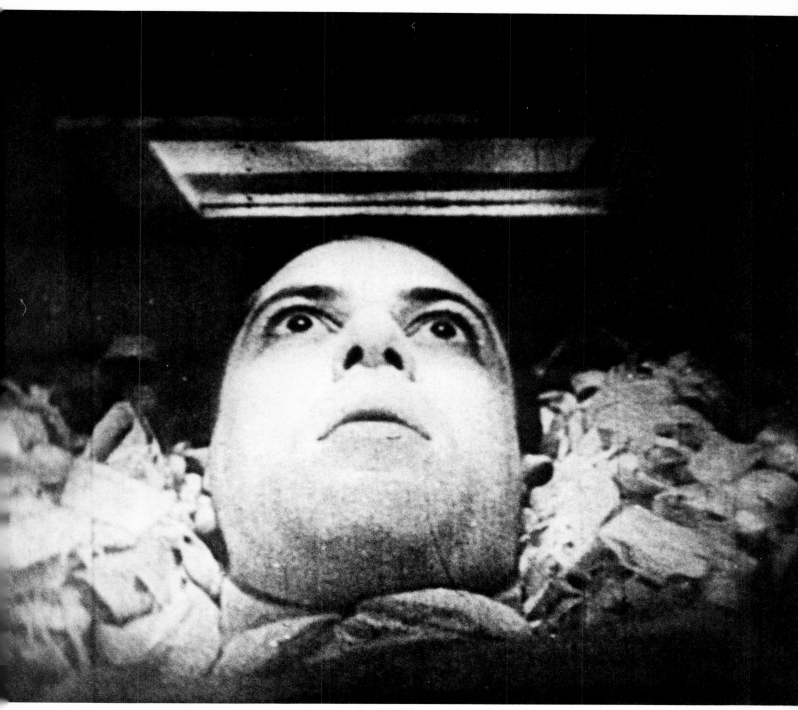

Julian West, as David Gray, dreams of his own funeral.

white flour, instead of drowning in black mud), but it also added to the dreamlike and even Freudian quality of the narrative. Not only were all the actions seen in the indistinct world of twilight, but they were seen through a white haze. It created that old and terrifying dream sensation of trying to escape from unseen pursuers through water, and having one's flight impeded through intangible forces, unseen, yet all around. It is almost symbolic of the film's visual ambiguity that one of its most famous and oft-used stills (a closeup of the dead policeman's face, after he has fallen down some stairs) is *always* printed upside down, and retains its hypnotic power, even though a mandolin seems to be suspended from the ceiling rather than propped up on the floor!

But with all of its stylized photography, careful pacing, and brilliant use of non-actors in key roles, *Vampyr's* most chilling moment is a deceptively simple closeup of Sybille Schmitz, a superb German actress, who plays one of the Vampire's victims. She sits, weakened from loss of blood, tended by her innocent, bewildered sister. Suddenly, the Vampire's influence begins to make itself manifest. The face awakens, and in one magnificent single-frame shot, the head slowly turns from right to left, the facial expression changing from one of love and gratitude to animal cunning, then hate, and—as

Sybille Schmitz as the vampire's victim

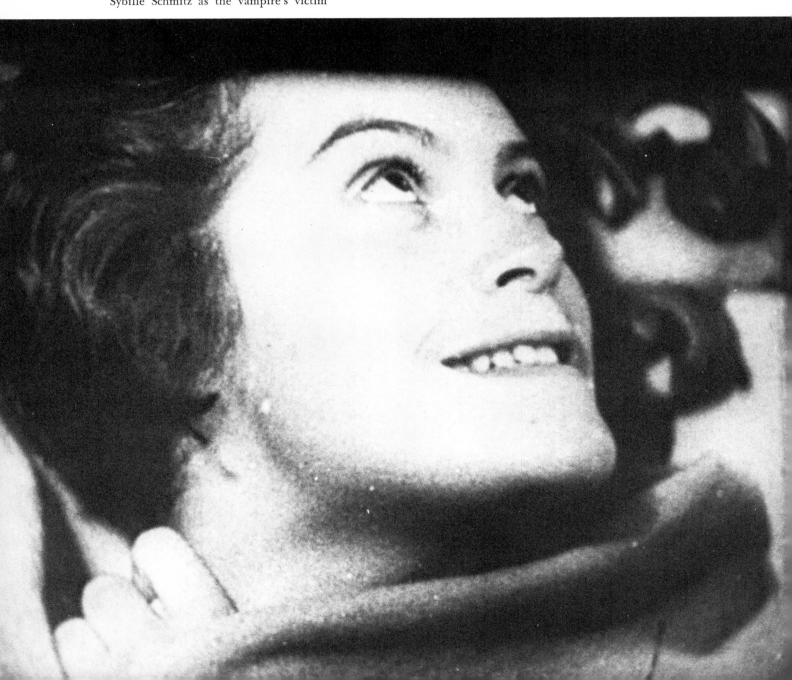

the lips part to reveal strong white teeth and a tongue licking them in obscene blood lust—a final reversion to self-disgust and shame, as the sister, watching in horror, realizes what thoughts are passing through her mind.

It's typical of Dreyer's compassion that he is able to make us fear the stricken sister and yet feel profoundly sorry for her at the same time. The old Vampire is a tool of the forces of evil, almost against her will, and being frail and subject to the unreasonable and rigid restrictions of the supernatural (which, like the world of fairy tales, is unbending in its adherence to the rules) is therefore vulnerable and deserving of our pity. (Conversely, in his later *Day of Wrath,* Dreyer directs all our compassion to the plight of the frail old woman, condemned to be burned as a witch—then allows her a sudden, near-diabolic outburst of defiance which makes us fear her too, and for the first time injects the possibility that she may indeed be a witch!)

Perhaps the key element of *Vampyr* is the uneasiness it creates, and this even extends to the people that Dreyer used. Only Sybille Schmitz and Maurice Schutz were professional actors; the other players were recruited by Dreyer because of their faces, and perhaps because of some ambiguity in their makeup. The fawn-like heroine was actually a nude model, a profession of somewhat less repute then than now. The thoroughly evil doctor was a kindly journalist—and yet Ebbe Neergaard, a Danish critic and friend of Dreyer, has pointed out that there was something innately, if unwittingly sinister about him, something that the camera picked out without his being aware of it. An atmosphere of uncertainty and uneasiness pervades the whole film. Even when the film has finished and hero has rescued heroine, and they have escaped to a safe and happy land, one has the chilling feeling that while these two have escaped, largely by their innocence, the land of phantoms remains behind them—decimated by one Vampire and a handful of human aides—but with the graves still full of further Vampires who will continue their onslaught against the living. One sees the whole film with the sense of someone just behind one's back, and not infrequently one tends to turn and look. There is nothing there of course—nothing *tangible* that is—but such is the power of the film, that one soon turns again, just to make sure!

5 Murder by the Clock

Lilyan Tashman turns her seductive wiles on Lester Vail in a decidedly unromantic locale.

(Paramount, 1931) Directed by Edward Sloman. Screenplay by Henry Myers, from an original story by Rufus King and Charles Beahan. Camera, Karl Struss.

With William Boyd, Lilyan Tashman, Irving Pichel, Regis Toomey, Sally O'Neil, Blanche Frederici, Walter McGrail, Lester Vail, Martha Mattox, Frank Sheridan, Frederick Sullivan, Willard Robertson, Charles D. Brown, John Rogers, Lenita Lane, Harry Burgess.

Murder by the Clock created quite an impact on its original release, perhaps because it drew atmosphere from the just-beginning cycle of horror films to beef up the generally prosaic and talkative quality of the mystery films of the day. Its plot is a good one, even if there is a little cheating by the camera as it shows the tricks pulled by the villain to suggest that a dead woman has returned to life and is perambulating from within her own self-designed crypt. This anticipating-all-emergencies mausoleum not only can be opened only from the inside, but is also equipped with an eerie horn that can be turned on to proclaim that the occupant is not dead, or is at least still quite active!

Needless to say, the horn is heard only when the nerves of the protagonists—and the audience—are already stretched pleasantly taut by the mysterious goings-on. These include the colorful situation of the murderer of the old lady being murdered himself, and being revived by exceptional medical ministrations, only to be confronted by both his attempted killer and the apparent spectre of his own victim. Suffering this double shock, he understandably lapses back into a genuine and permanent death! It's a full-blooded film, and audiences of the time were thoroughly scared by the comparative realism of the tomb and graveyard scenes, and by the unrestrained menace of Irving Pichel, a lecherous giant of a half-wit, than by the more fanciful horrors of Vampires and Monsters.

Those who saw it then remember it fondly, and talk of it with an appreciative shudder; even those who cannot recall the title have never forgotten the horn in the crypt, and the nocturnal prowlings of Blanche Frederici. That it dates today, and fails to live up to one's memories, is perhaps to be expected. It is somewhat slow-paced, and the total lack of any incidental music emphasizes that. On the other hand, it is very much of a "fun" movie.

Lilyan Tashman implants the idea of murder in the brain of half-wit Irving Pichel.

The plot and characters are colorful, and no punches are pulled—especially by Lilyan Tashman, as a svelte modern Lady Macbeth, clad in precarious *derrière*-hugging evening gowns, and turning her sexy wiles on detective, lesser villains, and psychopath alike, when it serves her immediate purpose. The Tashman performance prevents it from being taken too seriously, but, on the other hand, without her tongue-in-cheek villainy, it would all be a good deal less diverting. Visually too (art direction, atmospheric sets, Karl Struss' camerawork), it is handsome, impressive, and always good to look at.

Director Sloman, a good silent director, keeps the film sufficiently on the move so that it avoids the leaden pace of so many of its contemporary talkie mysteries. Quite incidentally, the climax—in which the detective turns his lady over to the police to face murder charges—is quite surprisingly close to the denouement of *The Maltese Falcon,* which it followed into release by a bare couple of months. With the flamboyance of the Tashman and Pichel villainies cornering most of the limelight, it's good to note that the conventional romantic cutaways between Regis Toomey (a cop on the case) and Sally O'Neil (a maid in the house) are virtually just that—editorial cutaways, to establish change of time or locale—and are never given enough footage to get in the way of the enjoyable parade of murder, madness, lechery, and wanderings in the family crypt.

6 Dr. Jekyll and Mr. Hyde

Fredric March in the 1932 version

(Paramount, 1932) Directed by Rouben Mamoulian. Screenplay by Samuel Hoffenstein and Percy Heath, from the story by Robert Louis Stevenson. Camera, Karl Struss.

With Fredric March, Miriam Hopkins, Rose Hobart, Holmes Herbert, Halliwell Hobbes, Edgar Norton, Tempe Piggott, Arnold Lucy.

There have been a dozen or more authentic and respectable versions of the Jekyll and Hyde tale, and in the later years of relaxed censorship, the story was harnessed for sex exploitation purposes as well. But the Fredric March version of 1932 is the best remembered of them all, even though unseen for some 20 years, due to MGM's having bought the property from Paramount to protect its own Spencer Tracy version. During those years, it received no exhibition at all, except—infrequently— at European archives and, as so often happens with "lost" films, generations who had not seen it began to build its reputation in absentia. Fortunately, the film was good enough to survive even this; when it did become available again in the early 1970s, albeit, with a couple of censor cuts, inflicted for a post-Production Code reissue in the 30s, it more than lived up to its reputation, and even managed to surpass it.

Certain juvenile-oriented monster magazines, clearly not having had access to the film for decades, had had the temerity to "apologize" for its transformation scenes, because the film was made before the slick changeover techniques employed by Universal in their Wolf Man and other Monster movies. Quite apart from the subtlety of construction in the changeover scenes, with a subjective camera recording the experience from Jekyll's point of view, the physical depiction of the transformation—already applied makeup becoming visible only when subjected to infra-red light—is far more convincing than the stop-motion techniques, with various stages of makeup, employed in the Wolf Man films. Director Rouben Mamoulian had a tremendous visual sense and an obvious enchantment with the possibilities of the film medium. He didn't even mind appearing banal if he could do it visually. To him, it was more important than appearing intelligent in a literary fashion. His absorption with style for its own sake made his films occasionally seem self-conscious when re-appraised much later. As a result, he is not universally liked by critics and theorists on film, but his contribution in the early days of talkies—when there were too few stylists at work—was enormous. *Dr. Jekyll and Mr. Hyde* (actually a 1931 production, though released in 1932) was only his third film, and is still a remarkable achievement.

While legal and copyright problems were largely responsible for keeping the film in limbo for so long, it is highly probable that certain aspects of the Hyde characterization, which at times took on characteristics of Negro stereotype mixed with Oriental dialect, may—in later, racially more delicate times—have discouraged attempts to overcome those legal problems. Although it is undoubtedly ultra-stylish *Grand Guignol,* in a sense it falls a little short of the 1920 version with John Barrymore, which for pure story-telling is probably the definitive *Jekyll and Hyde.* Even though it took decided liberties with the original story, it pioneered the idea of introducing two women—one sexy and promiscuous, the other pure—to parallel

John Barrymore in the 1920 version

74

7 Freaks

Director Tod Browning with some of his cast

(MGM, 1932) Directed by Tod Browning. Screenplay by Willis Goldbeck, Leon Gordon, Edgar Allan Woolf and Al Boasberg from Spurs *by Tod Robbins. Camera, Merritt B. Gerstad.*

With Wallace Ford, Leila Hyams, Olga Baclanova, Henry Victor, Roscoe Ates, Harry Earles, Daisy Earles, Rose Dione, Daisy Hilton, Violet Hilton, Edward Brophy, Albert Conti, Matt McHugh, Murray Kinnell.

The wedding feast: Harry Earles (back to camera), Olga Baclanova, Henry Victor.

Monsters and monstrosities have almost ceased to qualify as horror factors in this jaded age. An estate overseer, at the beginning of Tod Browning's *Freaks* (1932), refers to the circus sideshow Freaks as "monstrosities that should have been killed at birth," an attitude that the film is quickly at pains to correct. *Freaks* is unfairly regarded (and maligned) as one of the most unpleasant horror films of all time, and it was initially subjected to much editing and censorial harassment. It may once have been more physically repellent, since for road show engagements it did include what one might term a "hard core" sequence of the more grotesque Freaks.

Its climactic reel, a veritable nightmare sequence, does justify its classification as a horror film. But the main problem with *Freaks* has always been that of over-reacting to advance publicity and word of mouth. Audiences, at their first exposure to *Freaks*, are automatically on the defensive, steeled not to be repelled by what they see, sitting rigidly, and prepared to ward off shocks to the sensibilities. And though the shocks don't come (at least, not from the Freaks) it is too late to revise one's attitude, and the short film is over before one can re-adjust. However, on second viewing, a miraculous transformation occurs: almost from the first moment, the Freaks—childlike perhaps, certainly not menacing—take on a surprising warmth. The film is about their world, and it is the "normal" people who become the outsiders.

Admittedly, the normal villains (Olga Baclanova and Henry Victor) are so offensive and almost obscene that one looks forward to their "comeuppance" at the hands of the Freaks, and when that actually happens, the catharsis of approved violence is almost as spectacular as in Sam Peckinpah's *Straw Dogs*, which came much later. Apart from being Tod Browning's warmest and most humane film (probably his only film to justify those ad-

jectives), it is also one of his best in purely film terms, and it is interesting that it completely repudiates the structure of almost all of his other films.

It starts on a fairly prosaic, non-visual level, in which the exposition is verbal and not even particularly enticing—as opposed to silent films like *The Blackbird* and *The Show*, which begin on visually fascinating shots, which are dropped as soon as they have served their purpose of grabbing the collective audience attention. From its beginning *Freaks* builds steadily to a first climax (the bizarre wedding ceremony wherein the big trapeze star marries the midget, while the Freaks drink their health and chant that she is "one of us, one of us!"). Then, instead of relaxing its tempo, it builds at a newly accelerated pace to the final climax. Unlike most Browning climaxes, the finale is visual and largely exterior, in contrast to his typical climaxes where, even in silent films, the characters talk their way to a solution in a claustrophobic interior set. Too, the climax is anticipated, and is not a sudden, ironic twist.

In terms of its nightmare quality—the circus caravan in a thunderstorm at night, the villain trying to murder both hero and heroine, the Freaks, lit by sudden flashes of lightning, slithering through the mud to the rescue—it is full scale *Grand*

Guignol, but with an interesting mixture of realism and fantasy. The hero comes off badly in the fight, is outmatched, doesn't always fight "clean," and is human enough to scream in pain when pinioned against a hot stove. On the other hand, the shots of the Freaks are designed more for their shock impact. An armless, legless torso squirming through the mud with a knife between his teeth doesn't present much of a menace in realistic terms, and it is hard to understand why the able-bodied and long-legged Olga Baclanova isn't able to outdistance her diminutive and handicapped pursuers as they chase her through the forest. But then, the ultimate solution—the transformation of Baclanova into a legless "feathered hen" sideshow Freak—is more nightmare than logic, too, and the film sensibly fades out on shock, not on explanation.

Olga Baclanova as the trapeze star who plans to marry midget Harry Earles for his money

The freaks are aware of the "big woman"'s attempts to poison her husband

The revenge of the freaks: Olga Baclanova as the Feathered Hen

8 The Old Dark House

Boris Karloff, Eva Moore

(Universal, 1932) Directed by James Whale. Produced by Carl Laemmle, Jr. Screenplay by Benn W. Levy with additional dialogue by R. C. Sheriff, from the novel Benighted, *by J. B. Priestley. Camera, Arthur Edeson.*

With Boris Karloff, Melvyn Douglas, Charles Laughton, Raymond Massey, Ernest Thesiger, Gloria Stuart, Lillian Bond, Eva Moore, John Dudgeon, Brember Wills.

The Old Dark House, last seen theatrically in the early 1950s, after which it was withdrawn to make way for William Castle's practically blasphemous "remake," is a film that almost invariably disappoints on its first viewing. In England, it made its first reappearance after a long absence during the later years of World War Two, when the censors had banned the release of new horror films, and older chillers were being reissued to fill the void. In the United States, it became available again—in a very limited way, via archives and film museums—only in the early 1970s.

Whole generations grew up, and knowing only its title, and tantalized by wonderfully atmospheric stills and the reputations of Karloff and James Whale, assumed it was one of the greatest of all horror films. In many ways it is; it is certainly the apotheosis of all "Old House" chillers, and a virtual climax to such works as *The Bat, The Cat and the Canary, The Gorilla, Seven Footprints to Satan,* and other silents and early talkies. Nothing better in this vein has been done before or since. However, on the basis of its name, stars, and reputation, expectations run high—and when one first sees it, those expectations are not altogether fulfilled. Nothing really seems to happen, despite the predicament of five travelers, cut off by floods and landslides and forced to spend a night at the most mysterious of old houses, presided over by the most bizarre of households!

The disappointment was compounded for British audiences. The distributors jazzed up their set of stills by including a genuinely gruesome scene from the old, and then quite forgotten Columbia thriller *Night of Terror,* giving the impression that meaty scenes had been cut from the reissue. But, fortunately, *The Old Dark House* is the kind of film one wants to see more than once, and from the second viewing on, it gains tremendously. One has time then to forget about its lack of spectacular

thrill set-pieces, and just sit back and admire its mood, its style, and its wit. James Whale, a former stage actor and director, handles the film much like a play: it is a series of dramatic entrances and exits; Karloff crashing through a heavily timbered door, a hand appearing on the bannister at the top of the stairs, staying there until it is almost forgotten, then its owner making a dramatic appearance on a near-empty stage; moments of genuine shock providing a form of "curtain," to be followed by a "buffer" scene of tranquility before the next thrill sequence develops. But if the methods are those of the stage, the execution is pure cinema, with a wonderfully mobile camera, Whale's typically effective use of short, sudden closeups, and beautiful lighting. (Arthur Edeson was one of Hollywood's best cameramen, and he did some of his finest work for James Whale.)

Priestley's original novel was rather uneven; he was generally much more at home with his "social," semi-political books and plays—or with his simple, regional comedies of manners, like *When We Are Married,* which dealt with the people and class-distinctions of Yorkshire that he knew so well. Elements of both schools of writing seem to be forced into *Benighted,* and get in the way of the melodrama too often. The one major difference between novel and film was that Priestley killed off his hero, Penderell, whereas the film lets him live—although there are definite indications in the film that this might have been a last minute decision. The well-knit scenario is carefully balanced, pitting the five inhabitants of the house against the five guests. In a very rough kind of way, each has an opposing counterpart, and the night of terror brings out the best (or worst) in all of them, solving all their problems, just as dawn automatically banishes the insoluble fears and dangers of a nightmare. (Somehow, it is a little difficult to consider oneself free of problems with Karloff's semi-mad butler still lumbering around!)

More than just a delightful example of its *genre, The Old Dark House* is a prototype in reverse; a belated blueprint and summing up of all that had gone before in this kind of film, distilling the best from all of them, yet adding so much that was uniquely James Whale's. Despite the many colorful ingredients, it works best when it eschews the grim exterior set and the fearsome Karloff figure. The plot is really just a basic situation, and the highlights bear little relation to what plot line it does have. There's a marvelous sequence in Eva Moore's

Raymond Massey, Boris Karloff, Gloria Stuart

lack of music. Apart from a few notes of highly evocative music in the main titles, there is no music, but the constant sounds of wind, rain, thunder, flapping shutters, billowing curtains, forms its own kind of symphony. Moreover, the film is so tightly paced (it runs a little less than 70 minutes) that there are none of those awkward pauses where one becomes aware of the absence of music.

Photographically, it is superb; the first glimpse of the House, seen through mud and lightning flashes, is one of the most effectively ominous establishing shots ever created. (Again, Whale deliberately downplays it by having Raymond Massey deliver a beautifully underplayed line, "It might be wiser to push on!" a piece of understatement that he exceeds later on, when he tries to soothe his wife's fears about "this awful house" and agrees, "It isn't very nice, is it?")

The sets are splendid, yet they still need a man of Whale's taste and imagination to get the best out of them. Universal later rented the same sets to small independent companies for their cheap thrillers, and yet they were almost unrecognizable since so little was done to exploit them in terms of camera placement and lighting. A few shots are superbly designed miniatures, and Whale wisely

cluttered, claustrophobic Victorian room, in which she talks about the sin and debauchery of an earlier day, and makes the baleful influence of the past far more menacing than the bogeymen of the present. Later, there's a lovely little vignette (predating many similar Val Lewton scenes) in which the scared Gloria Stuart tries to cheer herself up by making shadows on the wall, and is interrupted by the unexplained shadow of Eva Moore. James Whale's always sardonic sense of humor is very cunningly employed. A "shock" closeup of the principal menace on his initial introduction was always an unwritten law in this kind of film, and Whale dutifully supplies it for Karloff's introduction. But then he follows it up with a comedy line of dialogue which squashes the Karloff menace, and suggests that a tongue-in-cheek approach is under way. To an extent it is. The audience is nicely lulled into a sense of false security, heightened by a deliberate anti-climax near the end, only to be outsmarted when Whale plays his final act completely straight.

Unlike *Dracula*, and so many other early horror films, *The Old Dark House* does not suffer from a

Ernest Thesiger, Eva Moore, Charles Laughton, Lillian Bond, Boris Karloff

never gives us a really good look at the exterior of the House in daylight. Thus, even though the human menaces are explained away, the House itself, as a kind of baleful embodiment of evil, can remain undiluted in our memories.

Notwithstanding the pictorial splendor of the film, or the Karloff diversions, perhaps the greatest joy of the film lies in the teamwork of Eva Moore and Ernest Thesiger as the Femms, owners of the House, and in their beautifully written and delivered dialogue. It's unquestionably Thesiger's best role, and I'm not forgetting his colorful Dr. Praetorius in *The Bride of Frankenstein*. There's just the right mixture of fear, pride, potential insanity, and mordant humor in everything he does. While the camerawork and specific angles stress his thin, bird-like body and features as he walks into the camera, his contempt for the characters surrounding him seems to extend to the film crew and theatre audience as well! "My sister was on the point of arranging these flowers!" he remarks cheerfully, at one point, immediately transforming his benign smile into a sneer as he tosses the bouquet into the fire. On another occasion, as bluff, hearty Charles Laughton tries to add some merriment to the occasion by getting everybody to talk about themselves, pointing out that they're all together, all friendly, yet know nothing about each other, Thesiger promptly dumps them back into a spirit of gloom again by sniffing "How reassuring!" However, none of his marvelous lines match the combination of contempt, miserliness, and distrust that he manages to inject into the simple line, "Have a potato," as he hosts his uninvited guests to a singularly frugal meal.

The casting of Eva Moore as his sister was almost an accident. A familiar character actress in minor roles in British and American films of the 30s and 40s, she had come to Hollywood the year before, not really seeking work, but accompanying her daughter, actress Jill Esmond, then married to Laurence Olivier, and looking (quite successfully) for Hollywood work herself. Her casting by Whale was a stroke of fortuitous genius. She is perfection itself as the kind of aging hangover from Victorian days that was a surprisingly common national type in England of the 30s. Whale knew and understood such people, and one finds them turning up quite frequently in his films—in *One More River*, for example, although more warmly there, and with no sinister undertones. I still remember the feelings of mixed awe and mild fear I had when, in the

Gloria Stuart, Brember Wills

mid-30s, I was (frequently) taken to visit such an old lady, who apparently never emerged from a parlor that contained gaslight fixtures, who kept the thick velvet curtains permanently closed against the sunlight, refused a radio or other modern contraptions, and filled her room to overflowing with stuffed birds and butterflies in glass containers.

To further complete the image that Whale recreated so accurately in *The Old Dark House*, a large solemn portrait of Queen Victoria hung on the wall, together with one of the daughter of the house who had been forced into a life as Captain in the Salvation Army. In all probability they're still there, with a horrid secret hidden in the upstairs attic, awaiting the rising waters of a James Whale storm to sweep them away.

9 White Zombie

Robert Frazer, right, and zombie

(United Artists, 1932) Directed by Victor Halperin. Screenplay by Garnett Weston. Camera, Arthur Martinelli.

With Bela Lugosi, Madge Bellamy, Joseph Cawthorne, Robert Frazer, John Harron, Clarence Muse, Brandon Hurst, Dan Crimmins, John Peters, George Burr McAnnan.

White Zombie was once described in a responsible film magazine (by a less responsible "critic") as "a horror film for idiots." This rather neatly disposes of such notable historians as Carlos Clarens and Arthur Lennig, as well as Bela Lugosi himself, who had a tremendous fondness for the film. To admit its flaws immediately: it *is* an oldfashioned film (not always to its disadvantage) and it sometimes approaches silliness through trying too hard to horrify its audiences. At a time when horror films were generally restrained, it anticipated the Hammer *modus operandi* of physical shock and repugnance via its closeups of repellent Zombies and their bullet-ridden torsoes. The Victorian literary flourishes of the dialogue, and such incidentals as the heroine's pre-wedding posing in be-ribboned lace underwear further tend to date the film.

It was already an anachronism in 1932, and its slightly primitive production techniques make it seem a far older film than such contemporary horror films as *The Old Dark House* and *The Mummy*. But technical expertise is hardly all, and in its mood and effect, *White Zombie* is one of the most satisfying films of its period, as well as being the "definitive" voodoo film—not that there have been more than a handful of films in that category. Its *Beauty and the Beast* and *Sleeping Beauty* sub-motifs also give it something of the magical quality of the true fairy tale. Producers Victor and Edward Halperin strongly believed in the visual aspect of film, and at the time stated openly (such an approach to film was then most unfashionable) that they were trying to recapture the "look" of the best silents. Although important information is conveyed by dialogue, it is a wholly pictorial film. Not only the composition of the frame itself, but also the use of glass shots, elaborate optical wipes, and split-screen effects, add to its visual elegance.

The Zombies are glimpsed first in extreme long shot, as black silhouettes stumbling down a hillside at night. Lugosi's first appearance is achieved via a full-screen closeup of his eyes, from which the

camera tracks back rapidly, the increasingly smaller eyes superimposed over a long shot of Lugosi's gaunt figure waiting by the roadside to greet travelers in a coach. There is a meticulous, almost ornamental composition of the frame throughout: Zombies parade silently behind latticed windows, scenes that are almost Dreyer-like in their pace and design. Lugosi and Madge Bellamy frequently move into a scene by being framed through apertures in masonry, or staircase bannisters, the resulting scenes being almost literal equivalents of the old, laboriously handwritten books, where the first letter of the first word of a new chapter would be elaborately enlarged and illuminated.

The pictorial values are outstanding throughout, and are backed by solid looking sets, an imaginative use of light and shadows, and a sustained use of music. Admittedly, this music is melodramatic and oldfashioned. Most of its themes were developed during the silent period, and in the early years of sound, and then farmed out as "canned" music to independent producers who had neither the budget nor the creative necessity for original scoring. On

Bela Lugosi

Madge Bellamy and zombie

the other hand, there is a rich, larger-than-life flourish to this kind of music. It was used to punctuate or to highlight action or melodrama; the pieces are played through from beginning to end, often without any kind of accompanying dialogue or sound effects, and they help to provide a necessary rhythm to such deliberately slow-paced sequences as Lugosi's burning of a wax Voodoo effigy of the heroine during her wedding ceremony. While the dialogue is sparse, it is also very rich. Each line is made to cover in compressed, florid style what would take several lines to accomplish if the style was more realistic. In this respect, it is interesting to compare the film with the Val Lewton-Jacques Tourneur *I Walked With a Zombie,* which is certainly an intelligent and literate horror film.

Because of its more naturalistic and restrained approach, it has to use a great deal of dialogue, none of it with the theatrical bravura of *White Zombie. White Zombie* contains some of Lugosi's best written and best delivered dialogue, but so carefully is it integrated into plot that—unlike some of Lugosi's choicest lines from *Dracula* and *The Raven*—it cannot really be torn out of context and quoted as an example of "juicy" or theatrical writing styles. Lugosi's line to Robert Frazer—"Well, well, we understand one another *better* now!"—conveys nothing to anyone who has not seen the movie; in context, as the key line of a protracted cat and mouse sequence, delivered with a curious mixture of malevolence and smug paternalism, and climaxed by an elegant and underplayed gesture of Lugosi's hand, it becomes almost the definitive illustration of the revenge motif so dominant in horror movies. Incidentally, the Voodoo necromancer provided Lugosi with his most sinister role, reveling in evil for its own sake, and without even the token sympathy one sometimes felt for the Vampire. Moreover, with comparatively little dialogue to deliver, and less to react to, Lugosi seemed to understand his dialogue much better. (In other films, he was frequently thrown by an excess of dialogue, and knocked off balance by the wisecracking repartee of Wallace Ford or similar heroes.) Here, there is no comedy relief to upset the rhythm of his performance, and his own sardonic sense of humor comes through occasionally in lines which he delivers with wit and menace.

Independent producers Victor and Edward Halperin never again made a film as rich as *White Zombie,* but all of their relatively low budget

86

Lugosi carves a wax voodoo replica of Madge Bellamy while zombie-in-the-making Robert Frazer watches helplessly.

Madge Bellamy, Bela Lugosi, Robert Frazer

horror films were interesting and had certain common denominators. Chief among these was a rather morbid preoccupation with the ritual of death. *White Zombie* spends a great deal of time on the funeral of the apparently dead heroine, and later on, talking about it. The funeral itself is played for its grief and sense of loss, not for potential horror; one remembers the harsh sound of the wooden coffin as it scrapes against the flagstones, and the light being blotted out as the coffin is slid into its place. This fascination with the mechanics of death turns up again in the Halperins' *Revolt of the Zombies* (an unexciting attempt to cash in on *White Zombie* by suggesting a sequel, which it was not; it had some later topical interest in that it was set in Cambodia and used its horror framework to provide an anti-war message), *Supernatural,* an extremely interesting programmer for Paramount, dealing with the possession of the living (Carole Lombard) by the spirit of an executed murderess, and even in *Buried Alive,* a prison melodrama with much death-house ritual, and even a great deal of grisly "black" humor about executions!

A scene from *Supernatural,* one of the Halperins' other horror films: Vivienne Osborne, H. B. Warner, Carole Lombard, Randolph Scott

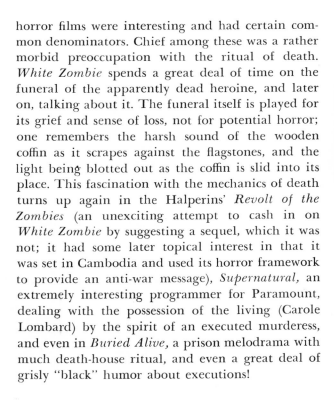

10 The Mummy

Karloff

(Universal, 1932) Directed by Karl Freund. Screenplay by John L. Balderston from a story by Nina Wilcox Putnam and Richard Schayer. Camera, Charles Stumar.

With Boris Karloff, Zita Johann, David Manners, Edward Van Sloan, Arthur Byron, Bramwell Fletcher, Noble Johnson, Leonard Mudie, Eddie Kane, Henry Victor.

Although there have been a dozen or more *Mummy* films, only one of them, the 1932 original, can lay claim to being a classic. The reasons are not difficult to fathom. For one thing, there is no ancient mythology to lend even temporary credence to the notion of an Egyptian mummy walking our earth once again. The literature, folk-lore and myths of the world do tend to substantiate either a minimal belief in werewolves and vampires and their local variants, or at least an understanding of the superstitions that made fear of such supernatural creatures explicable. Egyptian folk-lore is admittedly filled with mysterious intangibles, of curses striking down those who defiled ancient tombs, but the mythology of the revitalized Mummy must be credited solely to Universal Pictures' enterprise in striving to find a successful Karloffian follow-up to *Frankenstein*.

Discarding for a moment the Mummy's lack of history and tradition, there is the important fact that filmically he is not a particularly menacing figure. Apart from his novelty value in having been raised from the dead, he is not really a supernatural figure and is eminently vulnerable to sundry modes of destruction. His normal Egyptian stamping grounds are so far removed from our own environments as to very literally keep his menace at a distance, and transporting him to America was a clumsy and unworkable contrivance. Furthermore, stiffened with age and hampered by bandages, he is so slow-moving that escaping from his clutches is child's play—and his movie victims invariably had to edge themselves into corners and paralyzed with fright, patiently wait for him to lumber up to them and dispatch them with a one-handed stranglehold.

His only expression of vitality was in his libido, surprisingly virile in a creature of his years, and he was quite spry in taking off after young maidens (Peggy Moran, Virginia Christine, Elyse Knox, Ramsay Ames) whom he assumed to be reincarnations of old girl friends. Sequels to the original

The Mummy (1932): A fine closeup study of Karloff's makeup

The Mummy quickly fell into a standardized rut of maraudings and chases, as stereotyped as those of the Western, but with a good deal less pep. So unmenacing was the Mummy himself, that there invariably had to be a human villain as well—usually a High Priest in the form of George Zucco, John Carradine, Eduardo Cianelli or Turhan Bey—to keep the action even tolerably exciting. Hammer's later remakes in color, despite added budgets, found the same problems in keeping interest alive. The action was just too restricted and repetitious—and the only suspense that could have been eked out of the standardized plots would have been for someone to unwrap the bandages!

Karloff, Arthur Byron, David Manners

The Mummy's Hand (1940):
Tom Tyler takes over Karloff's Mummy role

However, the original *The Mummy* instinctively sensed these problems, and aimed not at creating *greater* thrills than *Frankenstein,* but different ones. *The Mummy* offered uneasy thrills, not shocks. The finest sequence in the film is when the Mummy comes back to life—and does nothing but claim a scroll that will enable him to be reincarnated in human form. All that is shown is the Mummy's hand reaching for the scroll—and then the tattered ends of a bandage, trailing behind him as he staggers out into the night. It is a superbly underplayed scene, and a totally convincing one. It is enough to drive a witness to the event, Bramwell Fletcher, quite mad. It is also perhaps the only scene in the entire 40-year Mummy saga that is genuinely horrifying. For the rest, the original *The Mummy* can be interpreted as a love story almost as much as a thriller. The menace lies not so much in what the Mummy does, as in the intangibles of Egyptian religion and science that make such happenings possible. Moreover, Karloff's reincarnated Mummy is a being of dignity for whom one feels some compassion, and his ultimate destruction is tragic as much as it is a triumph for the traditional forces of "good."

The film is beautifully directed by Karl Freund, formerly (and subsequently) a cameraman—and it is a cameraman's film rather than a director's, indicating more than once how much better a film *Dracula* might have been had Freund directed it instead of just photographing it. It is leisurely and unsensational, the camera prowling through a deserted museum at night, rising upwards for powerful crane-shots, and accompanied by an equally unhurried yet evocative musical score which combines Egyptian themes with motifs of menace that are yet mystical and romantic at the same time. Karloff's excellent diction and controlled playing, backed by the outstanding makeup designed by Jack Pierce, creates one of his finest roles. (Pierce's Mummy makeup was rightly praised, but it appears only briefly, whereas the quite different and perhaps superior makeup that Karloff wears in his reincarnated form is usually ignored.) There are some chilling closeups of Karloff's face and eyes as he kills and hypnotizes from afar merely by a tremendous exertion of will, and an impressive flashback sequence to ancient Egypt. Even though Freund is using economical sets and some familiar outdoor locations, he has the uncanny knack of *really* evoking ancient Egypt in these scenes (just as he convincingly evoked Transylvania on Universal's

Karloff, Zita Johann

91

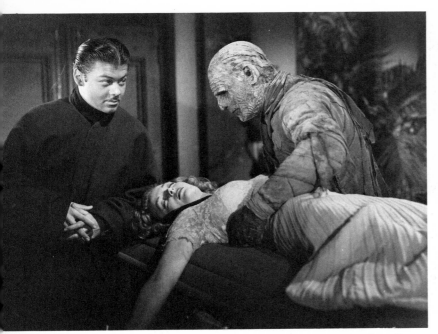

The Mummy's Tomb (1942): Turhan Bey, Elyse Knox, Lon Chaney, Jr.

The Mummy's Curse (1944): Last of three cheapies in which Lon Chaney Jr. wound up the Mummy series

The Mummy's Hand: with George Zucco masterminding the Mummy's villainy

The Mummy's Hand: Tom Tyler, Dick Foran

Curse of the Mummy's Tomb (1964): After Christopher Lee resurrected the Mummy, the role in this follow-up was passed on to a non-star name.

back lot for *Dracula*) to the extent that this whole sequence really looks as though it was taken from a much earlier film. Indeed for many years the belief (unfounded) persisted that it might have been lifted from a silent German film. (These powerful scenes were reused in most of Universal's later *Mummy* programmers, and they always remained the highlights of those films, their real style contrasting with the slick but sleazy look of the rest of the productions.)

Karloff's performance, Freund's direction and Charles Stumar's expert photography are virtually the whole show, but the suporting cast is an exceptionally able one, ranging from the type-casting of Edward Van Sloan in a typical Van Helsing role (with some grandly appropriate dialogue) and Noble Johnson in another of his faithful servant specialities, to the more off-beat utilization of such players as Zita Johann, Arthur Byron and Bramwell Fletcher. Considering how early it came in the horror film cycle, it is surprising how restrained and unsensational *The Mummy* is. On the other hand it is that very restraint that helps to make it a classic. If one accepts *The Bride of Frankenstein* for its *theatre* and *The Body Snatcher* for its literacy, then one must regard *The Mummy* as the closest that Hollywood ever came to creating a poem out of horror.

93

The bizarre experiment designed to recreate the conditions of the murders

(First National, 1932) Directed by Michael Curtiz. Screenplay by Earl Baldwin and Robert Tasker from a play by Howard Comstock and Allen C. Miller. Photographed by Ray Rennahan and Richard Tower.

With Lionel Atwill, Fay Wray, Lee Tracy, Preston Foster, George Rosener, Leila Bennett, Arthur Edmund Carewe, John Wray, Tom Dugan, Harry Beresford, Robert Warwick, Willard Robertson, Thomas Jackson, Harry Holman, Mae Busch, Selmer Jackson.

For years, *Dr. X* was one of the most elusive of all the major horror films of the early 30s, steadfastly refusing to turn up either on television or in theatrical reissue. Because one always expects too much of the apparently unattainable, it would be easy to be disappointed by *Dr. X*, but when it did become available again, it held up surprisingly well. It remains one of the most enjoyable thrillers of its period, and if it doesn't have quite the Gothic style or the comic subtlety of James Whale's films, it nevertheless has the slickness, pace, and recognizable visual style (with its stress on shadows and sharp, angular images) that distinguished all of Michael Curtiz' work.

Although made in two-color Technicolor, the film, alas, is known mainly via black and white versions. This dates back to its original release when, after press shows in Technicolor, it was released largely in black and white, color prints being reserved solely for key opening dates here and in Europe. This procedure has never been satisfactorily explained, although the belief is that Warners made the film in color, not from choice, but because they had a number of contractual commitments with the Technicolor company. Until that point, color had been used (and extensively by Warner Brothers) almost entirely in musicals. But the vogue for musicals had been over-exploited, and the *genre* was temporarily dead; the novelty of color had worn off, too, and at this stage it had no appreciable box office value. Horror films, on the other hand, were at a peak of popularity. Warners may have reasoned that *Dr. X* was good enough to succeed on its own merits without the added and expensive gimmick of color—just as many of the later 3-D films of the 50s were released in flat versions once the novelty of stereoscopic film had gone. One rather worn 35mm color print of

Dr. X did surface in 1973, and shows that the film was almost as imaginative in its use of color as its more elaborate followup, *The Mystery of the Wax Museum.**

The eerie shots of the moon and, particularly, the grim climax, in which the human Monster is transformed into a blazing torch, exploited color for both atmospherics and shock value. The laboratory scenes, with their relatively sparse equipment and great expanses of space, likewise lent themselves well to color, while several of the Old House sets —particularly a corridor stretching off into an obviously painted infinity—seemed far less artificial in color. In any event, *Dr. X* is a grand chiller of the old school, replete with clutching hands, a weird laboratory, a hooded killer, gas jets, secret panels, a wonderful group of suspects—and, on the debit side of the ledger, the inevitable wisecracking reporter-hero, tiresome in concept, but at least amusing in execution, thanks to Lee Tracy's verve and seemingly impromptu dialogue delivery. (Too, he was a hero human enough to be scared, his unreliability thus emphasizing the menace confronting the heroine.) Anyone who couldn't guess the identity of the hidden killer within fifteen minutes deserved to be drummed out of the theatre in disgrace . . . but guessing *who* still didn't mean knowing *why*, and suspense on this front is well maintained.

Most of the action takes place in an appropriately spooky old mansion atop the cliffs at Blackstone Shoals, allegedly on Long Island. It's based on a play and shows it, particularly in rather protracted comedy-relief inserts, but so much happens and the dialogue is delivered so fast that it never slows down to a stagey walk. While it doesn't pull any punches in the strong laboratory and Monster scenes, there's no sick emphasis on gore and blood. Indeed, most of the real unpleasantries are conveyed by dialogue. And, of course, in this kind of a show, who better than Lionel Atwill and Fay Wray to preside?

Miss Wray, on the verge of being menaced twice more by Atwill, and once apiece by King Kong and Count Zaroff, makes a most prophetic entrance into the horror *genre*. Barely a couple of frames into her first scene, she lets out a piercing scream at the unexpected appearance of

* *The Mystery of the Wax Museum* may also have been made primarily to use up a Technicolor commitment, but its use of color was so essential an ingredient that there was never any question of its being released in black and white.

Lionel Atwill in the title role

her father, with whom one would assume she was sufficiently familiar for such a reaction to be justified. And Lionel Atwill . . . with what zest and aplomb he delivers all of his meaty lines. How his eyes light up, like Satanic neons, when a fellow scientist reveals casually that he is "on the verge of the secret of life," or when he delicately hesitates before telling the police that Dr. So-and-so is beyond suspicion and reproach, other than for that one slight lapse in taste when circumstances forced him into cannibalism! But nothing sums up the goodnatured horror of the whole film better than the classic scene in which a doctor unscrews his artificial arm before the shocked gaze of the police. Like a teacher ushering his infant charges on to the next exhibit in the zoo, Lionel cheerfully announces, "Come along, gentlemen, there are many more interesting things to see!"

Officially, the same original play inspired the scenario of a much later Karloff film for Warner Brothers, *The Invisible Menace*. It was a routine melodrama with no horror content; the plot lines of both films overlapped but once, and only slightly at that. The much later (1939) *The Return of Dr. X,* a more traditional horror film, and smoothly done, without any appreciable effort to raise it from its humble programmer status, was in no way a sequel or a remake, and certainly John Litel's thoughtful, but rather stodgy Dr. Xavier couldn't hold a candle—or an electrode—to Lionel Atwill's original creation.

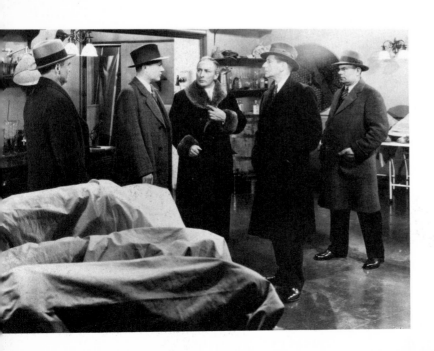

Detectives Willard Robertson and Robert Warwick flank Dr. X (Atwill) as they investigate moon murders.

12 King Kong

Kong enamored of his blonde captive

(RKO Radio, 1933) Directed by Ernest B. Schoed-sack and Merian C. Cooper. Executive Producer, David O. Selznick. Chief Technician, Willis O'Brien. Camera, Edward Linden, Verne Walker, J. O. Taylor. Screenplay by James Creelman and Ruth Rose from original story ideas by Merian C. Cooper and Edgar Wallace. Music, Max Steiner.

With Robert Armstrong, Fay Wray, Bruce Cabot, Frank Reicher, Sam Hardy, Noble Johnson, James Flavin, Steve Clemento, Victor Wong, Leroy Mason, Ethan Laidlaw, Dick Curtis, Vera Lewis, Leigh Whipper.

While there's no doubt that *King Kong* (1933) is the greatest of all Monster movies, its position in the hierarchy of screen horror has always been debatable. Initially, it was designed and sold as a stunt thriller rather than as a horror film, but its shock value was such that it certainly could not be discounted as a horror film. In fact, in England, where local censor boards could overrule the classifications of the National Board, *King Kong* was in the unique position of playing to adults only in some areas, while in others, children could see it unaccompanied.

Audiences of today have, of course, become jaded by the kind of Monster movies of which *Kong* was the forerunner. The novelty has worn off, the limited plot lines have been repeated incessantly, and too many cheap entries have stressed their artificiality by special effects work considerably less expert than that pioneered by Willis O'Brien and Ray Harryhausen. In fact, the flood of artificial Monster movies from Japan—devoid of thrill and horror, depending instead on action and the inherent delight we all share in scenes of mass destruction—have come to be designed more and more for juvenile audiences, giving the Monsters cute, Disney-like qualities (one would hate to say "personalities," since they remained patently unreal toys, totally devoid of the real personalities, temper tantrums, and sly sense of humor with which Willis O'Brien endowed his creatures). Godzilla, for example, has degenerated into a kind of reptilian Lone Ranger. One no longer looks for any kind of horror in this fare, although oddly enough, the rather hidebound British censors still insist on giving them an "Adults Only" classification, disappointing the thrill-seeking audiences that *do* go to them, and frustrating the juvenile audiences for which they were originally made by

denying them! At the very most, in the occasional films of Ray Harryhausen, one looks for (and usually gets) incredible technical expertise, and an amazing illusion of reality.

King Kong, however, not only was virtually the first of its kind (Willis O'Brien's silent predecessor *The Lost World* was notable, but far less successful, perhaps because it lacked the important elements of sound effects and music), but remains the only example of its kind that still has the power to *scare* an audience. The incredible technical skills apart, the enormous importance of Max Steiner's score notwithstanding, what really makes *Kong* work so well is its meticulous construction. Almost the first half of the film is *buildup.* One gets to know the characters, to care about them and what happens to them; because *they* fear what is on the island, so do we. And once Kong makes his initial, fearsome appearance, the pace changes totally. It becomes hysterical, hammering home shock upon shock, never giving the audience more than a few moments to relax.

One frequently notices audience laughter in the second half of *Kong* at exactly the same time in each screening—as the sailors, those who survived the dinosaur's attack in the swamp, rush madly through the jungle trying to escape. There is nothing funny about the scene, even unintentionally; nor is it the laughter of amusement that accompanies this scene. It is near hysterical laughter, a need to release tensions that have been built up and given no opportunity to be relieved. It's interesting that, despite audience familiarity with *King Kong* through reissues and TV exposure, any theatrical showing before a substantial audience still produces this same result, at this same moment, a tribute to the almost mathematical precision with which *Kong* was put together. Much later Monster movies—*The Beast from 20,000 Fathoms,* for example—proved the value of the *Kong* formula by repudiating it, introducing their Monsters too soon and too casually. The one later Monster movie—though not necessarily a horror film—that repeats the *King* formula, is the carefully made and much underrated *20 Million Miles to Earth* (1957), one of the best of the Ray Harryhausen films, and also one of the few that had the wit (and the ability) to make the Monster sympathetic as well as menacing.

United States audiences, unfortunately, have not had the chance to see *King Kong* at its full powers since its initial release. On the occasion of its first reissue, and on subsequent occasions, too, it has

98

Fay Wray, Bruce Cabot

The stark main title card of *King Kong* which, backed by a chord of Max Steiner music, heralded the greatest monster movie of them all.

100

been increasingly trimmed to meet more exacting censorship requirements. Some of the cuts were dramatically sound: shots of *Kong* casually chewing natives, or trampling them underfoot just for the sheer hell of it, lost him a great deal of audience sympathy. His character, and the film as a whole, works better without those scenes, fascinating though they are. On the other hand, removal of the scene where a curious *Kong* undresses Fay Wray, not only robbed the film of one of its most complex and convincing pieces of technical *tour-de-force*, but it also detracted from the human side of Kong's nature, and it was a shortsighted decision indeed.

Far more damaging than individual cutting, however, was the decision to change the pictorial *timing* of the film, so that later printings from the same negative made the film much darker. (With so much complicated matte and process work, it was already darker than the average film to begin with.) This was done to minimize the detail of blood and torn flesh in the Monster-fight scenes, but instead of darkening just those sections, RKO merely had the whole film printed several points darker, often totally obscuring skillful and convincing detail that Willis O'Brien and his crew had labored long and hard to perfect. One sees almost nothing now of the incredibly lifelike movements of the water snake as it attacks Kong; and when Kong stalks through the streets of New York (accompanied by the most evocative high points of Steiner's score, as witness the perfect combinatiin of notes to herald the approach of the elevated subway train), one sees only the larger essentials, not the fantastic detail of people peering from windows, scurrying back to safety, and then drawn to the windows again by sheer curiosity.

Even the giant wall outside the native village is

Unaware that it is not a meat-eater, the dinosaur pursues and devours one of the hapless sailors

Ghidrah (1965: One of the best of the generally not very good Japanese imitations of *King Kong*

almost a total loss; one sees *Kong* at the bottom of the frame, the natives atop the wall, and an inky black mass in between. Originally, one could see every detail of that wall: the indentations in the rock, different textures, vines and foliage growing from its crevices. RKO Radio have always taken a very cavalier and disrespectful attitude towards their established classics, cutting and shortening such films as *Follow the Fleet, Gunga Din,* and *The Lost Patrol,* on general principles. But their desecration of *King Kong,* which depends so much on its visual detail, must surely top the list. Television

exposures, of course, cuts down visibility even more, and adds the handicaps of time-slot editing. However, for the rest of the world, the mighty *Kong* is still, fortunately, intact—complete, uncut, well lit, and as great as ever. *King Kong* is unique, too, in being the only major Monster movie to escape alliance with the science fiction *genre*. From the 1950s on, which is, after all, where one finds the bulk of this kind of film, the Monster almost takes second place to the real villain—impersonal science—which has released or created him, usually through nuclear experimentation or interplanetary travel.

Rodan (1957): Another destructive but ultimately sympathetic Japanese monster

13 Mystery of the Wax Museum

Atwill and assistant Allen Vincent watch as Mathew Betz and Arthur Edmund Carewe (to right of casket) unveil the new Joan of Arc.

(Warner Bros., 1933) Directed by Michael Curtiz. Screenplay by Don Mullaly and Carl Erickson, from a story by Charles Beldon. Camera, Ray Ranahan. Art Director, Anton Grot.

With Lionel Atwill, Fay Wray, Glenda Farrell, Frank McHugh, Arthur Edmund Carewe, Allen Vincent, Holmes Herbert, Monica Bannister, Edwin Maxwell, Gavin Gordon, DeWitt Jennings, Pat O'Malley, Thomas Jackson, Claude King.

For virtually a quarter of a century—from the mid 1940s until the late 1960s—*The Mystery of the Wax Museum* was missing from the American scene, and presumed lost forever. During those years, its reputation—to use contemporary terminology—escalated to such a degree that the film became accepted as a masterpiece of screen horror, and its neglect virtually a cultural disgrace. To a degree, this was understandable. Many of us who saw it in the 30s remembered it well and in detail. Its impact at the time was considerable, and not only for its rich melodrama and highlight thrill scenes. It was the first really "modern" horror film; that is to say, one set against the bustling reality of a 30s milieu: New York, Broadway, busy newspaper offices. (Other current horror films such as *Dr. X* had certainly been contemporary in period but they had removed most of their action to traditional Old House backdrops.) Another striking innovation of the film was its use of Technicolor for such a background; not until the satirical comedy *Nothing Sacred,* in 1937, was Technicolor again used for a New York story. In addition, the 1953 remake *House of Wax* jogged our memories a little more, and enabled us—by a process of comparison—to recall how superior the original film was.

The film's "loss" was certainly accidental. Warner Bros. in England maintained an excellent original 35mm Technicolor print, which they used constantly as a stop-gap booking in the early 40s. When, in 1946, Warners' London office staged a special festival to celebrate the 20th anniversary of sound, *The Mystery of the Wax Museum* was one of three early features (the others: *42nd Street* and *I Am a Fugitive From a Chain Gang*) shown to the public as part of the exhibition. Tickets were free, and the theatre, though full, was never packed. Perhaps it might have been if people had been aware of how long it would be before the film would reappear. The print, a nitrate copy beginning to show signs of decomposition, was withdrawn from

theatrical release thereafter, and in 1954 it was destroyed. Thereafter, when new distributors, taking over the old Warner Bros. films for television and reissue, sought to find a copy of the horror classic in order to put it back into distribution, it appeared that the London copy had been the last one in existence

The remake, a new cycle of horror films, and renewed interest in the old ones combined to stimulate fresh interest in the original film. The new owners, convinced that it could make a profitable reissue, made a "no questions asked" reward offer for anyone turning up a print. There were rumors of a black and white print still circulating commercially in Czechoslovakia, but they came to nought. Finally, and totally unexpectedly, in the very late 60s, an original 35mm color print, slightly worn but otherwise in good condition, was found, in Jack Warner's private vault. Amid a flurry of excitement, it was unearthed, distributors, archives, and the American Film Institute all jockeying for position in an effort to be the ones to copy and preserve it. But on initial screenings the reactions—both culturally and commercially motivated—were all so disappointing that everyone then sought to back away from the offers of preservation money.

A faithful copy of an original, somewhat shrunken, two-color print—making first a negative, and then preservation prints—would have taken a lot of meticulous lab work, and a great deal of money—money that might be better spent on other preservation projects. (It was unfortunate, too, that James Whale's superb *The Old Dark House* re-emerged at the same time; its overall superiority and undated qualities threw the shortcomings of *The Mystery of the Wax Museum* into even sharper relief.) Finally, because it was, after all, a usable property, the distributors did make a copy negative —but as cheaply and with as little effort as possible, thus robbing the film of its one major asset, its rich and often creative pastel coloring. In the prints that have since been made for television use, the film looks almost like a black and white film, *artificially* colored; single tones—blues or ambers—tending to dominate for whole reels at a time. The flaming reds of the fire scenes, or the eerie greens of the bubbling wax, had vanished entirely. Indeed it would have looked better in straight black and white; a diminished reputation was thus dealt a death blow.

Let it be said right away that, disappointing as it may well be today, seen in its original form (and sporadic showings still take place of that one surviving original print), it is still an interesting and often impressive film; a relative classic, if not a consummate one. Why, then, the disappointment? The film disappeared only 13 years after its production (in the United States, it probably vanished earlier than that), at a time when horror films had still not become a mass-produced commodity like the Western, and when screen horror had turned more to the sophistication and subtlety of the Val Lewton and *Dead of Night* school. In the 40s, when Hollywood product was so slick and glossy, nothing seemed quite as old as the rough-hewn films of the early 30s. They were not yet old enough (as were the silents) to take on any kind of historical perspective, but they were old enough for the differences in technology to be apparent. (Differences should not be read as inferiorities.) Thus, *The Mystery of the Wax Museum* really seemed to reflect the robust vitality of a breed of horror film, seemingly gone forever, and to be one of the best of its breed. When in 1953, the 3-D remake, *House of Wax,* came along—a careful enough remake for those with good memories to make direct comparisons—we all felt that it took too many obvious, easy ways out, and rejected the subtlety of the original. For one thing, it took its story back to a period setting, all dark alleys, mists, cloaked figures, and the trappings of Victorian *Grand Guignol.*

The original film had seemed far subtler in its contrasting of the Old and the New. It created an unreal nightmare world of wax amid modern New York, so that merely stepping from Broadway through the doors of the Museum was like stepping into a whole new world of unseen terrors. (In the remake there was no such contrast, the streets as menacing as the Museum.) Furthermore, the original's restrained and limited use of the Monster made it less apparent that he and the sculptor (Lionel Atwill in the original, Vincent Price in the remake) were one and the same, and thus the final classic unmasking had surprise, as well as shock, in the first version. Somehow it was all handled much too abruptly and casually in the remake. Horror films had still not reached the deplorable stage where they relied for much of their effect on physical repulsion; hence the scene was not played for its purely physical effect. Nor, since it had long been apparent that Monster and sculptor were the same, was it played for suspense or surprise. It was a dramatically effective scene, true, but only a shadow of the original, in which Fay Wray first hits at the face in self defense, recoils in horror as it

Lionel Atwill

cracks, beats at it again, and then rips off the remnants of the mask to reveal the gnarled, burnt walnut face beneath it. The remake did point out one or two definitely superior aspects of the original, but it also allowed us—mentally, and unwittingly—to "re-direct" the original. There was thus a tendency to remember the original as it could and perhaps should have been, but, unfortunately, not as it really was.

The one major flaw of *The Mystery of the Wax Museum* is the scenario's determination to live up to its title. It is constructed far more as a mystery than as a horror film, with so many characters and sub-plots that too much time is taken away from the basic story line—especially with a brief running time of only 73 minutes. In this respect, the remake is neater and more cohesive, concentrating on

House of Wax, the remake: Vincent Price, Phyllis Kirk

a compact if more oldfashioned plot line, with no extraneous side issues. For example, in the original, Atwill's partner, the man who destroys the wax museum for its insurance (Edwin Maxwell; Roy Roberts in the remake), turns up later as an all-around petty criminal. Apart from the supplying of bodies to the wax museum, he is also a dope pusher, and via this means has one of Atwill's minions (Arthur Edmund Carewe) under his domination. The dope angle is quite explicit, incidentally, and the breaking down of the addict by a harsh police interrogation has a surprising parallel in Fritz Lang's *The Testament of Dr. Mabuse.*

In both films, the police interrogation is used as a suspense cutaway while the principals are in danger, and in both cases it is the addict's confession which paves the way for the final police roundup. However, the similarity is doubtless coincidental; Lang's film, though earlier, had not been shown in the United States by the production date of the Curtiz film. One of the film's two nominal heroes is discovered in jail on a murder charge that is vaguely related to the story, but that eats up footage to no great purpose. Fay Wray is brought into the film quite late (she has far less footage than Glenda Farrell, the wisecracking reporter who finally cracks the case), and has really nothing to

107

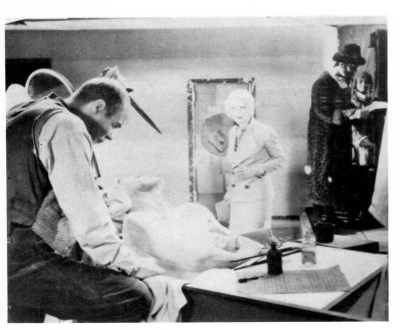

Mathew Betz, Glenda Farrell

Lionel Atwill (in wheel chair) opens his new wax museum in New York

do other than providing a luscious victim for Atwill in the closing reel. Miss Wray is first seen doing her exercises in sweater and brief shorts—looking most fetching in Technicolor. She also doubles for the wax figure of Marie Antoinette in the opening reel—none too convincingly. Why Curtiz didn't shoot a few feet and then freeze-frame it, is somewhat of a mystery; the shot goes on for so long that Miss Wray can be seen all too clearly to be breathing, moving her eyes, and even twitching!

All in all, the original is subtler than the remake, but disorganized and surprisingly lethargic at times, its potential never fully realized. What dates it far more than anything else is its total lack of background music. How much *The Mummy* gained, for example, by its use of slow, almost funereal music, as the mobile camera prowled restlessly through the deserted museum. Even the climactic face-smashing scene, though better done than in the remake, isn't quite the peak of terror that memory told us it was. Fay Wray has recalled, in a recent interview, how the scene was under-rehearsed, and that when it came to actual shooting, the wax mask didn't crack the way it was supposed to. Without a standby mask on hand, they had to make the best of it, and the scene doesn't build as it should. It seems incredible that such a key scene, handled by a craftsman as meticulous as

Curtiz, should not have been better prepared or protected, but Miss Wray's recollections, if accurate, would certainly explain the disappointing quality of the scene today. Rather surprisingly, it is the film's less ambitious forerunner, *Dr. X,* that stands the test of time better. Even though it is more conventional, it is tighter, better-paced, and its comedy not only dates less, but adds a nervous, staccato quality to the film that enhances its excitement.

But with all its shortcomings, seen in the light of perhaps over-critical 1970s reappraisals, the original *The Mystery of the Wax Museum* still has a great deal going for it. The makeup of the sparsely seen Monster is not only startling, but consistent with the explanation finally provided. It makes Glenda Farrell's description—"He makes Frankenstein look like a lily"—no exaggeration, even if it does repeat the irritating merging of Frankenstein and his Monster into one entity. The soft hues of the old, two-color Technicolor were also a tremendous asset to the original version; especially in the scenes of the museum fire where the flames dissolve the wax models, and the smiling, serene figures of Voltaire, Marie Antoinette, and the others disappear in rivulets of molten wax, the eyes appearing to grow wider and bigger with astonishment as the faces distintegrate around them. (Both films shared the disadvantage of open-

108

Gavin Gordon, Glenda Farrell

Claude King, Holmes Herbert, Lionel Atwill

ing with this fire scene, which was so dynamic that it was difficult for the rest of the film to sustain its quality.) The restrained, yet slightly unreal color hues added to the nightmarish quality of the final laboratory scene too, creating erotic as well as terrifying effects with its contrast of the pink flesh tones of an (implied) nude Fay Wray strapped to an operating table, with the bubbling green fluid in Atwill's wax-embalming vats.

A handsome production in every way—Anton Grot's sets were not only imaginative, but they made extremely effective use of space; Atwill's laboratory, for example, being fairly limited in spectacular equipment, but nicely "filled in" by a bordering catwalk—*The Mystery of the Wax Museum* was also extremely well served by its cast. Glenda Farrell and Frank McHugh, as the newspaper reporter and her boss, not only added pace in their brisk conversations, but also tied the Gothic story firmly into a 30s milieu. Arthur Edmund Carewe, a master at playing suspects, red herrings, and vicious henchmen, was fine as Atwill's second-in-command, while oily, cigar-chewing Edwin Maxwell, Hollywood's number one purveyor of fat, lecherous money-grubbing, was marvelous as the fast buck operator who burns down Atwill's museum for its insurance. Much later, in Atwill's new museum, he comes tumbling out of a casket right

Lionel Atwill as the sculptor, before his hands are destroyed in a fire.

109

The moment of truth in all horror films: Atwill offers immortality to a reluctant Fay Wray.

into the camera, one of many corpses transformed into a wax replica of an historical figure.

It was Fay Wray's misfortune to be an exact double for Marie Antoinette, thus arousing Lionel Atwill's creative instincts and allowing him to trot out his theories and promises of "eternal life," while the wax is boiling away and bubbling higher and higher in the immediate proximity of an understandably unenthusiasitc Miss Wray. Never before

or since, has Atwill enjoyed such a perfect part. With his props of dignified beard, wheelchair and crutches, plus some rich dialogue, it offered him a genuinely bravura role. Moreover, it was the kind of role usually allotted to Karloff—the fiend, who is, nevertheless, almost totally sympathetic, and whose life and work have been ruined by the blunders and greed of others. Atwill's flamboyant acting style, his steely eyes, and his lecherous chuckle

110

stood him in good stead in many expert and traditional villain roles, but his superb performance in *The Mystery of the Wax Museum* transcended the undemanding requirements of the horror *genre,* and was high calibre acting by any standards. It was unfortunate that he was to become almost as typed (and later, wasted) as Bela Lugosi, and while he often scored in character roles in non-horror films, he was never again to get a starring role that so enabled him to interweave subtle pathos with menace.

Echoes of *The Mystery of the Wax Museum* have continued to have their effect on other movies down through the years. After *House of Wax,* a further remake was planned, but as *Chamber of Horrors,* a TV pilot expanded to theatrical length, it bore little resemblance to its inspiration. The wax figures from the Museum turned up frequently in Warner films of the 30s; a large photographic blow-up of an Atwill-Wray scene was used as a theatrical background in *The Florentine Dagger,* doubtless at the instigation of director Robert Florey, himself a buff, devotee, and occasional director of horror movies. Atwill's Monster makeup has

been plagiarized several times. The original ads for the film made extensive use of a big head of Atwill, composed—on closer examination—of the bodies of women. It was a gimmick that was copied exactly, and applied to Vincent Price, in the ads for his much later *Masque of the Red Death.* And even if the film does disappoint today, critics still remember it fondly and use it as a yardstick for measuring screen horror. At least one British critic praised the 1973 horror film *Horror Hospital* by calling it an obvious "homage" to Curtiz and *Wax Museum.* The elements common to both films were extremely slight, and producer Richard Gordon assures that no homage was intended. (Very much an admirer of the original film, as well as being an astute producer, he would certainly have left no doubts about it if the film had been intended as a nostalgic recall of the earlier film!)

We should be grateful indeed that *The Mystery of the Wax Museum* is back with us after a 25-year hibernation, and is not the "lost" film we have for so long thought it to be. That it is also not quite the classic that we remembered is one of the hazards of such re-discoveries.

House of Wax: Caroline Jones' body is stolen from the morgue to be transformed into a Joan of Arc wax figure.

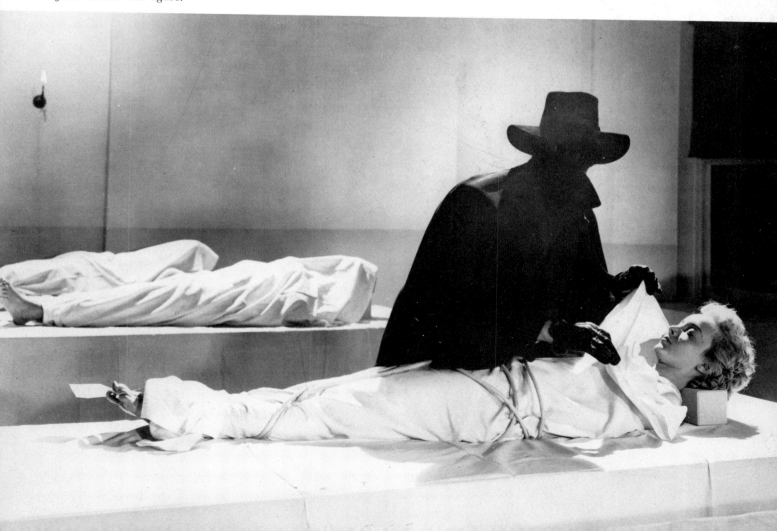

14 Murders in the Zoo

Lionel Atwill and faithless wife Kathleen Burke

(Paramount, 1933) Directed by Edward Sutherland. Screenplay by Philip Wylie and Seton I. Miller. Camera, Ernest Haller.

With Lionel Atwill, Randolph Scott, Charlie Ruggles, Gail Patrick, John Lodge, Kathleen Burke, Harry Beresford, Edward McWade.

Made at the height of the horror film cycle of the early 30s, *Murders at the Zoo* garnered little attention at the time mainly because, like Paramount's other horror film of the period, *Island of Lost Souls,* it was considered rather tasteless and certainly lacked the genuine Gothic style of that cycle. Tastelessness is a matter of relativity, however; in comparison with the physically repellent obsession with gore and clinical detail that has marked recent horror films, *Murders in the Zoo* seems a model of decorum, and if there is any tastelessness at all, it is primarily in the healthy vulgarity of some of Charlie Ruggles' comedy. (Example: having been petrified with fear by a marauding mamba snake, he asks plaintively for the whereabouts of a laundry!) Even so, *Murders in the Zoo* is sometimes quite grim stuff; on its original release, many local and state censor boards removed chunks of footage, including the villain's climactic death; later, television showings usually made cuts as well.

The plot is inconsequential, and like the format of so many contemporary horror films, merely an excuse for a series of horrors. Lionel Atwill plays a wealthy zoologist/sportsman, using animals—and his knowledge of them—to kill off his wife's actual or suspected lovers. With such a limited plot, and a director, Edward Sutherland, who was a good all-around man, but a specialist in comedy, the film gets most of its punch from the suave villainies of Atwill and the atmospheric photography of Ernest Haller. Primarily of course, it is a showcase for the bravura nastiness of Lionel Atwill, who, apart from relishing every line and nuance, also managed to suggest general tendencies towards unspecified depravities which his scripts never intended. The gleam that came into Atwill's eye, the sneer of his lips, his quick dismissal of unspeakable things that had happened off-screen before the story got under way, all of these little acting ploys somehow turned him into an unwholesome killer as well as an illegal one! (The single notable exception was *Mystery of the Wax Museum,* where his villainy was partially

justified, his character decidedly sympathetic, and his unhinged horrors so devastating as not to need the backup of suggested depravity!)

Atwill gets matters off to a colorful start in *Murders in the Zoo;* in the opening sequence he is seen in the jungle, just concluding a neat job of sewing up his victim's lips after the manner of headshrinkers, and leaving him trussed up in the jungle at the mercy of maurauding wild life. Later, when his unsuspecting wife asks if her erstwhile lover left her any message before "leaving," Atwill replies with honesty, nonchalance, and a superbly timed, pregnant pause, "He didn't say—anything." Atwill's dominance of the film is so assured that it seems rather unfair that Charlie Ruggles gets top-of-the-cast billing over Atwill, but this may have been for purely legal and contractual reasons, since Ruggles was a Paramount star, Atwill merely a lethal visitor.

It's a slick, fast-paced and well cast production, though that excellent actor (and later, Governor of Connecticut) John Lodge is rather wasted as one of the wife's paramours. The wife, Kathleen Burke, is toppled from an ornamental bridge into a crocodile pool so totally unprotected that one can only muse, with appalled horror, at the number of tots, old ladies, invalids, and drunkards who must have fallen into it from time to time.

Moments before the end of a marriage: Lionel Atwill, Kathleen Burke

15 Island of Lost Souls

Dr. Moreau's creatures turn on him.

(Paramount, 1932; released 1933) Directed by Erle C. Kenton. Screenplay by Philip Wylie and Waldemar Young from The Island of Dr. Moreau *by H. G. Wells; Camera, Karl Struss.*

With Charles Laughton, Richard Arlen, Bela Lugosi, Leila Hyams, Arthur Hohl, Kathleen Burke, Stanley Fields, Paul Hurst, Tetsu Komai, Bob Kortman, John George, Hans Steinke, Jack Burdette, Duke York.

Richard Arlen, Leila Hyams, Charles Laughton

Despite being billed by Paramount as "H. G. Wells' surging rhapsody of terror," and ballyhooed by a spectacular stunt advertising campaign built primarily around the Panther Woman, for whom a well publicized search had been conducted, *Island of Lost Souls* was a comparative commercial failure at the time, although released at the height of the horror film boom. Its rather tasteless story concerns itself with the evolution experiments of Dr. Moreau, who on his own private island seeks to speed up the development process of changing animal into man, and also to investigate the results of mating his creations with humans. H. G. Wells was outspoken in denouncing the film as a travesty of his original which, while containing horror ingredients, was far from the lurid *Grand Guignol* of the movie. In England, along with *Freaks*, the film was banned outright by the censors—and only after some thirty years were both films finally released there.

The basic problem with *Island of Lost Souls* (and it must have been especially apparent in 1932, when horror films had such style) is that, like the Hammer chillers of the 50s and 60s, it has all the ingredients but little of the mood required. One is often repelled by the film, but rarely convinced by it—even within the limited powers of conviction of most horror films—and thus, one is never really frightened by any of it either. Although the sets and locations (mainly Catalina Island) are effective, there is not a note of background music to help create mood, and there is a listlessness in direction which is telegraphed by the casual and almost disinterested introduction of Dr. Moreau.

Perhaps, inadvertently, Charles Laughton is partially to blame. He gives a marvelous performance, but it never quite seems to match the rest of the film. His lines are polished and matchlessly delivered—some of the best of them almost thrown away—but despite his Satanic beard, he rarely suggests anything much worse than a medically curious

Captain Hook. After showing us the human monsters that represent successful scientific operations, he refers casually to some caged and deformed creatures as "my *less* successful experiments!" Every so often he relaxes into a mischievous, cherubic grin, like a schoolboy playing with test tubs in a fourth-form lab. This macabre humor worked wonders for Ernest Thesiger in Whale's *The Bride of Frankenstein,* but here, everything—operations, cannibalism, attempted matings of human and monster—is so grimly straightforward that the elements of humor, so beneficial to horror films, never get a chance to mesh.

Nevertheless, visually, the film does have a good deal to offer and many scenes have a curious power, especially the crane shots of Laughton, God-like, addressing his creatures with a staccato speech that seems like a deliberate perversion of Kipling's child-like *Jungle Book* language. Lugosi, in an incredibly minor role, gives a surprisingly good performance as an Apeman, while the climax itself (in which the creatures overpower Dr. Moreau and vivisect him in his "House of Pain") is a real shocker, a nightmarish and savage episode comparable only to the climax of Tod Browning's *Freaks*.

Director Kenton, in the 20s a pleasing second-string Lubitsch, was here essaying his first horror film. Later on, in *The Ghost of Frankenstein,* he was rather more efficient. With *Island of Lost Souls* he misfires, but he does so in an interesting fashion.

Island of Lost Souls: An interesting closeup of Bela Lugosi's wolfman makeup

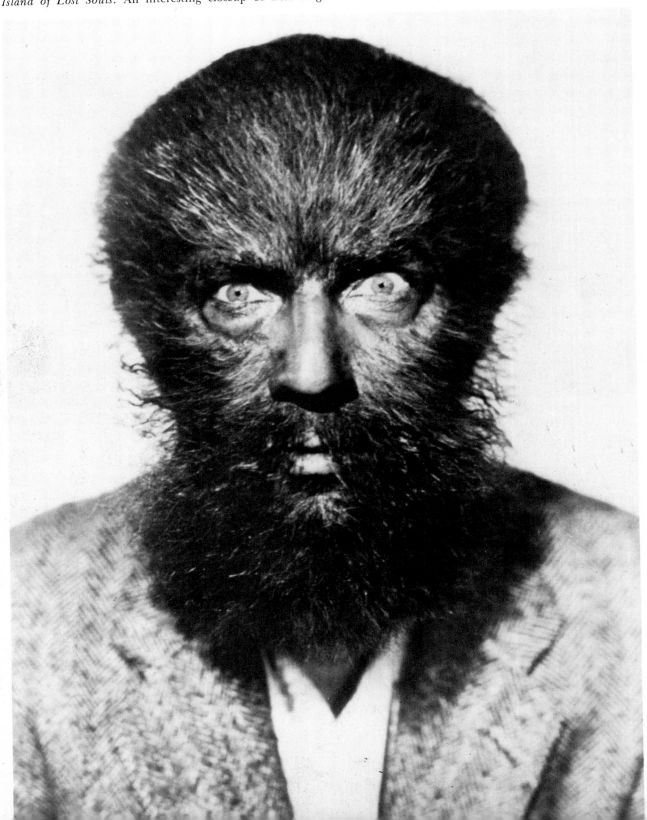

16 The Ghoul

On his death-bed, the dying Karloff gives last-minute burial instructions to his man-servant, Ernest Thesiger

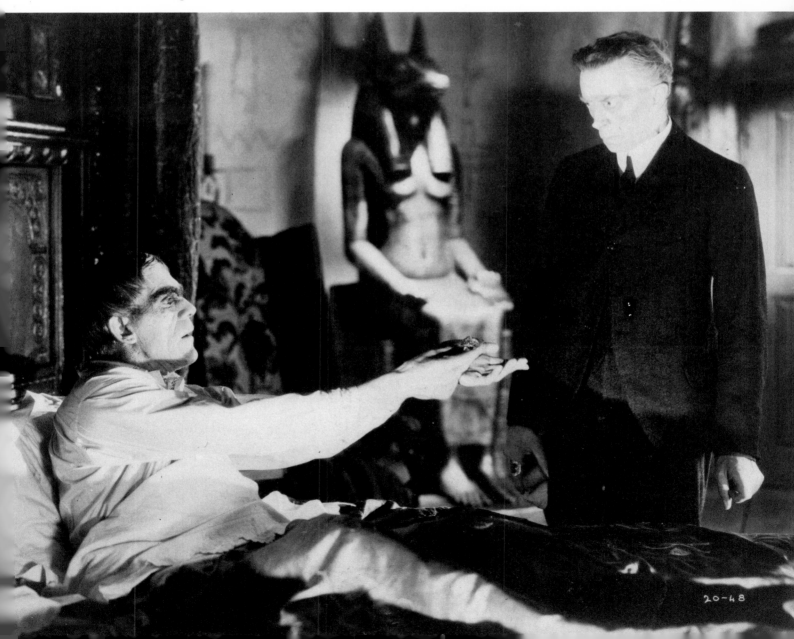

20-48

(Gaumont-British, 1933) Directed by T. Hayes Hunter. Screenplay by Rupert Downing from the play and novel by Dr. Frank King and Leonard Hines. Camera, Gunther Krampf. Editor, Ian Dalrymple.

With Boris Karloff, Dorothy Hyson, Sir Cedric Hardwicke, Ernest Thesiger, Ralph Richardson, Anthony Bushell, Kathleen Harrison, D. A. Clarke-Smith, Jack Raine.

For years *The Ghoul,* while perhaps not the most in demand, has been the most elusive and mysterious of all the "lost" horror films. Elusive because, until 1969, it had never shown up once since its original release, and even in England it disappeared from distribution within a very few years. No prints are known to have survived in this hemisphere, and even the tattered and unprojectable print held in England by the Rank Organization—the negative having decomposed, that print was all that was left —is now no more. Every few years, as with the complete *Greed,* its rediscovery has been hailed— and invariably, of course, it has always turned out to be the much later and more routine *The Mad Ghoul.*

Mysterious—because little was ever really known about the film; no reputable historians appeared to have seen it, only a handful of mouth-watering but not very informative stills seemed to have survived, and most of the original reviews tended to cancel one another out. One acclaimed it as a triumph for British studios, matching Hollywood standards of horror, while another dismissed it as silly and amateurish. One referred to Boris Karloff playing "a kindly old gentleman" in his first sympathetic role, while yet another said that Karloff wore no makeup—both statements being spectacularly at odds with the facts. Karloff himself tended to minimize the film, and even went so far as to express the hope that it would stay lost, but this attitude is easier to understand. Karloff appears (albeit to tremendous effect) only in the opening two and closing two reels, and his dialogue is quite limited. To an actor, it must have seemed no more than a standard bogeyman role, and coming right on top of some of his best and most literate thrillers for Universal, it probably represented a time-killing retrogression for him.

Happily, however, on re-examination, the film proves to be a very pleasant surprise. (A tattered but nonetheless welcome print was discovered in an East European archive, and a copy was made for the Theodore Huff Memorial Film Society, a New York group that made it available to students from late 1969 on.) It was made right after Karloff's Universal films, *The Old Dark House* and *The Mummy,* and is a rather interesting combination of themes and moods from both films. As the first major British effort to cash in on the big horror cycle, it is remarkably effective, and in terms of production value, sets, and atmosphere, generally up to the average if not the best Hollywood standards of the day. It may not be another *The Old Dark House,* but a comparison with *Murders in the Rue Morgue* would not be inapt. The sets are handsome, the Gothic mood well sustained by the stylish camerawork of Gunther Krampf, and there is even a very effective musical score.

Karloff plays Professor Moriant, a rich eccentric who has dabbled so much in the Egyptian occult, that his mind has become partially unhinged. Near death, he is convinced that the burial with him of a priceless jewel, "The Eternal Light," will bring about his resurrection and eternal life by the Egyptian God Anubis, a statue of which is next to his bier in the crypt. He is buried in a grim, torch-lit ceremony, and an appropriate collection of scavengers descends on the household for the reading of the will: genuine heirs, a grasping lawyer, and sinister, Oxford-educated Egyptians, anxious to reclaim the jewel for their own country.

While the element of mystery and suspense is maintained, these middle portions of the film—denied the Karloff presence—tend to bog down a little in their obligatory nods to a bickering hero and heroine who finally find love, and the comedy relief of Kathleen Harrison, genuinely funny as a sex-starved spinster who seems to have formed her ideas of romance from old Valentino movies, and who makes thinly veiled suggestions to the Egyptian that she is available for love and domination. The jewel is stolen from Karloff's body, and at the next full moon—in a genuinely terrifying sequence, well up to the best Hollywood standards—he rises from the grave and stalks his old house, seeking both revenge on the defilers of his tomb, and the regaining of the jewel, so that he may gain his eternal life.

Since so many malefactors are after the jewel, it becomes highly mobile. At one point, it accidentally turns up in the hands of the heroine—allowing for the expected Monster-and-the-girl confrontation, even though Karloff had loved the girl (his niece)

Karloff returns from the grave when his tomb is defiled, and recovers a ceremonial jewel accidentally in the possession of Dorothy Hyson

in life, and presumably would have little real reason for trying to throttle her now. Ultimately, Karloff does regain his jewel, and in a grim sequence (especially by British standards), stands before the statue of Anubis, carves sacrificial symbols into his chest with a knife, and dies again after having had the satisfaction of seeing the statue come to life to accept his gift of the jewel. However, there is one more plot gimmick as yet another villain is revealed—the most considerate, kindly and least suspicious of the entire motley crew—and he and the

hero grapple before the crypt goes up in flames. Quite incidentally, since there are at least two lesser villains who physically steal the jewel from Karloff's body, and a third who tries, technically, it is they who qualify for identification with the film's title, since a Ghoul is a grave-robber and defiler of the dead. Nevertheless, it was understandably good showmanship to suggest, in the initial advertising, that Karloff played the title role, and in later years such generally uninformed publications as *Famous Monsters* not infrequently published stills from the film with the specific caption, "Karloff as *The Ghoul*."

In terms of plot, the film (based on a novel and play) is dangerously close to farce at times. Were is not for the Karloff presence, it might well teeter more in the direction of *Thark* (a famous British stage and film farce) than *The Old Dark House*. In fact, in 1961 it was remade as a knockabout comedy, impure and simple, by some of the "Carry On" gang. Titled *What a Carve Up* in England (a slang expression that had a double pun application to the film's content), it was retitled *No Place Like Homicide* for the United States. Its distribution was sparse, and served to make it legally as well as physically impossible to get at *The Ghoul!* Even the original has its pronounced comedy elements, and some of the performances (particularly that of Sir Cedric Hardwicke, grotesquely made up like a Dickensian caricature as the scheming lawyer) were so overdrawn as to suggest that the actors were having a little fun on their own. For the most part, however, the dominating influence of Karloff manages to keep the levity in check. His makeup is still genuinely horrific, and there are several grim closeups with stress on gaunt, hypnotic eyes. It's never quite explained why a scholarly if eccentric English gentleman should look and walk like the Frankenstein Monster, but that is perhaps the only major loose end.

Despite all the red herrings and the casual intermingling of the occult, the supernatural, and the plain melodramatic, the plot (within the wide boundaries of its *genre*) is quite a good one, with satisfying if not entirely convincing explanations made in the last reel. The cast, of course, is a standout, with Karloff and Thesiger, fresh from *The Old Dark House,* stealing all the honors. Despite the limitations of the role, Karloff still manages to extract a good deal of audience sympathy from it, without in any way lessening his menace. *The Ghoul* is certainly no classic rediscovery, but as a piece of sheer horror hokum it

survives rather well, especially since T. Hayes Hunter, a prolific but undistinguished director of the 20s and 30s (and incidentally, before that, D. W. Griffith's successor at Biograph), was at best a journeyman director. In fact, the major weaknesses of *The Ghoul* are all ones that a really good director could have sidestepped. Ernest Thesiger's role is a case in point: it is inconsistent not only in details (a club-footed limp that comes and goes, and is never properly exploited for menace or bizarre visuals), but also in conception. James Whale would have directed this part for both macabre humor and real terror; Hunter seems to give Thesiger no direction at all, leaving him floundering much of the time. Thesiger is still a fascinating enough performer to be superficially one of the best things in the film, but the potential of the role (with its opportunities for menace, sardonic humor, and quivering terror) is all but thrown away.

Next to Karloff and Thesiger, one of the film's major assets is the lovely and graceful Dorothy Hyson—then a young actress apparently on the threshold of a career that somehow never materialized. (Attention to marriage and raising a family perhaps militated against the aggressive pursuit of the right roles, so essential to a British actress.) However, her screams while collapsing in Karloff's clutches would not have shamed Fay Wray! Incidentally, Miss Hyson possesses a rare set of production stills from the film which stress the ingenious effects achieved with very little. The set for the exterior of the tomb, for example, was just a simple flat thrown up in the middle of a field, looking for all the world like the sparse but extremely atmospheric sets constructed for so many silent German films of the 20s. One suspects from these stills that cameraman Krampf and his (unbilled) German art director probably had a good deal more to do with the physical design—and success—of the film than director Hunter.

17 The Black Cat

Boris Karloff, Egon Brecher

(Universal, 1934) Directed by Edgar G. Ulmer. Screenplay by Peter Ruric and Edgar G. Ulmer, suggested by Edgar Allan Poe's short story. Produced by E. M. Asher. Camera, John Mescall.

With Boris Karloff, Bela Lugosi, David Manners, Jacqueline Wells (Julie Bishop), Lucille Lund, Egon Brecher, Anna Duncan, Albert Conti, Henry Armetta, Andre Cheron, Harry Cording, George Davis, Alphonse Martell, Tony Marlow, Paul Weigel, Albert Polet, Rodney Hildebrant, Paul Panzer, John Carradine.

The first of the three bonafide Karloff-Lugosi co-starring vehicles (they often appeared together later, but never in such showcase films, and usually with Lugosi in a lesser role), *The Black Cat* was in many ways the best of the trio, and the only one in which both stars had equal opportunities. (In *The Raven,* Lugosi dominated, and in *The Invisible Ray,* it was Karloff.) Although allegedly based on the Poe story, it has no relationship to it whatsoever, any more than the equally Poe-credited *The Raven,* or a much later film called *The Black Cat* did. Actually it draws its inspiration far more from the career and personality of Aleister Crowley. However, in its mood and in its oppressive, claustrophobic, and generally unhealthy atmosphere, it does evoke a very definite feeling of Poe—allied perhaps with a Kafka-esque sense of entrapment, futility, and hopelessness. It is slow and stately, an aura underlined by its deliberate use of classical music in place of original scoring, the macabre story of devil worship imbued with a sense of death and decay, furthered by some extremely literate and well delivered dialogue. It may be considered one of the most successful attempts to transfer Poe to the screen, even though it transfers only a mood and not a plot. And the weaknesses of the script, decidedly vague and contradictory actions and motivations, while probably accidental, add to the perversity of the film.

Karloff's screen performances generally fell into one of three categories: those where he genuinely respected the film and the role and gave of his best; those, like both versions of *The Raven* and *The Mask of Fu Manchu,* where he realized that the roles could never be taken seriously and approached them in a bravura, tongue-in-cheek style; and the *Voodoo Island* and *Frankenstein 1970* roles where he merely walked through the films without undue effort, apparently on the theory

that for such junk the prestige of his name and presence was contribution enough. *The Black Cat* falls into the first of these categories, and together with *The Mummy, Frankenstein,* and *The Body Snatchers* must be considered one of his finest characterizations. With his black costume, Satanic haircut, intentionally obvious use of makeup, and his beautifully modulated and accented dialogue, his Hjalmar Poelzig is a marvelous incarnation of evil for its own sake. Lugosi, too—never as good an actor as Karloff, hindered by his lack of understanding of the subtleties and nuances of the English language, but capable of extremely good things at times—rises to the occasion with one of his best performances. It is a concentrated duet all the way, and supporting players matter little. Henry Armetta's comedy interlude is largely unnecessary, but certainly brief. It does at least serve a constructional function in stressing the hero/heroine predicament, and in allowing for a relaxing of tempo from a peak that it would have been hard to sustain, in order that it can begin to build all over again. David Manners is a typically useless hero, being knocked out and locked up after only token resistance, but there are some interestingly depraved faces among both household retainers and devil-worshipping disciples.

The camerawork is sometimes too tricky for its own good—an eiderdown drawn up over the bed provides a black screen transition to another shot, causing audiences to be disoriented both in a story-

Bela Lugosi, Jacqueline Wells, Boris Karloff

sense and technically, since curiosity about the mechanics of the shot is stronger than involvement in the story at that point! On the other hand, the striking, pictorial quality of the film creates a decidedly non-Hollywood and non-stereotyped horror film. The milieu and backgrounds are unusually convincing; its incidental background and establishing shots have the same look of subdued melancholy as many authentic East European films of the period (*Extase,* especially), and while one or two shots may have been lifted from European productions, the style throughout is consistent. The cold, modernistic sets, the rich quality of eroticism (often involving the change of focus within a shot to give added sexual emphasis), and the slow, gliding camerawork of John Mescall are all helped in their creation of mood by a brilliant musical score which draws very heavily on the classics, and particularly on an imaginatively orchestrated arrangement of Liszt's *Piano Sonata in B* and Schumann's *Quintet in E Flat Major, op. 44*—with a few effective chunks of Tschaikowsky here and there. The visual stateliness, and the "equal time" given to both protagonists (Karloff is evil yet magnetic, while Lugosi's hero is sympathetic and well-intentioned, yet also callous and dominated by some far from admirable traits) make it difficult—even within the undemanding confines of the horror film—to "identify" with either faction.

The overall effect is rather like that of experiencing a nightmare that one *knows* is a nightmare. Because the horrors are so unpredictable and so calmly presented, it is the fear of the *next* horror—unseen, unimaginable—that works best. The audience is placed in the position of a spectator who fears getting caught more than getting involved, but is fairly secure in the knowledge that the nightmare is bound to end before that can happen. Incidentally, the literally nightmarish story (punctuated by a stress on *black*; black clothes, black trees silhouetted against a darkening sky, even black lipstick makeup on Karloff's mouth) is a sadistically "sick" and complicated one. Karloff—who marries both Lugosi's wife and his daughter (consecutively, not concurrently)—winds up as Bela's father-in-law. Thus, Bela's ultimate revenge (skinning Karloff alive on an embalming rack, prior to blowing him up) is not only medically drastic, but paternally tactless, to say the least.

Since *The Black Cat* runs a mere 65 minutes, it is technically a "B" picture, although quality rather than length was always the deciding factor in a

Boris Karloff, Bela Lugosi, Harry Cording

film's billing status in the early 30s. All in all, it is almost certainly the best film of that interesting but overrated director Edgar Ulmer, whose corner-cutting efficiencies in the cheapest of PRC "B" melodramas have raised the *Cahier du Cinema* cultists to the heights of rhapsodic ecstasy, but whose real style and evocation of atmosphere here has somehow left them cold, perhaps because they were backed up by a decent budget and solid production values, thus somehow violating the rules.

Apart from its visual flair, one of the real pleasures of *The Black Cat* is its exploitation (in a creative sense of the word) of the speech patterns and dialogue delivery of its two stars. Dialogue in the film is relatively sparse, but the lines conceived for Karloff and Lugosi, quite apart from their theatrical bravura, seem almost to have been story-boarded to take advantage of their accents, and to extract the maximum from those lines via skillful cutting. At one point, the rather ingenuous romantic lead, David Manners, dismisses a macabre theory as "superstitious baloney," to which Lugosi—breaking up an ordinary line into an orchestration of musical syllables—replies, "Superstitious, perhaps, *baloney,* perhaps not!"—each of the five words underlined by the slightest shift in facial expression.

The Black Cat: In the chart room of Karloff's remodelled fort, Lugosi finds the preserved
body of his dead wife.

In the same sequence, Karloff, explaining the
phobia that has just caused Dr. Vitus Verdegast
(Lugosi) to throw a knife at and kill an intruding
cat (the only reference to Poe's title), delivers a
beautifully spoken little monologue about the "extreme form" of the phobia, climaxed with the
explanation that Lugosi suffers from ". . . an all-
consuming horror—of cats." Karloff's diction adds
immeasurably to the effectiveness of the lines; the
word "horror" is emphasized, given a sensual and

menacing intonation, while a pregnant pause, and
a lifting of the eyes upwards in a mock-religious
expression, a slight hissing in the final sound, gives
the simple phrase "of cats" a genuinely frightening
connotation. The music too, subdued to give dominance to the dialogue, matches the mounting climax
of Karloff's diagnosis. It is a superbly played and
directed moment, and *The Black Cat* is full of such
moments even if the whole film as a unit doesn't
quite match them.

18 Mark of the Vampire
London After Midnight

Mark of the Vampire: Bela Lugosi, Carol Borland

(MGM, 1935) Produced and Directed by Tod Browning. Screenplay by Guy Endore and Bernard Schubert. Camera, James Wong Howe.

With Lionel Barrymore, Elizabeth Allan, Bela Lugosi, Lionel Atwill, Jean Hersholt, Henry Wadsworth, Donald Meek, Jessie Ralph, Ivan Simpson, Leila Bennett, Carol Borland, Holmes Herbert, Michael Visaroff.

LONDON AFTER MIDNIGHT

(MGM, 1927) Directed by Tod Browning. Scenario by Waldemar Young from an original story by Tod Browning. Camera, Merritt Gerstad. Art Direction, Cedric Gibbons and Arnold Gillespie. Produced under the title The Hypnotist.

With Lon Chaney, Marceline Day, Henry B. Walthall, Percy Williams, Conrad Nagel, Polly Moran, Edna Tichenor, Claude King.

For years, discussion (and comparison) of Tod Browning's most famous silent film, *London After Midnight,* and its sound remake, *Mark of the Vampire,* has been hampered by the non-availability (and so the legend went, non-existence) of the silent version. As is often the case, its reputation was boosted out of all proportion (helped along by non-authoritative and non-critical accolades in the horror movie magazines, designed for consumption by a primarily eight-to-sixteen age group). One easy way to inflate a reputation is to downgrade the competition, and *Mark of the Vampire* has consistently been slighted as a silly, inferior pale shadow of its original.

In view of the legend surrounding the original, and the apparent current impossibility of refuting it by actual evidence, protestations that the first film wasn't actually a very good film have been futile. Chaney's grotesque makeup—the wide staring eyes, the filed vampire teeth, the costume of top hat and opera cloak—plus the admittedly appetizing stills, promising much in the way of bizarre sets and lighting—seemed to sweep away all criticism. Even if the film had nothing but Chaney, his makeup, and the pictorial atmosphere, the argument seemed to be, it couldn't help but be anything less than great! *Mark of the Vampire,* on the other hand, was usually dismissed, even without discussion, because of its "cheater" ending.

London After Midnight: Lon Chaney

Actually, *London After Midnight* and *Mark of the Vampire* are virtually identical: the plot weaknesses of one are to be found in the other, the continuity is almost scene for scene the same, both films have the same brief running time (a minute or two over the hour). Given the rapidly reinforced suspicion (one is tempted to say "proof") that the greatness of the Browning-Chaney vehicles is a myth, *London After Midnight,* if eventually located, may well be the last nail in their filmic coffin. (Both Chaney and Browning were indisputably great; but Chaney achieved his greatest without, and *before,* his collaboration with Browning, whereas Browning's best films came *afterwards.*) Audiences of 1927 undoubtedly felt less cheated by the film's denouement. After all its limitations, the film was one of the better Browning thrillers, and the dynamic Chaney personality—with a utilization of makeup

second only to his fearsome *Phantom of the Opera* face—was certainly enough to rivet attention. Moreover, in that pre-*Dracula* period, audiences (only a small portion of which could have been exposed to the German *Nosferatu*) were not conditioned to expect sensational thrills from the promise of a Vampire story. Indeed, the stress on mystery and a "logical" ending may have been far more acceptable then.

Not so with the virtually unchanged remake. At this late stage, it can surely be giving away no secrets to reveal that the story of both films deals with an apparent plague of Vampires, and that the solution reveals the whole thing to have been a put-up job, the phony Vampires and their castle merely props to force the confession of a·murderer. (The only substantial difference in the two films was that in the original, the detective—Chaney—also posed as the leading Vampire, while in the remake, the roles were split, Lionel Barrymore essaying a Professor Van Helsing role as the investigator, Bela Lugosi playing the Vampire who is revealed at the end to be a ham actor.) In 1935, the title, the teaming of Lugosi and Atwill (with their respective

Mark of the Vampire Carol Borland, Elizabeth Allan

Dracula and *The Vampire Bat* still well remembered and constantly in circulation), and general audience unfamiliarity with the plot did cause the film to be regarded as somewhat of a let-down. The shocking waste of Lugosi for red-herring purposes (he had only one short line of dialogue in the entire film, and that a mild gag line for the fadeout), coupled with the fact that 1935 also offered such genuinely classic horror films as *The Bride of Frankenstein* and *Mad Love,* made the betrayal seem even more arrogant.

Today however, when we have been inundated with a whole decade of over-exposure to Vampire films from America, Britain, France, Germany and Italy, the film can be seen in a different perspective. For all of its misleading action, the film never really cheats: cunningly, all of those scenes of Vampires performing supernatural functions (changing from bat to human form, for example) are actually illustrated *recitals,* events described by someone who saw them, and merely a part of the campaign against the real murderer (a campaign so costly, elaborate, and time-consuming—it is spread over a period of years—that one seriously doubts any police department's spending taxpayers' money quite so recklessly). Logic, of course, is *not* a strong point. Since the authentic Vampiric activity is nil, the villagers' total belief in them is a little hard to swallow. And James Wong Howe's camerawork builds up such a meticulously created nightmare world of crumbling castles, gnarled trees, constant mist, spooky graveyards, and sinister peasantry— that one wonders why anybody should choose to live in such an environment, and also what the reaction will be when sunlight and normalcy return following the investigators' departure. One is also tempted to raise an eyebrow at the enterprise of the actor-Vampires who contrive (presumably by theatrical props and pulleys) to "fly" in their castle for the benefit of casual eavesdroppers who may be peering through the windows.

But since the whole film is a charade, one really cannot in fairness quibble at details. The atmosphere is flawlessly evoked (one wishes that Browning had managed to evoke an equal atmosphere for the final two-thirds of *Dracula*), individual scenes achieve moments of real terror, the cast is thoroughly professional, and the whole film has that care and gloss so typical of MGM, even when they were basically ashamed of their product. (One has the feeling that MGM never really wanted to make

Mark of the Vampire: Lionel Barrymore, wolf-bane, and Jean Hersholt

horror films and made a minimum contribution to the field only because they were in business to make money, and horror films were commercial in the 30s. By their short running times and lack of showmanlike exploitation, MGM seemed to be trying to ignore their presence; yet cognizant of the fact that they had a reputation to uphold, they still gave them superior casts and production trappings.)

With all of the film's wild plottings, the final revelations hold water, if not logic. All, that is, but the revelation of the *mode* of murder. The killer has somehow contrived to drain the victim of blood in order to sustain the illusion of supernatural, Vampiric participation. This deception does not fool the perceptive Lionel Barrymore, who deduces what has happened merely from spotting a large goblet among the murderer's accoutrements. When a baffled assistant asks what it is for, a smugly satisfied Barrymore gives the brief explanation, "Why, to cup the blood of course!"— thus sidestepping awkward discussion of a murder *modus-operandi* that must have been long, laborious, tedious, utterly impractical, and finally, rather messy.

19 Mad Love

Peter Lorre, Frances Drake and director Karl Freund between takes

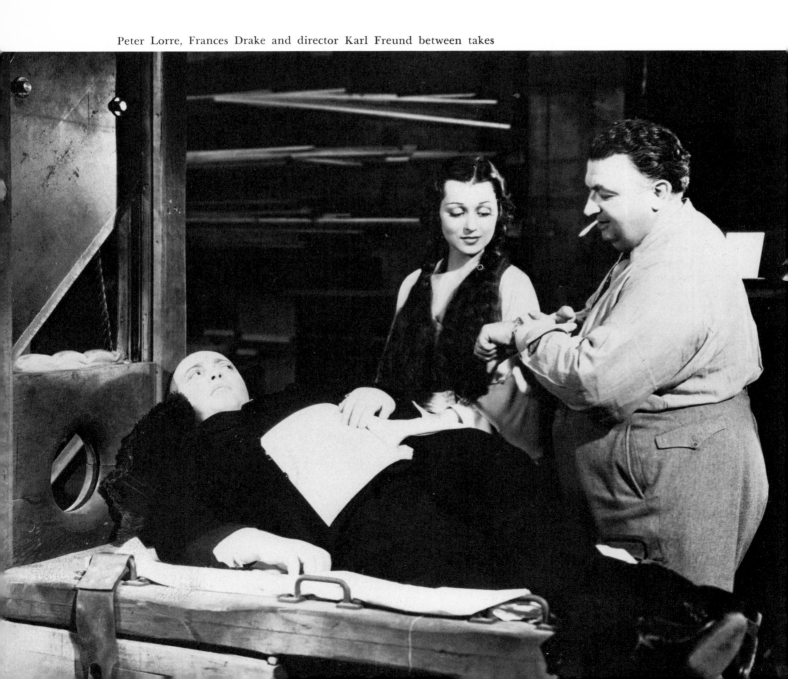

(MGM, 1935) Directed by Karl Freund. Screenplay by Guy Endore, John Balderston and P. J. Wolfson from The Hands of Orlac *by Maurice Renard. Camera, Gregg Toland and Chester Lyons. Music, Dmitri Tiomkin.*

With Peter Lorre, Colin Clive, Frances Drake, Ted Healey, Sarah Padden, Edward Brophy, Henry Kolker, Keye Luke, Ian Wolfe, Charles Trowbridge, Murray Kinnell, May Beatty, Rollo Lloyd, Philo McCullough, Edward Norris, Isabel Jewell, Harvey Clark, Frank Darien, Billy Gilbert, Clarence Wilson, Sarah Hadden, Cora Sue Collins.

Mad Love, long unseen, its release to television long withheld, in 1970 began to stir up some belated intellectual interest, thanks to Pauline Kael's references to it in her well circulated and controversial articles on *Citizen Kane.* In them she equated Welles' makeup as Kane with that of Lorre as Dr. Gogol in *Mad Love,* and also suggested that some of Toland's German expressionist style may have derived from his earlier work on this film—although the much later (and much closer to *Kane) Son of Frankenstein* is far more marked in its Germanic photographic style. But if her remarks serve, like a TV teaser, to whet the appetites of those who might otherwise consider the film beneath them, all well and good. For *Mad Love,* coming at the apex of Hollywood's big horror cycle (1935 is also the year of *The Bride of Frankenstein* and *Mark of the Vampire),* is one of the best Hollywood chillers.

Its plot, originating with a French author, is so bizarre and out of touch with its contemporary locale as to more properly belong in the more fanciful German silent films of legend. In fact, it saw its first movie incarnation as one of director Robert Wiene's several interesting but unsuccessful attempts to find a commercial framework for the films of stylized fantasy that he had pioneered with *The Cabinet of Dr. Caligari.* It concerns a world famous concert pianist, Stephen Orlac, whose hands are totally destroyed in a train wreck. The hands of an executed murderer are grafted on to his arms, and while he finds it very difficult to regain his musical skill, he finds it distressingly easy to throw knives with unerring accuracy.

Unlike many other horror films of the period, this is no tongue-in-cheek affair. While there is some levity in the film, it is largely limited to unobtrusive inside joking. Karl Freund, a superb

cameraman who dabbled briefly in direction, and in 1932 directed the fine Karloff film *The Mummy,* repeats, in similar context, one of the key lines from that film, "It went for a little walk!" (referring to the Mummy originally, and a wax figure here).

And there's rather contemptuous humor in starting the whole film off in the framework of a grisly *Grand Guignol* performance of a play dealing with the torture-chamber branding of an unfaithful wife. Not only does it establish Dr. Gogol (Peter Lorre in his first American film) as a distinctly unhealthy personality, fascinated both by pain and sadism, and the sexual coveter of the star of the show (Frances Drake), even though she is another man's wife, but it also maliciously tweaks the noses of audiences that dote on gruesome horror—namely, the audiences that have paid to see *Mad Love.* But apart from that, there is (rightly) little humor in the film, and Freund manages to overcome even the comedy-relief formula casting of Ted Healey as the wisecracking newspaper reporter who had become such a fixture in early 30s horror films. Healey (a bluff, unpolished, unattractive comedian could

Peter Lorre

be tremendously funny and effective in purveying vulgarity and other unsympathetic traits) does have an occasional, very funny line, but for the most part his role is distorted so that it provides pace and punctuation, at times even propels the story forward.

While the film is a visually handsome production with some extremely good sets, it is much less of a cameraman's film than was *The Mummy*. If anything, though much more erotic and more uneasily chilling, it absorbs a good deal of the stately Gothic style of James Whale. (It's poetic justice, too, to see Colin Clive, the erstwhile Dr. Frankenstein, himself the victim of an enterprising Mad Doctor!) The story is a good one that has seen service many times, both in official remakes and in tangential variants that include a London stage version, starring John Mills. This screen adaptation, fashioned by those specialists in the macabre, Messrs. Endore and Balderston, is quite the best movie version, though with several justifiable changes. The emphasis this time is shifted from the long suffering hero to the sexually frustrated psychopathic villain. In the silent German version, Conrad Veidt played the pianist on such a sustained note of hysteria and madness that there was no room for his "deterioration"; furthermore, the sets for even the most commonplace of locations (a restaurant, for example) were so gloom- and doom-laden that there was no hint of normalcy about any of the milieu, and the film took on the aspects of a nightmare. Conversely, a more recent version (with Mel Ferrer and Christopher Lee) tried so hard to be respectable and psychological (even to having the idea of the grafted hands turn out to be a falsehood nurtured by the Doctor in order to drive his victim to madness or suicide) that it eased out all of the thrills.

Mad Love, on the other hand, plays all of its thrill material to the utmost: even though the audience knows that Dr. Gogol is manipulating Orlac in order to get his wife, the hand-grafting theme is no trick, and the suspicion that Orlac may indeed have murdered his own father is not allayed until quite late in the proceedings. There's a genuinely frightening sequence in which Gogol, disguised in black cloak, metal substitute arms, and surgical neck brace, convinces Orlac that he is the resuscitation of the executed Rollo brought back to life by Gogol's medical skill. Instead of the film's tempo relaxing after this grim sequence, it actually builds and increases as Gogol descends further into giggling madness and tries to kill Frances Drake, who has replaced the wax effigy of herself in Gogol's chambers, and acts out the pretense of a Galatea coming to life. Ironically, it is Orlac's unwanted and Gogol-implanted knife-throwing skill that ends Gogol's life, just as he is strangling her with the braids of her own hair.

Mad Love has its mistakes, certainly; one of them is the casting of Edward Brophy as the killer who is guillotined. Even within the context of the film he is entirely too likeable and human (but especially now, when he is even more familiar as a comic performer and Disney model) to suggest exerting a baleful influence from beyond the grave. This miscasting is more than offset by the tortured, neurotic expertise of Colin Clive, the lecherous, heavy-breathing, giggling mania of a totally bald Lorre, and the serenity and beauty of Frances Drake. And the climax, while neatly disposing of the villain, does tend to gloss over the fact that the hero is still left with a plethora of personal problems—debts, inability to perform as a pianist—the only profession he knows—and most of all, the rather embarrassing ownership of hands that insist on throwing knives at people!

The film as a whole is so satisfying, however, that perhaps one shouldn't quibble—unless it be to complain that Karl Freund didn't see fit to go all the way, and leave this black thriller with the suggestion that the hero will in fact, in time, kill his adoring wife, thus fulfilling the old quotation (of which Gogol had earlier reminded us) that "each man kills the thing he loves."

Colin Clive, Peter Lorre

Frances Drake, Peter Lorre

The Hands of Orlac: A 1964 remake of *Mad Love* with Mel Ferrer

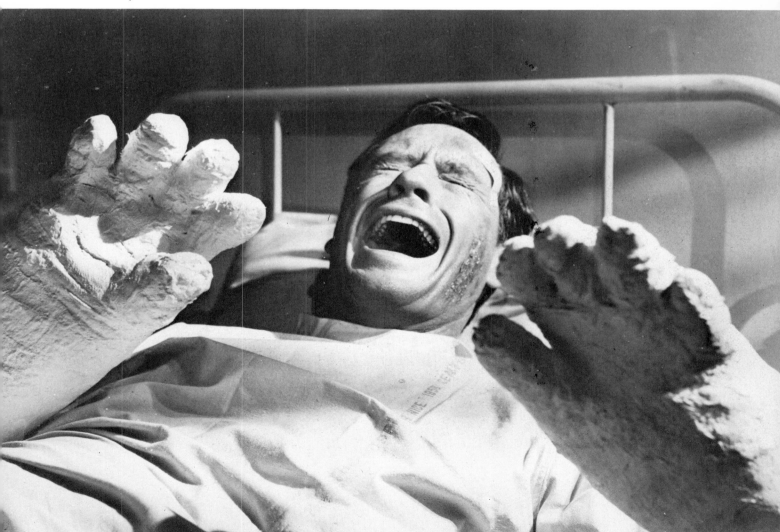

20 The Black Room

Boris Karloff

(Columbia, 1935) Directed by Roy William Neill. Original story by Arthur Strawn. Screenplay by Arthur Strawn and Henry Myers. Camera, Al Siegler.

With Boris Karloff, Marian Marsh, Robert Allen, Thurston Hall, Katherine DeMille, John Buckler, Frederick Vogeding, Torben Meyer, John Bleifer, Henry Kolker, Edward van Sloan, Egon Brecher, Lois Lindsey, Herbert Evans, Colin Tapley, John George, Robert Middlemass, Michael Mark, Sidney Bracey.

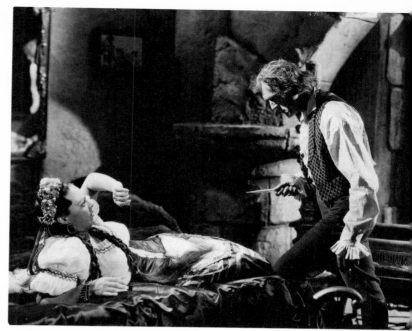

Boris Karloff, Katherine deMille

With a plot line, much in the Wilkie Collins–*The Woman in White* tradition, and a little of *The Man in the Iron Mask* thrown in for good measure, *The Black Room* is a curious one-shot horror film for Columbia. Karloff plays a dual role as twin brothers, one kindly and thoughtful of his feudal tenants, the other evil, murderous and lecherous. The scenario, though an original for the screen, manages to suggest that it might be drawn from some Victorian classic melodrama, for it is replete with a prologue, a family curse, and the sinister, hidden Black Room of the title. It is equipped with a deep pit into which enemies, competitors and discarded mistresses can be dropped to their doom. Needless to say, the evil brother murders the good one, masquerades as him (even to duplicating his paralyzed left arm) and is exposed (by the good brother's loyal mastiff) just in time to prevent his marriage to the innocent heroine, and the wrongful execution of the hero.

Superficially, at least, it is almost as stylish a production as James Whale's films for Universal, and Columbia never again did anything quite like it. Certainly, their quartet (quintet, if one includes the spoof *The Boogie Man Will Get You*) of Karloff horror films in the early 40s, though interesting, didn't match the quality of this earlier film. With its traditionally Victorian story of prophecy, sealed rooms, and family curses, and effectively Gothic pictorial castle, church, and cemetery scenes, it is the kind of (serious) melodrama that has virtually disappeared from the screen. Many of the exteriors, with their painted brooding skies and distorted trees, are deliberately non-realistic, as were the woods and rocky hills in Universal's first three *Frankenstein* films.

Karloff turns in an excellent performance, and the editing in his dual role scenes is particularly neat. The musical themes throughout are first rate, interestingly speeded-up in the climactic reel, and

Boris Karloff, Marian Marsh

Boris Karloff, Katherine deMille

transformed from macabre *mysterioso* motifs into all-out *agitato* music. In this speeded-up form, the themes were later used as standard fast action chase music in the serial *The Secret of Treasure Island,* and other serials and Westerns. Roy William Neill, who directed, also made all but the first of the Universal Sherlock Holmes mysteries, another neat Columbia "Old House" chiller, *The Ninth Guest,* and *Frankenstein Meets the Wolf Man.* He was stronger on pace and movement than on atmospherics, but in *The Black Room* he managed both with distinction.

21 The Walking Dead

Finding peace only in a cemetery, he is murdered there by gangsters.

(Warner Bros., 1936) Directed by Michael Curtiz. Screenplay by Ewart Adamson, Peter Milne, Robert Adams and Lillie Hayward from an original story by Ewart Adamson and Joseph Fields. Camera, Hal Mohr.

With Boris Karloff, Edmund Gwenn, Ricardo Cortez, Marguerite Churchill, Warren Hull, Barton MacLane, Henry O'Neill, Joe Sawyer, Addison Richards, Joseph King, Eddie Acuff, Ruth Robinson, Kenneth Harlan, Miki Morita, Adrian Rosley, Milt Kibbee, Bill Elliott.

An always underrated Karloff vehicle, *The Walking Dead* is far more intelligent, thoughtful, and directorially stylish than its rather sensational title and a misleading, gruesome trailer would lead one to expect. The plurality of the title suggests a film about a *group* of Vampires or Zombies, but actually, only one dead man is reactivated, and not until the second half of the film.

Karloff is an ex-convict, framed by a gang of mobsters who kill off the judge who originally sentenced him, in order to save their own higher-ups from certain conviction by the same incorruptible judge. They also browbeat into silence the only witnesses who can prove Karloff's innocence. He is tried and electrocuted—but brought back to life by scientist Edmund Gwenn. His grim, spectral appearances among the gangsters causes each of them, one by one, to bring about their own deaths, and he finally dies again himself, his last words describing the death that he had known and returned from as "peace." A good, if grim thriller, rather than a traditional horror film, it is quite devoid of the vulgarity and cheap shocks that characterized *The Monster and the Girl,* a poor Paramount horror film of the early 40s with a generally parallel plot. (So muddled was its plot line, and so vague the many characters involved, that most audiences still don't realize that the racket the villains were involved in was white slavery!)

Apart from one major concession to the horror image—a laboratory sequence in which Karloff's makeup and Mohr's cunningly angled shots contrive to make Karloff look suspiciously like the Frankenstein Monster—the film never really *tries* to scare its audience. It would be difficult anyway, since audience sympathy is immediately with Karloff. Hero, heroine, "good guys," and innocent bystanders are never in jeopardy, and the audience is automatically rooting for the successful comple-

138

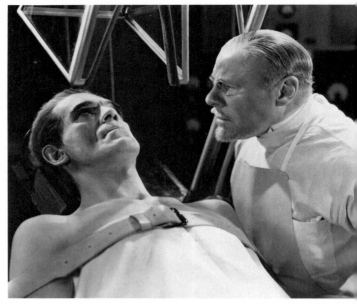

Unjustly executed, Karloff is brought back to life by scientist Edmund Gwenn

Karloff's campaign of retribution brings death to those who had wronged him

Music is the one joy that the man from the dead finds in his new life; in the background, Marguerite Churchill

tion of Karloff's series of destiny-supervised deaths. Not having to worry about scaring his audence, the versatile Michael Curtiz—who dashed this one off quickly and efficiently before getting down to more serious matters with *Stolen Holiday* and *The Charge of the Light Brigade*—concentrates instead on pace, mood, good performances from an often quite literate script, and helping to keep Mohr's camerawork sharp, well varied, and incisive. (It is often difficult to ascertain where the responsibility for the actual on-screen image ceases to be that of the director and becomes that of the cameraman; but all of Curtiz' horror films and melo-

dramas have such similar use of design and lighting that it is apparent that he worked very closely with his art directors and cameramen, injecting his own pictorial style into every film he made.)

Curtiz was too good a showman not to use such reliable props as rain, and thunder, and graveyards, but he uses them as dramatic backdrops to already taut situations, rather than as lazy devices to beef up dull scenes. In many ways *The Walking Dead* is one of Karloff's most interesting and satisfying films, and oddly enough, it is the only horror film in the quintet of starring vehicles that he made for Warners.

22 The Man Who Changed His Mind

The final experiment: Anna Lee (assisted by Cecil Parker, rear) performs the brain transference operation which saves hero John Loder

(Gaumont-British, 1936) Directed by Robert Stevenson. Screenplay by Sidney Gilliat and John L. Balderston, from a story by L. duGarde Peach. Camera, Jack Cox. Released in the United States as The Man Who Lived Again, *and later reissued as* The Brain Snatcher.

With Boris Karloff, Anna Lee, John Loder, Frank Cellier, Lyn Harding, Cecil Parker, Donald Calthrop.

Never as well known or as appreciated as it deserved to be, and perhaps now never likely to be, since the lack of really good or complete printing materials preclude the probability of a reissue or television sale, *The Man Who Changed His Mind* is in many ways the best and most sophisticated of the trio of horror films that Boris Karloff made in Britain in the 30s. *The Ghoul* was more in the Hollywood mold, and *Juggernaut* probably seemed like a good idea at the time, in that it got Karloff away from stereotyped menaces into a more sensible kind of villain role, but it was so stiff and unexciting that years later it was remade as a straight drama.

The Man Who Changed His Mind, however—the subtlety of the semi-pun title was clearly lost on the American distributors, who changed it to *The Man Who Lived Again*—was and is quite unique. One has a clue to its special qualities by noting its two scenarists: reliable John Balderston, deadly serious screenwriter of many stage-derived chillers of the early 30s, *Dracula* among them, and Sidney Gilliat, writer for Hitchcock and Carol Reed before becoming a writer-director himself, and one of Britain's best to boot. Gilliat's special *forte* was wit, the well-turned phrase cropping up at precisely the right moment to punctuate and give added flavor to a thrill or suspense sequence.

The plot premise is quite a good one. Karloff, as Doctor Laurience, is working on experiments whereby (as in the much later *The Fly*) matter can be dissolved, transmitted and reassembled. The focal point of this experiment is to exchange brains within bodies, with the praiseworthy aim of prolonging the useful life of creative brains which would normally die when their bodies aged. (Presumably the success of such an experiment could also lead to a lively black market in youthful bodies!) Progressing from monkeys to humans, Karloff successfully transposes the brain of his crippled and dying assistant (Donald Calthrop) to the body of a financial wizard and potential backer (Frank Cellier). Cellier, inheriting the old, worn-

Boris Karloff

out body, dies himself, of course—but audiences in the depression-ridden 30s had little sympathy for financial wizards. Cellier's son (John Loder) investigates, and falls in love with Anna Lee, Karloff's charming and able assistant. Ultimately, Karloff transposes his own mind to Loder's body, and the Karloff body (with Loder's mind) falls from a window as the police close in. Loder is near death, but the resourceful Anna Lee forces Karloff to submit to a reversal of the operation. Loder is restored to his former self, and Karloff dies quite happily, asking forgiveness, and suggesting that, his theories proven, it might now be better for mankind if his notes and apparatus were to die with him.

Doctor and assistant; Karloff and Anna Lee

Between them, Gilliat and Balderston come up with a beautifully balanced screenplay which allows the well-staged laboratory scenes and other thrill highlights to be played straight, but much of the intermediate material to be tongue-in-cheek. Before his demise, Frank Cellier's board meetings allow for some pungent dialogue and some witty political barbs. The *genre* itself is kidded in an affectionate way. When, at the beginning of the film, Anna Lee arrives at a deserted region in rural British suburbia and asks to be taken to Karloff's house, the cabbie reacts with all the superstitious horror of a Transylvanian coachman ordered to drive to Borgo Pass on Walpurgis Night. Karloff's own defensive descriptions of his scientific aims include several genial variations on the "You think I'm mad?" clichés.

Like all Gaumont-British films of the period (successful at home, and aiming at the American market), it is a goodlooking production all the way,

with atmospheric art direction for the exteriors and laboratory scenes, and the overall polish and elegance of Hollywood standards. Karloff seemed totally attuned to the aims of the film, playing his menace straight, but never dehumanizing himself to a bogeyman level, so that there were no jolting lurches as the mood shifted from thrill to light comedy. Robert Stevenson, who directed, was, next to Alfred Hitchcock and Victor Saville, Gaumont-British's most valuable asset. He never had time to specialize, being shunted from action-adventure (*King Solomon's Mines*) and suspense-thriller (*Non-Stop New York*) to comedies and romances, without a breather. Ultimately, like Hitchcock and Saville, he went to Hollywood. *The Man Who Changed His Mind* was his only horror film, which is a pity, for—backed up, of course, by a solid script—he brought a civilized sophistication to the *genre* which it all too rarely displayed, or even thought necessary.

142

23 The Devil Doll

Raffaela Ottiano

(MGM, 1936) Directed by Tod Browning. Screenplay by Tod Browning, Erich von Stroheim, Garrett Fort and Guy Endore from the novel Burn Witch Burn *by Abraham Merritt; Camera, Leonard Smith.*

With Lionel Barrymore, Maureen O'Sullivan, Frank Lawton, Henry B. Walthall, Lucy Beaumont, Robert Greig, Arthur Hohl, Grace Ford, Pedro de Cordoba, Rafaela Ottiano, Juanita Quigley, Claire du Brey, Rollo Lloyd, E. Allyn Warren, Billy Gilbert, Eily Malyon, Egon Brecher, Frank Reicher.

Tod Browning's second-from-last film shouldn't be confused with two much more recent British thrillers, an unrelated *Devil Doll*, which has its inspiration in the ventriloquist sequence of *Dead of Night,* and a *Burn Witch Burn,* which is actually only the American release title for *Night of the Eagle,* and which derives not from Merritt's science fiction novel, but from Fritz Leiber's *Conjure Wife.*

Browning's films, many of them long unseen, some of them only recently available for re-appraisal, have recently become the center of a rather curious cult, developed and sustained by young film students, all of them born well after Browning's last film was made. Their enthusiasm and dedication to tracking down facts, to say nothing of often profound analysis of the films themselves, is certainly laudable, and doubtless at least one good and definitive Browning book will emerge from all this overlapping investigation. One's sympathies, however, go out to the few remaining survivors of the Browning "team" (mainly stars, such as Robert Young and Maureen O'Sullivan) who have been subjected to non-stop siege by the Browning investigators, one following on the heels of the other, and all with the same basic questions! The fascination with Browning is difficult to understand: the Browning films' common denominator is more in content (a stress on irony and cruelty, and an obsession with the morbid) than in style, and they work more in isolation than as part of a mass of work. Browning's work *in toto* would seem to both confirm the *auteur* theory, and also pose severe doubts as to the advantages of being an *auteur*. In theory, the more one learns about Browning, the less one should appreciate his achievements, yet this does not seem to have been the case.

Apart from their plot lines, often unhealthy almost for the sake of it, Browning's films have usually had one major flaw: a dynamic and bizarre opening that is both disturbing and attention-getting (*Dracula* with its extended opening sequences at Dracula's castle is, of course, the perfect illustration of this), and then a steady decline into stagey and talkative melodramatics, with no return to the motifs or suggested plot developments by which those opening shots held such promise. Not a few of his films, but especially the silents, *The White Tiger* and *The Show,* and the early talkie *Outside the Law,* not only didn't live up to their pregnant openings, but even contrived, at a little past the halfway mark, to get all of the principal characters locked up in a single room, talking their way to a climax, so that the final denouements were claustrophobic as well as static. His silent films, at least, suggested that Browning had a greater talent as a weaver of ironic and macabre tales than as the director of films based on them. His reputation is based almost solely on his silents, and specifically, those in which he teamed with Lon Chaney.

One wonders idly how he might have fared in collaboration with a director who took the opposite tack, starting slowly, then building steadily towards a strong climax. A Browning partnership with a John Ford or a D. W. Griffith might have been rewarding indeed. But if the Browning silents have been extolled beyond their true values, then his talkies have been maligned in equal exaggeration, tossed aside casually as representing a great talent in total disintegration. Yet the more one sees of his work *en masse,* the more one is forced to the conclusion that his sound films, or at least the best of them, are his best works. Certainly none of his silents had the warmth or compassion of *Freaks,* and none of them had the steadily mounting excitement of *The Devil Doll,* possibly his very best thriller.

To an extent, *The Devil Doll* falls into some of his usual traps. The opening scenes are beautiful: mysterious, abstract credits dissolving into a scene of eerie menace that is not immediately identified. But thereafter, thanks no little to the careful spacing of the big trick sequences, suspense and story values are maintained throughout. Despite Merritt's source novel, the screenplay seems to be inspired in equal part by Browning's own twice-filmed *The Unholy Three,* and Dumas' *The Count of Monte Cristo.*

Lionel Barrymore plays an unjustly imprisoned financier, who breaks out of Devil's Island after a 20-year incarceration, in the company of his friend and fellow-prisoner, scientist Henry B. Walthall. Walthall survives to reach his hideout, demonstrates his scientific discovery (the ability to reduce

Henry B. Walthall, Lionel Barrymore

Lionel Barrymore, Arthur Hohl

animals and humans to doll size), and then suc-
cumbs. Barrymore decides to use the formula to
revenge himself on the three partners who framed
him, and to make life easier for the daughter who
has grown up believing him a criminal. Masquerad-
ing as an old lady with an enterprising line in dolls,
Barrymore manages to reduce two of his former
partners to living dolls; the third, terrified, con-
fesses and proves Barrymore's innocence. His work
done—but complicated by the hate and insanity of
Rafaela Ottiano, Walthall's old partner—Barrymore seeks oblivion. He cannot reveal himself to
his daughter, but satisfied with her new-found happiness, he disappears to a clearly implied off-screen
suicide. Presumably, the Production Code prevented
this being spelled out more clearly; presumably, too,
the Code was ambiguous enough to permit it, since
it expressly forbade "suicide in plot solution"—
and the plot was neatly wrapped up without it.

Considering the quartet of bizarre writers who
collaborated on the screenplay, the fantastic story
values are surprisingly restrained. There's a typical
horror film cliché when Henry B. Walthall delivers
the standard, "You think I'm mad?" speech (although that fine actor manages to make it seem
fresh and sincere), and a glorious moment when
Rafaelo Ottiano hisses, "We'll make the whole
world *small*." But for the most part, the not unworthy scientific experiment (of dubious practical
application, the advantages of a world needing

only a tenth of its normal food supply somewhat
outweighed by the inconveniences of living in a
world where everything is designed for normal-
sized people) is treated in a non-wild and woolly
manner. The photography, lighting, set design, and
matching up of furniture, etc., in the sequences with
the dolls are all beautifully done and infinitely
superior to the cheaper, simpler work in the similar
Dr. Cyclops and *The Incredible Shrinking Man*.

Apart from mild echoes of *The Bride of Frankenstein*, there are more specific throwbacks to Browning's own *The Unholy Three*, in the use of "dolls"
to burglarize a house (in the earlier film, it was a
midget who "passed" as a baby), and in Barrymore's
masquerade as a kindly old woman. It's a pity that
the inspiration (or the budget) didn't extend to
Ethel Barrymore's playing the role of this masquerade, since Lionel's voice would hardly fool
anyone.

Unfortunately, one can only conjecture as to
Erich von Stroheim's participation in the script.
Individual components have much of a Stroheim
look, particularly, the idea of having tragedy and
evil played out against a Christmas tinsel motif
(something he did in both *Greed* and *Walking
Down Broadway*), while the detective's line that the
city is full of religious fanatics around Christmas
also sounds like a typically sour Stroheim line. Most
of all, there is the question of final atonement;
although the climax *seems* rather gentle, especially

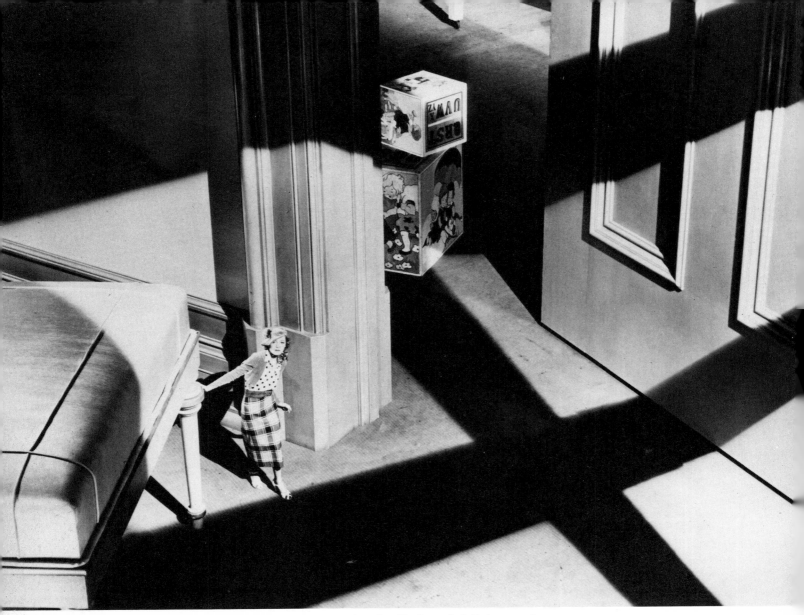

Example of the enlarged props and set to give the illusion of doll-size people

by 1936 censorial standards, examination of the film shows that everybody more than pays for his sins, if not legally, then certainly morally. This excessive expiation was always a Stroheim characteristic. But —to be fair—it must be stressed that these are mere guesses; knowing how MGM worked in those days, it is possible that Stroheim's contribution to the final film was minimal. Coincidentally, as with all films that Stroheim was associated with, there are signs of post-production tampering. The voice of Wilfrid Lucas (an actor not otherwise in the film) is used several times to dub in voice-over lines for players who are off-screen, or whose backs are to the camera.

146

24 The Devil Commands

The grim climactic laboratory scene: Karloff, daughter Amanda Duff, and friends borrowed from the cemetery

(Columbia, 1941) Directed by Edward Dmytryk. Produced by Wallace MacDonald. Screenplay by Robert D. Andrews and Milton Gunzburg from the novel The Edge of Running Water *by William Sloane. Camera, Allen Siegler.*

With Boris Karloff, Amanda Duff, Richard Fiske, Ann Revere, Ralph Penney, Kenneth McDonald, Dorothy Adams, Walter Baldwin, Shirley Warde.

Although it is considered something of a disappointment by those to whom William Sloane's original novel is a minor masterpiece of subtle horror, *The Devil Commands* is, nevertheless, by far the best of the quartet of decidedly economical horror films that Boris Karloff made for Columbia in 1939-40. (The others, in order of production, and surprisingly for a "B" series in *reverse* order of merit, were *The Man They Couldn't Hang, The Man With Nine Lives,* and *Before I Hang.*)

Its story line, regardless of how much it may compromise the original, is the least hackneyed of the group, and its director, Edward Dmytryk (still a new and vigorous filmmaker, turning out much better movies on the whole then than in his later days of bigger and "important" films), managed to give it far more style than Nick Grinde was able to impart to the other three. Unfortunately, it was the last of the series and, as always with such wrap-up films, the budget allocation was virtually threadbare. While the others had been cheap, they had enjoyed the benefits of decent sets and such useful supporting players as Edward Van Sloan, Evelyn Keyes, and Charles Trowbridge. Apart from some quite good laboratory equipment—inexpensive, but made to look rather impressive by cunning angling, lighting, and photography—Columbia provided Dmytryk with virtually no production facilities at all. Except for a short stretch of road, the few "exteriors" were all studio interiors; the sets were so cheap that Dmytryk was forced to an unsubtle over-use of darkness and shadows to hide their lack of substance, and while the opening model shot of Karloff's cliff house served its purpose well enough as an establishing night scene, camouflaged by narration, music, and sound effects of wind and thunder, it couldn't—and didn't—stand up to the scrutiny of use in a daytime scene. All of this was doubly harmful, since the plot—involving Karloff's initial experiments to record the thought waves of the human mind, and his accidental stumbling into a possible way of communicating with the dead—was basically a good one. It even had the wit to debunk the commercial artifice of spiritualism, but to admit that mediums *can* possess a psychic power after all. Since the world of the spiritualist is at least closer to one's own experience than the world of the Monster or the Mad Doctor, and since all of us, in varying degrees, are fascinated by and afraid of death and the unknown, the film could have manipulated audience emotions to a remarkable degree. Thanks to Dmytryk's skill, it did anyway—the audience did a lot of the work, scaring themselves with their own fears, but the production itself was too cheap and artificial-looking to be really convincing. The story certainly warranted upper-bracket production; with a longer running time, decent sets, and a greater use of actual locations to stress the juxtaposition of the next world with the reality of the present, this could have been a genuinely frightening film, bringing to the motif of spiritualism the same mood of utter conviction that *The Uninvited* brought to a story of a haunted house.

But even with its severe limitations, the film plays chillingly well. A past-tense narration by Karloff's daughter brings a doom-laden atmosphere to the film even before it is under way, though the underplaying of her lines results in some unintentionally hilarious moments. "Why are they afraid?" she inquires petulantly, telling the audience about the villagers who fear to go near her father's now

Karloff as the scientist who mixes electricity with spiritualism

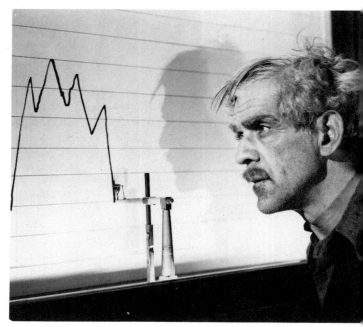

deserted house, while the picture on screen and the sound-effects track are working furiously overtime at creating an image of the darkest of old dark houses, perched over crashing breakers, and surrounded by halos of lightning flashes! Other moments are subtler, however. There is a casual introduction of Karloff's wife when she comes into his laboratory during a thunderstorm, her face momentarily hidden by the hood of her black raincoat. Later, after her death, there is exactly the same casually introduced shot of her daughter coming into the laboratory—identically angled, and likewise wearing a black raincoat and hood. Without shock-cutting or crashing music, the audience gets almost as great a jolt as Karloff. The seance sequence, dominated by Ann Revere, has an enjoyable queasiness to it, and the laboratory sequences, in which Karloff's weird, robot-like machines (manned by the corpses acquired in off-screen graverobbing) vibrate to the current produced by his apparatus, are genuinely weird. One sequence in which a nervous maidservant is locked in with and killed by the suddenly activated machinery is a particularly strong and well done episode.

The "seedy" quality of the decor and sets (Columbia *was* capable of the lushest of visual looks, as is apparent in such specials as *Gilda*) unfortunately extends down to a more personal level as well. Kar-

loff appears to be using old studio-wardrobe clothes rather than his own; his makeup (even in the earlier scenes, before the script has him become something of a physical wreck) is careless, and the camerawork hardly shows him to advantage. He looks ten years older here than in a contemporary and more polished Universal horror film, *Black Friday.* Nevertheless, it is a classic example of how one good director, one good actor, and a basically good story can combine to produce something worthwhile despite a plethora of obstacles and a dearth of advantages. A measure of its effectiveness is that one always tends to take it reasonably seriously, even when Karloff—convinced of the presence of his dead wife—straps his frightened daughter to a chair, surrounds her with weird machines and sundry corpses, and chidingly admonishes her not to be nervous!

Unlike *The Man They Couldn't Hang*—in which Karloff was allowed to prove his formula by bringing his daughter back from death, before dying himself and taking his secret with him—*The Devil Commands* doesn't provide that ultimate satisfaction before he, his machines, and his workshop collapse in a very budget-conscious holocaust. And his years of work are dismissed with the rather defeatist remark, "There are things that human beings have no right to know."

Karloff, then playing on Broadway in *Arsenic and Old Lace,* arrives at Times Square's Rialto Theatre where *The Devil Commands* is having its premiere.

25 Man Made Monster

Lon Chaney, Jr., Anne Nagel

(Universal, 1941) Directed by George Waggner. Screenplay by Joseph West, from an original story by Sid Schwartz, H. J. Essex and Len Golos. Camera, Eldwood Bredell. Special Effects by John Fulton.

With Lon Chaney, Jr., Lionel Atwill, Anne Nagel, Frank Albertson, Samuel S. Hinds, William B. Davidson, Ben Taggart, Connie Bergen, Ivan Miller, Chester Gan, George Meader, Frank O'Connor, John Dilson, Byron Foulger, Russell Hicks.

Man Made Monster is a special kind of "classic" —or perhaps "model" would be a better word for it. It was little more than a "B" picture, a classification underlined by its mere 59-minute running time. Yet it was eminently superior to Universal's earlier (1940) foray into a "B" horror film with *The Mummy's Hand*, a slick little film, with far too much comedy padding, until it got down to serious business in its closing reels. Yet *Man Made Monster* had a couple of distinct advantages going for it. First, it was designed as a trial run for the studio's proposed new horror star, Lon Chaney, Jr., and thus, was given far more care than the average "B." (It more than succeeded in its aim of establishing him, and *The Wolf Man* and *The Ghost of Frankenstein* were immediate and more elaborate followups.) Second, it benefited from the revamped utilization of an old, but never filmed, Karloff-Lugosi script, and had literary qualities at least a notch or two above the average. Chaney, a fairground sideshowman, whose act involves playing around with electricity, is the sole survivor when a bus crashes into an electric pylon, and medical examination shows that he has somehow built up an immunity to electricity. Unfortunately, his opportunities to exploit his talents, either in show business or in the world of medicine and electronics, are short-circuited when he falls into the eager hands of Lionel Atwill.

Atwill is his usual amiable, over-zealous self as a Mad Doctor who seeks to build a race of supermen. (Atwill's scientific experiments were usually singularly lacking in point, and devoid of the at least partially sound medical foundation that characterized Karloff's work). As Atwill's guinea pig, Chaney—not exactly the life of the party to begin with—is systematically drained of his energy and transformed into a Zombie-like slave to Atwill's will. The increasing use of dark eye makeup, and Chaney's disturbing talent for electrocuting pet goldfish, cause a certain uneasiness among his

Lionel Atwill as Dr. Rigas

friends, but no outright suspicion. However, when Samuel S. Hinds—Atwill's superior, and the heroine's father—stumbles upon the truth, Chaney, acting under Atwill's dominance, murders him. Chaney is tried and sentenced to death in the electric chair, much to Atwill's delight, for this will provide a supreme (and if successful indisputable) proof of Atwill's theory of electrical supermen.

Chaney absorbs all the current that the executioners can provide, breaks out of the death chamber, murders the warden, and stalks through the countryside literally glowing. Atwill takes him in tow, fits him up with an energy-conserving rubber suit, but unfortunately, comes a cropper when the heroine denounces him as being mad—a tactless remark at the best of times, but a downright fool-hardy one when trapped in a laboratory with him! Lechery taking over from science for a moment, Atwill straps the heroine (Anne Nagel, before Evelyn Ankers became Universal's resident lady-in-distress) to an operating table and chortles about the fascination of proving his theories on the female of the species. Chaney, however, recovers the innate decency that had been distressingly dormant when he was instructed to murder the lady's father, and disposes of Atwill in a shower of sparks, then takes off across the countryside, only to fall foul of a barbed wire fence, and have the electricity—and his life—slowly ebb through the tears in his insulated clothing.

In its own way, *Man Made Monster* was an expert little made-to-measure horror vehicle, delivering everything that the fans expected, including clichés that were still new enough to be welcome friends, and not—as they would be in just a few years—repetitious bores. Chaney, fresh from *Of Mice and Men,* and still considered essentially a character actor, played his fairly well written role for pathos and tragedy as much as menace, and came as close as he ever would to Karloff's genius for making an audience feel sorry for him even while they feared him. But it was Atwill's show all the way. He delivered all of his glorious lines with either bravura or understatement, depending on the situation, but *always* with relish. Just before Chaney is to be subjected to his first major experiment at Atwill's hands, he asks curiously why the rabbit isn't being used again. "Oh—well, the rabbit worked yesterday," explains Atwill, with a nervous hesitation which makes us all aware that we'll never see *that* rabbit again and at the same time bodes ill for Chaney's own future. Then, when Chaney is nicely strapped into the maze of electrical equipment, Atwill turns on his best bedside manner. "Relax!" he beams confidently, before turning up the voltage.

However, his real moment of glory comes when the heroine has the temerity to question his sanity. His eyes light up as though fueled by an internal laser beam, and he launches into the inevitable, always eagerly awaited soliloquy of the inspired Mad Scientist, rapidly ticking off the names of

Galileo, Marconi, and others, who were thought mad by their own generations, and indicating that his own experiment will provide a spectacular climax to their humble beginnings. Even Samuel S. Hinds has his own cliché-highlight when, confronting Atwill with his perfidy, he utters that time-honored invitation to destruction—"You're mad!

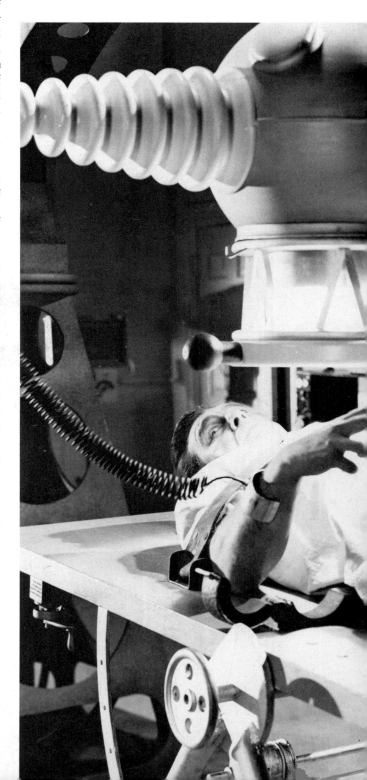

I'm going to notify the police!"—and is a good enough actor to look surprised when he is promptly liquidated.

Man Made Monster aimed more at science fiction thrills than at real terror, and except for its lack of macabre comedy, somewhat resembled *The Invisible Man*. The laboratory scenes were spectacular and exciting, and made good use of low-key lighting for closeups of Atwill and Chaney, but it was a clean and ultra-efficient laboratory, with none of the musty decay and cobwebs of Dr. Frankenstein's workshop. The few exteriors—as in Chaney's final nocturnal prowl—were naturalistic, in contrast to the unreal stylization and dead trees of *Son of*

Lon Chaney Jr. (on table) and Lionel Atwill

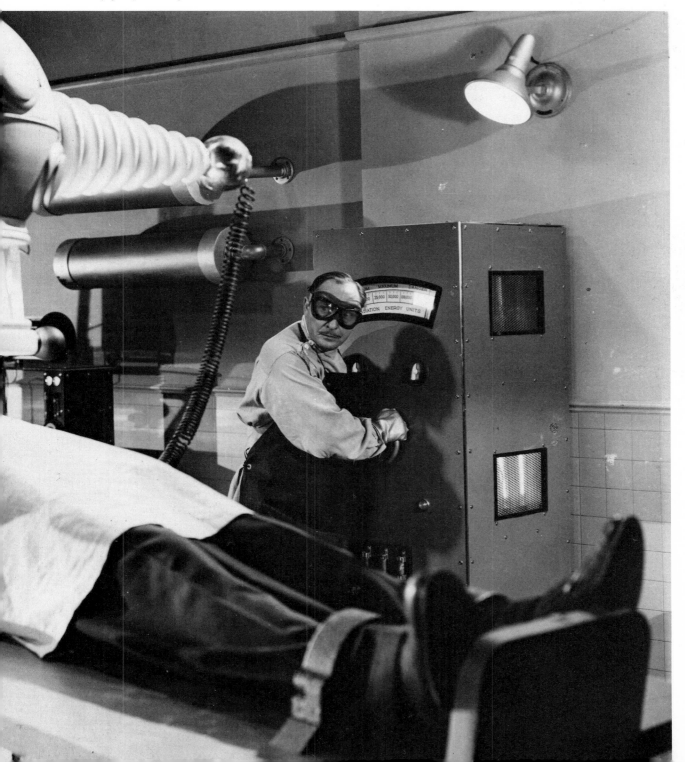

The Mad Ghoul (1943): Evelyn Ankers, Turhan Bey and
David Bruce.

Frankenstein. Other scenes were sleek and cheerfully lit, ranging from the hero's modern roadster
to the heroine's expensive house and sunny garden.

Atmospherics were mainly a matter of Hans J.
Salter's musical scoring. However, it was made at
an interim stage in Universal's horror program; its
success would pave the way for a more aggressive
attempt to scare audiences in subsequent movies.
Even as it stood, it was considered too grim by the
British censors, although the cutting of most of the
deathhouse sequences was mainly a matter of taste.
The British censors have always frowned on the
often over-morbid Hollywood stress on ritualized
execution scenes. Moreover, there was a wartime
ban on all horror films in England, so the dis-
tributor's decision to make minor cuts and to
change the title to *The Electric Man* was a way
of sneaking it through as a thriller, rather than a
chiller. (During a later American reissue, the film
also picked up a third title: *The Atomic Monster*.)

Despite being a successful model of its kind—
packing two star names, good production values,
and a solid story into a "B" picture running less
than an hour—*Man Made Monster* was not emulated by Universal. With horror films back on their
schedule, they clearly differentiated between reasonably expensive "A" efforts and increasingly standardized "B"s. It is hard to realize that only a couple
of years (and a great deal of talent) separate *Man
Made Monster* from 1943's *The Mad Ghoul*, a
singularly pointless, nonatmospheric and pedestrian
bore, redeemed only by the vitality of George
Zucco's Mad Scientist. One British critic commented that "to be a ghoul must be disconcerting
enough, but to be a *mad* ghoul must be the height
of personal embarrassment."

26 The Night Has Eyes

The Night Has Eyes: Joyce Howard, James Mason

(Associated British-Pathé, 1942) Written and directed by Leslie Arliss. Produced by John Argyle. based on the novel by Alan Kennington. Camera, Gunther Krampf. Music, Charles Williams. Art Director, Duncan Sutherland. United States release title, Terror House.

With James Mason, Wilfrid Lawson, Mary Clare, Joyce Howard, Tucker McGuire, John Fernald, Dorothy Black, Amy Daley.

Although Pathé was one of the most conservative of British producers, specializing in rather outdated romance and comedy, they very occasionally let themselves go with an all-out thriller. Lugosi's *Dark Eyes of London* was one, and *The Night Has Eyes*, a mating of *The Old Dark House* and *Jane Eyre*, was another. Its success as a chiller proved an unexpected embarrassment to them. With good reviews and a prestige name in James Mason (then on the threshold of being Britain's biggest star), it was booked into the huge Odeon circuit as a booster to support a disappointing "A" film. Suddenly, the British censors (who were illogically strict on horror films during the war years) had second thoughts, and reclassified the film "H"—a horror film to which under-sixteens were strictly forbidden. This meant a wholesale cancellation by the circuit houses (then reluctant to play films which couldn't draw on the entire family trade), hurried replacements and interesting reissues all over London, and an unexpected bonus for the independent cinemas, which suddenly had first crack at a classy and commercial thriller.

Although its horror content is limited to key sequences, it is still a powerful and quite grisly chiller, fairly obvious in its plotting perhaps, but no less effective for all of that. Gunther Krampf, who had also photographed *The Ghoul*, made more than the most of the handsome but economical sets, particularly in the earlier sequences of two girls trapped on a bog-ridden moor at the height of a thunderstorm! The dialogue is crisp, mature and well written (except for a single moment, when the heroine turns on the villain, and gasps, "Why, you're EVIL!"). The film also boasts two of those standbys of wartime British movies—the piano concerto theme music, and the disillusioned, Mr. Rochester-derived hero. Since any patriotic Englishman would naturally be in the Armed Forces, there was quite a spate of heroes who were either going blind, possessed fortuitous (but not obvious) injuries, or were cynical through experience in prior wars.

James Mason in *The Night Has Eyes* is a more brooding parallel to Melvyn Douglas in *The Old Dark House*. The sets—lonely house, moors, quicksand—are effective in the stylish if studio-bound manner of *The Hound of the Baskervilles*, and the film's only real drawback (a minor one, and less jarring than in *Dark Eyes of London*) is its insistence on obtrusive "American" comedy relief. However, this is more than offset by the macabre humor provided by the delightful and openly dirty-minded villainy of Wilfrid Lawson.

27 Dr.Cyclops

Albert Dekker

(Paramount, 1939; released 1940) Directed by Ernest B. Schoedsack. Produced by Dale Van Every. Screenplay by Tom Kilpatrick. Camera, Henry Sharp, Winton Hoch. Music by Ernst Toch, Gerard Carbonara, Albert Malotte.

With Albert Dekker, Janice Logan, Thomas Coley, Charles Halton, Victor Killian, Frank Yaconelli, Frank Reicher, Paul Fix.

In a year overrun with the cloying ministrations of *Dr. Kildare* and *Dr. Christian,* the medical malpractices of *Dr. Cyclops* somewhat restored the balance. An interesting stunt shocker, part of the big new horror cycle that had started with *Son of Frankenstein,* it marked Ernest B. Schoedsack's return to the horror field after some curiously empty and wasted years in which the glories of *King Kong* had given way to pleasant programmers like John Barrymore's *Long Lost Father,* and the Jack Holt melodrama *Outlaws of the Orient.* Moreover, it represented the first attempt since *The Mystery of the Wax Museum* to harness Technicolor to the service of screen horror. In a sense, it could be considered the first deliberate attempt to use color to serve the ends of horror, for while those ends certainly had been served earlier by Warner *Brothers,* and very creatively too, the motivation was commercial rather than artistic, the use of color then dictated by contractual obligation.

The return of Schoedsack, the use of color, the novelty of the subject matter—veering more to science fiction than most of the other horror films of the 1939–1940 years—perhaps justify the inclusion of the usually ignored and frankly disappointing *Dr. Cyclops* in a discussion of horror classics, although it is far from classic itself. Green is a color commonly associated with emotions of fear, and the dominating greens of *Dr. Cyclops* are certainly effective in the occasional laboratory scenes where the scientist uses radium rays to reduce humans to doll size. But for the most part, the use of green against a jungle background invariably produces the lush, cheerful effect that Paramount emphasized in their tropical adventure romances with Dorothy Lamour. The color made everything so bright and gay that it robbed the plot of menace or suspense, and it was helped in this by a jolly, frolicking musical score, almost Disney-like in its concentration on the novelty of the situation rather than its horror. (Quite incidentally, the storm sequence, which should have been genuinely night-

Dr. Thorkel (Albert Dekker) searches for his doll-size victims. This is a composite publicity still, and the scene in the film itself is less impressive. In addition, Charles Halton (2nd from the left) had actually been killed off before this sequence, and had no business being included in the still!

marish since it is the doll people's first experience with the outside world in their new size, is much inferior to, and certainly less frightening than Disney's similar storm sequence in *Snow White and the Seven Dwarfs.*)

Schoedsack, who prepared everything so carefully and mathematically in *King Kong,* is here bland and casual to a fault: everything starts too early, continues placidly on an even keel, and finishes with only the slightest buildup to a climax. There is not even the (one would think both obligatory

The murder of the professor (Charles Halton), the one really chilling moment of the film.

and essential) subjective view of the giant scientist from the doll people's point of view. The economical trick work is largely a matter of a few mattes and a lot of back projection; well enough done, the fakery minimized by the camouflage of color, but devoid of real imagination, and especially lacking the presence of Willis O'Brien. (What that superb technician could have done with the scenes in which the doll people find themselves menaced by cat, dog, and alligator!) Albert Dekker, then a relative newcomer, employs effectively sinister makeup and a few of the standard Mad Doctor punch lines, but has none of the verve of an Atwill or a Zucco. Thomas Coley's hero is singularly dull, and Janice Logan is pretty and ladylike, but a rank amateur in the bosom-heaving screams that call for the expertise of a Fay Wray. Charles Halton, as one of the professors, plays professionally, and

his death is a very chilling moment, not least because his acting momentarily turns the film from a colorful charade into something with a tangible grasp on reality. Too, in view of the general pussy-footing approach until that moment, his unexpected demise produces a much needed jolt.

Color (no longer a novelty, but not yet commonplace either, and good enough to be a box office asset in itself) was presumably the major cost factor with this film: the cast was inexpensive, the production values no more than adequate (though color always "dresses up" cheap productions), and the special effects decidedly cheap. As much money was spent on an admittedly striking advertising campaign as had been spent on the picture itself, and commercially, it undoubtedly paid off well for Paramount. It remains diverting hokum—but one of the major wasted opportunities among horror films.

28 Two Ghost Classics
The Uninvited
Dead of Night

Dead of Night: Michael Redgrave in the ventriloquist sequence

THE UNINVITED

(Paramount, 1944) Directed by Lewis Allen. Associate Producer, Charles Brackett. Screenplay by Dodie Smith and Frank Partos from the novel by Dorothy Macardle. Music, Victor Young. Camera, Charles Lang. Special Effects, Ferciot Edouart. Art Direction by Hans Dreier and Ernst Fegte.

With Ray Milland, Ruth Hussey, Gail Russell, Donald Crisp, Cornelia Otis Skinner, Dorothy Stickney, Barbara Everest, Alan Napier, · Jessica Newcombe, John Kieran, Rita Page.

The *serious* ghost story was virtually unknown in the cinema of the 30s—at least insofar as the English-speaking cinema was concerned. In the less realistic, more stylized milieu of the silent film, ghosts put in frequent and even casual appearances. But in the first decade of the sound film, when movies were supposed to have greater realism, it was felt that audiences would find ghosts either unacceptable or laughable or both. When they did appear, it was usually in a symbolic, literary, and non-contemporary sense, as in different versions of Dickens' *A Christmas Carol.* Even then, the very Hollywood MGM version made sure that audiences wouldn't laugh by making one of the ghosts a very buxom female spirit of substantial, Ziegfeldian proportions!

The war changed all this. Death of loved ones became a much closer threat, and the movies began to conjecture philosophically on the meanings and effects of death. Britain made a number of thoughtful, semi-intellectual films (*Thunder Rock, Halfway House* among them) which were certainly not horror films, though they had their macabre elements, in which past and present were interchangeable, and the spirits of the dead return to influence the living. These films led, indirectly, to one of the finest of all British ghost films, deliberately and very much a thriller, *Dead of Night.* Hollywood's war-inspired ghost stories were less fatalistic and far more romantic than Britain's. Initially, in short propaganda films, and then in the feature *A Guy Named Joe* (1943), they idealized death, softened the blow and showed the unscarred victims of war coming back after death to comfort wives, sweethearts, mothers and fathers, to assure them that their sacrifice had been worthwhile, and that they, the survivors, could find solace in keeping faith with the ideals for which they had died. The sentimentality in these tales was quite banal, but since the home front was far removed from the battlefront, and the grieving families had no first-hand knowledge of what war was really like, they probably filled a mildly useful and generally harmless niche. (It's significant that Britain, much closer to actual war, never tried to romanticize death in this way.)

In any event, the audience acceptance of ghosts on this artificial level undoubtedly paved the way for a romantic, but far more serious ghost story, in *The Uninvited.* (Interestingly enough, the producers maintained the English locale of the original novel, instead of switching it to Connecticut, as could easily have been done—presumably on the theory that if audiences didn't buy it on a serious level, the less familiar, older, and tradition-steeped English background would make it seem less outlandish!)

Like so many directorial "firsts," this initial film by Lewis Allen remains far and away the best film he ever made. It is also quite probably the movies' best ghost story, rivaled certainly by the mirror sequence in *Dead of Night,* but generally quite superior to *The Innocents, The Haunting, The Legend of Hell House,* and the very few other movies that have had the integrity to take their phantoms seriously without explaining it all away at the end, via natural or at least human agencies— as did this film's followup, *The Unseen,* an admirable thriller until its last-reel collapse.

To be sure, there are flaws in the film. In its determination to avoid mere sensation, it wisely underplays, and builds up a genuinely frightening web of intangibles which cannot be explained away. In that sense, it succeeds far more than *The Innocents,* which shows us the phantoms too clearly and too frequently, so that familiarity breeds if not contempt, then at least lack of doubt. But on the other hand, in avoiding visual horror it avoids most of the other visual elements too; too many things are *talked* about that could have been shown graphically and excitingly while still keeping the supernatural content to suggestion. Editing, camera-work, Victor Young's fine (if romantic) score, all are used to the full in the creation of tense atmospherics; but with one exception, nothing really happens that couldn't have been duplicated, in one way or another, on stage. (The exception is the eventual materialization of the ghost as a shadowy white mist. Some have felt this to be an unsubtle surrender to a need for at least

The Uninvited: Ray Milland, Gail Russell, Ruth Hussey

one special effect, but this seems an unfair criticism.)

After all, this is not a film about the possibility of the supernatural, or about suspicions; it is about ghosts, plain, simple, and uncontested, and there is no reason why, for this moment of extreme crisis, there should not have been a physical materialization. Too, and this may be partially the result of (1944) audiences having been conditioned to his suave comedy image, Ray Milland seems so much in control of the situation throughout that our own fears relax accordingly. Finally, the plotting gets just a little too complicated for its own good towards the end. The rather theatrical melodramatics that are introduced, via Cornelia Otis Skinner and her asylum, are not used to cheat or to find an easy way out, but they do tend to muddy waters that are clear and satisfying enough when they adhere solely to an investigation of the supernatural. Hitchcock gimmickry seems ever in the offing in the closing reels, and while it never materializes, the contrived complications, so suddenly introduced, do rob the film of some of its chilling simplicity. However, these are criticisms that are made only because the film as a whole is so effective. Its limitations are that it is rather like enjoying a good book, or a solid evening at the theatre, rather than watching a film that makes the very most of its potential. But good theatre and good writing are still attributes not to be sneered at, and on those levels the film succeeds remarkably

The Uninvited: Donald Crisp, Gail Russell

well. If it employs some of the literary clichés (such as the lonely old house on the Cornwall cliffs), it also avoids most of the usual ones (red herring characters and excessive ground mists). Above all, it convinces and chills.

Like Dreyer's *Vampyr,* it succeeds in creating the feeling that there is someone—or some*thing*—standing just behind you, silently watching. Its atmosphere is such that even on its fifth or sixth viewing, it still holds up as a fine piece of intellectual goose-pimpling. Those fortunate enough to see it now for the first time should find its impact quite stunning, not least because, for once, Hollywood's depiction of the English rural scene is quite remarkably convincing, but also because the far more graphic quality of the 70s horror films has conditioned us to expect unrestrained physical shocks. Thus, audiences today will undoubtedly be braced defensively against visual horrors that never come—and while the film, in its overall effect, will not let

164

them down, it will also benefit from the audience's unwitting collaboration.

Its persuasiveness is all the more apparent when the film is seen in direct comparison with the prolific output of ghost films from Japan in the 60s. Japan is a country that takes its ghosts quite seriously, albeit placing them in a legendary rather than a contemporary framework, and has afforded them a great deal of screen time in treatments ranging from the romantic and the mystic to the "hard-sell" horror approach. Yet there is a strange contradiction to them: the characters within the films accept the supernatural quite casually, often without question; yet it is obvious that the audiences are expected to be shocked and scared by these apparitions.

A film like *Kwaidan*—an equivalent of *Dead of Night,* in that it is a four-part compendium—may be fascinating visually in its bold use of color and imaginative sets, but (unless the Oriental is frightened by different things than the Westerner) it does virtually everything wrong in its attempts to create suspense and horror out of phantoms and apparitions. The stories, running for almost an hour apiece, are far too long for their own good. Since belief in the supernatural is established at the beginning, the stories don't have to suggest that there are ghosts, but merely confirm it. The last minute "surprise" twists are telegraphed miles in advance, and the heavy-handed, ponderously paced stories turn the ghosts into bores. Only one story works even reasonably well, and that because it is a semi-vampire tale (about a beautiful white lady who appears in the snows to suck the blood of freezing travelers), and the Japanese seem to be on less familiar terms with Vampires than with run-of-the-mill ghosts.

DEAD OF NIGHT

(Ealing Studios—England; 1945) Directed by Alberto Cavalcanti (The Christmas Story and the Ventriloquist Story); Basil Dearden (The Hearse Story and the Framing Story); Charles Crichton (The Golfing Story) and Robert Hamer (The Haunted Mirror). Produced by Michael Balcon. Music by Georges Auric. Camera, Jack Parker. Screenplay by Angus MacPhail and John Baines.

With Michael Redgrave, Mervyn Johns, Googie Withers, Ralph Michael, Frederick Valk, Sally Ann Howes, Basil Radford, Naunton Wayne, Mary

Merrall, Renee Gadd, Anthony Baird, Judy Kelly, Miles Malleson, Michael Allan, Robert Wyndham, Esme Percy, Hartley Power, Elizabeth Welch, Garry Marsh, Magda Kun, Peggy Bryan.

Dead of Night consists of five ghost stories told in the course of an evening by a group of guests at a lonely house, and linked by a sixth story of equally strong proportions, not merely a casual framing device as has become the fashion in such mass-produced, compendium horror films as *The Vault of Horror* or *Tales from the Crypt*. It was released in Britain at a time when audiences—their nerves sensitive from so many years of war—were ripe for such an unrestrained assault! Horror films had been banned by the British censors for the duration of most of the war, on the dubious supposition that audiences had enough real-life horror to keep them tense without the movies' adding to it. It was a somewhat unrealistic theory, since the grim footage of battlefield dead and concentration camp victims outdid anything that Hollywood could dream up. In any event, lesser horror films *were* released, with a few judicious cuts to reduce their impact, while the major horror films were stockpiled, to be released at the rate of one a month after the war.

Thus, *Dead of Night,* a brilliant film anyway, was doubly effective through being the first big "scare" film for several years. It was universally praised by the critics, but many felt that it was ill-timed, that its release should have been delayed until post-war tensions had subsided. The influential *Sunday Pictorial* even came right out and called for it to be banned. Certainly, the film deserved the censor's "H" certificate, designating a horror film for adults over sixteen only, a ruling rigorously enforced. In the past, the censors had frequently fallen back on the "H" rating to keep films with harrowing or controversial content away from juveniles, even though—like *Boy Slaves, Hell's Kitchen, A Child Is Born,* and, absurdly, *On Borrowed Time*—they were certainly not horror films. But an "H" certificate, at that time, severely limited a film's exhibition outlets, virtually denying it a circuit release, and the British censors were realistic enough to realize that this would be both unfair and financially ruinous to a fine film. So it was released with the standard "A" certificate, permitting children to see it so long as they were accompanied by an adult.

Like the Val Lewton films which certainly in-

fluenced it, *Dead of Night* avoids outright statement and concentrates on suggestion, using a skeptical psychiatrist (well played by Frederick Valk) as a figure of reason and scientific fact who, finally, cannot prevail against the unexplained forces of the supernatural. There is nothing of physical horror in the film stronger than a quick shot of a hearse waiting outside a window in the grey dawn, or a sudden, impulsive murder by strangulation in the closing reel. The horror creeps up on the audience slowly, engulfing it; the terror is by implication only, as in the story (charming, and chilling at the same time) of a Christmas party, where a teen-age girl (Sally Ann Howes) comforts a sobbing child in an isolated room—only to find out later that this was the ghost of a boy murdered by his sister.

The stories cover apparitions and premonitions, as in the case of the most celebrated story—that of a ventriloquist's dummy who comes to life and drives his owner to madness, the ventriloquist finally taking on the voice and mannerisms of the dummy that he has "killed." This, the longest,

Dead of Night: Sally Ann Howes in the Christmas Party sequence

Dead of Night: The haunted mirror sequence: Ralph Michael, Googie Withers

Dead of Night: The haunted mirror sequence: Ralph Michael, Googie Withers

most elaborate and climactic story, has been justly praised for its skill, but it has a cold, almost expressionistic quality, and since Michael Redgrave (as the ventriloquist) is obviously neurotic from the beginning of the story, there is no time for a gradual decline into madness to be observed, or for much sympathy to be created. And, unlike the traditional ghost story which poses a threat to everybody in a very general sense, the menace of this story is localized. Its eeriness is aloof, not contagious.

Far more successful—and indeed, perhaps the single most effective ghost story ever brought to the screen—is the second episode, that of a mirror bought from an antique store as a wedding present, which exerts a baleful influence on its new owner. Increasingly, he sees only the reflection of a different, much older room, in the glass. At first, by an effort of will, he is able to force the reflection back to what it should be, but ultimately, its fascination is too strong and he feels himself almost willingly being seduced and "claimed" by the mirror. Apart from the juxtaposition of the *wrong* reflection (oldfashioned bed, drapes, roaring fire) with the modern room (small, neat, compact), nothing is shown of the life beyond the mirror. Its ghostly story—its original owner paralyzed and driven to madness, murder, and suicide, cutting his throat while looking into the mirror—is told in flawless diction and magnificent ghost-story-telling style by Esme Percy (the antique store owner) to the wife (Googie Withers) of the new owner. Even the calm relating of the story—without flashbacks to the event, or even low-key lighting of the story-teller—is a chilling sequence. The wife rushes back to her husband, finds that he has been totally taken over by the mirror, and as he tries to strangle her she, too, sees the reflection of the old room in the glass, just before she manages to shatter it and destroy its influence. The whole episode is superbly —and subtly—done. It is helped by gentle humor (which constantly tries to minimize the possibility of such an event), by the restrained nervousness and tensely controlled calmness of Ralph Michael as the husband (Michael was a good, underrated, relatively little known actor, not a dynamic personality, and exactly the most believable kind of individual to be dominated by such a spectral mirror), by the subtlety of the camerawork (which in slow moving shots draws *us* to the mirror as irresistibly as the hero is drawn, and withholds the information within the mirror until he—and, subjectively, we—finally have the courage to look).

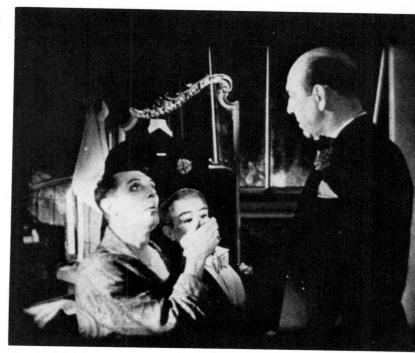

Dead of Night: Michael Redgrave, Hartley Power

Most of all, there is the brilliantly evocative score of Georges Auric. A French composer, who had worked extensively with Jean Cocteau, he was at his best with themes involving magic, fairy tales, or the supernatural. Auric created a genuinely Wagnerian style, characterized by two themes running in conjunction—a main theme, and an ominous undercurrent. The music (and the occasional deliberate withholding of it) is superb throughout *Dead of Night,* but never better than in the mirror sequence, where the music itself seems almost to emanate from the room behind the glass, to reach out, swell up, and engulf the victim (and the audience) looking in.

When released in the United States, *Dead of Night* was shorn of two stories: the Christmas party, and a droll and risqué comic interlude involving two golfers, one of whom is tricked into suicide and returns to haunt the other on his wedding night. These two deletions reduced the film to a tight, concentrated 77 minutes of thrills, but they did lessen the overall impact of cumulative horror. The comic sequence was no major loss, but the combination of charm, pathos, and terror that characterized the Christmas story was. Moreover, the climactic resolution, a nightmarish episode that

drew on scenes and locales from the preceding stories, became confused through its use of images totally new to U.S. audiences. Another unfortunate lessening of the film's power in the U.S. can be attributed to American projectionists. Originally, the film ended exactly as it began; the nightmare or the reality (one is never sure which) about to begin all over again. Several minutes from the beginning of the film are repeated until one is well into the story again, but repeated under a crawl listing of cast credits. Usually, as soon as projectionists saw the cast coming on the screen, they slammed on the house lights, turned off the projector, and drew the curtains—thus totally destroying both the meaning and the flesh-crawling impact of the film's climax. When the film was eventually released to U.S. television, complete and uncut copies began to make their appearance, and television thus made a minor compensation for its many crimes against the art of film.

There's something about the British milieu that makes the ghost story work—and not just because Britain is so old, so full of ancient buildings that belong in design and spirit to the past, that ghosts, rather than modern humans, would seem to be the logical inhabitants. There's a unique kind of melancholy to the English twilight, as though the day that has gone is forever beyond any kind of recapture or rebirth. England, even in its metropolitan centers, sleeps at night far more than does the United States. There's a quiet and a stillness to the English night, and in the cold and clear air one can see the moon reflected in the raindrops gathered on the twigs of trees and bushes. (Doubtless, one can see it reflected throughout the rest of the world, too—but somehow not in quite the same way.)

The English like their privacy, and curtains are usually drawn early, but a cheerful warmth somehow radiates through those curtains, to make the passerby seem more shut out than ever. (There are far fewer neon signs, restaurants and hotels competing for attention too!) Without any real reason for it, it is possible, and even easy, to feel sad and very lonely in England, and these senses (for the ghost story usually contains as much sadness as it does horror) feed and fertilize the land from which so many ghost stories spring. (England probably claims more authenticated hauntings than any other country in the world.) *Dead of Night*, with its sadness as well as its terror, its restraint, its casual acceptance of the supernatural, and its crisp black and white photography, catches all the nuances of the British ghost story as no other films have done.

Dead of Night: Frederick Valk, Mervyn Johns

29 The Lady and the Monster

Erich von Stroheim as the scientist, Richard Arlen as his assistant

(Republic, 1944) Produced and directed by George Sherman. Screenplay by Dane Lussier and Frederick Kohner from Donovan's Brain *by Curt Siodmak. Camera, John Alton. Music, Walter Scharf. Art Director, Russell Kimball. Special Effects, Theodore Lydecker.*

With Erich von Stroheim, Vera Hruba Ralston, Richard Arlen, Sidney Blackmer, Mary Nash, Helen Vinson, Charles Cane, William Henry, Juanita Quigley, Josephine Dillon, Tom London, Lane Chandler, Sam Flint, Edward Keane, Wallis Clark, Harry Hayden, Antonio Triana and Lola Montez (dance team), Maxine Doyle, Billy Benedict, Herbert Clifton, Harry Depp, Lee Phelps, Janet Martin.

In time, Curt Siodmak's classic horror story (horror does tend to dominate over science fiction, although it's a borderline case) may well turn out to be as venerable an inspiration for remakes and pirated copies as Richard Connell's *The Most Dangerous Game*. To date, there have been three official versions of *Donovan's Brain*, as well as such unofficial "borrowings" as *The Phantom Speaks*. Its plot is a complicated one, but in essence it deals with the brain of a dead criminal financial wizard that is kept alive by scientific experiment, and is of such dominant will that it eventually takes over the mind of a laboratory assistant, and forces him to complete the work left undone by the sudden death of the financier.

Despite its title, and undoubted horrific content, the film is perhaps only nominally a horror film, though certainly a superior one. Republic were never too meticulous about the meaning of their titles, so long as they were catchy and commercial, and it is a matter for conjecture whether the titular monster is Erich von Stroheim, or the brain itself, which proceeds to turn Richard Arlen into a form of Zombie. For box office purposes, the film tries hard to supply the superficial trappings of the *genre*, and horror devotees will not be disappointed. But Stroheim's Mad Doctor is not really mad (a trifle over-enthusiastic perhaps) and is definitely maligned by that inconsiderate title. The laboratory scenes are efficient but not markedly eventful (other than the look of loathing and repugnance that comes over Vera Ralston's face every time she is asked for a gigglisaw, presumably the instrument used whenever craniums are opened up), and there is little real menace in the usual sense. The film's major asset, of course, is its strong plot—a plot that

holds interest on a dramatic as well as a thriller level, and sustains that interest over a 9-reel length that would certainly be superfluous if it were merely a chiller. Medically, it even makes some sense, and for once the experimentation seems to have both point and justification.

Unusual care has been lavished on the production, and in fact, one of its flaws is that it is an *over*-produced movie. A dance number in a night club is quite unnecessary, and it seems unlikely that the decor in an ordinary Arizona hotel room would include an elaborate chandelier. Republic's familiar, slick, back-projection and studio "exteriors" smack of Hollywood a little too much, but Lydecker's miniature of Stroheim's wilderness castle (well matched up in partial sets) is a topnotch job. There were reasons for the budgetary generosity, of course; Republic Studios were then riding a box office crest, seeking to find acceptance as a major company, and were giving the "A" treatment to many properties that in other years would have been given run-of-the-mill "B" budgets.

More importantly, the film was designed to introduce Vera Hruba Ralston (later, the wife of Republic president Herbert Yates) as a new dramatic

Richard Arlen, Erich von Stroheim, Vera Ralston

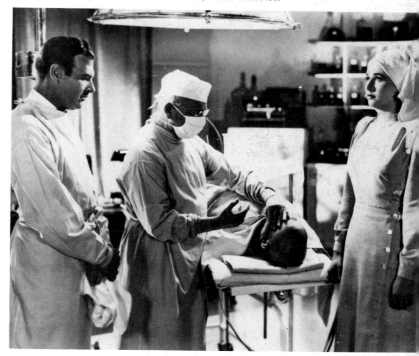

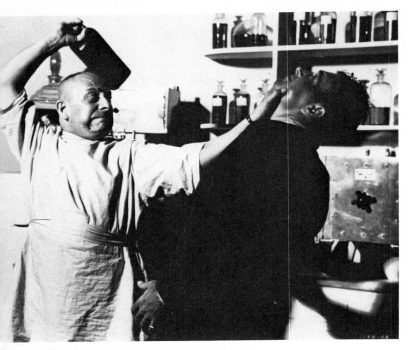

Erich von Stroheim, Richard Arlen

glamor photography and well-lit closeups, and to surround her with veteran actors. Curiously though, Republic didn't try to ease the acting load off her shoulders. Here they explain away her European accent by throwing in a one-liner about her father dying in Czechoslovakia, but she still has a lot of key dialogue, delivered in closeup. It was a rough chore to throw at her, and it is not to be wondered that one of the master scene-stealers of all time, Stroheim, and the veterans Richard Arlen and Sidney Blackmer, merely emphasize her lack of experience. (A followup, *Storm over Lisbon*, with the same three stars and the same director, treated her in the same way, but it was a much inferior film, with its "B" plot underlined by the excessive length and John Alton's superb lighting of glossy sets in which nothing really happened.)

In 1944, it was good to see Stroheim in a big role again, and John Alton, a top cameraman who was somewhat of a stranger to the Republic lot, created some good effects, though he was sometimes careless in matching the glamor closeups of Ralston with subsequent long and medium shots, and decidedly unsubtle in his use of low-key lighting for Arlen's face whenever he is dominated by the brain. In England, the film was shorn of some of its grimmer scenes and released as *The Lady and the Doctor*, and in the U.S. it was later cut down to second feature length and retitled *Tiger Man*, for reasons beyond explanation. George Sherman, a director brought up on fast Westerns, does not inject much Gothic style into it—not nearly as much, for example, as another Western specialist, Lambert Hillyer, brought to *Dracula's Daughter* and *The Invisible Ray*—but he does keep it briskly on the move, leaving it to dear old Erich to provide all the Gothic flavor one could ask for.

star, instead of just another second-string Sonja Henie. (Belita, another skating star, likewise found it difficult to duplicate the Henie success or to find a real place in dramatic roles.) The Republic method was to put Miss Ralston into as many varied roles as possible, to slant lines of dialogue calling attention to her staggering beauty, an assumption disputed by many, to co-star her with other big Republic names (John Wayne, Fred MacMurray), to give her the full treatment in

172

Charles Middleton and prospective victim, Rosemary LaPlanche. In the film itself
Middleton appears with far less clarity than in these publicity stills

(Producers Releasing Corporation, 1945) Directed by Frank Wisbar, from his own screenplay and original story. Camera, James S. Brown. Art Director, Edward C. Jewell.

With Rosemary La Planche, Robert Barrat, Blake Edwards, Charles Middleton, Effie Parnell, Nolan Leary, Frank Conlan, Theresa Lyon, Virginia Farmer.

During the 1940s, PRC enjoyed (if that is the word) and richly earned a reputation as representing the absolute nadir of cheap, independent products. True, such quickie outfits as Resolute, Ajax and Beacon, earlier in the 30s, turned out even scrappier and more threadbare products—but they made their films, literally, for a few thousand dollars apiece, in rented studios, sold their product to states' rights distributors, and were limited to stars who were either nonentities, occasionally talented youngsters on the way up and, sadly, once-important stars grasping at straws on the way down. Nobody expected quality from companies like that. But PRC at least had its own studios and distribution exchanges, a mass-production schedule which increased in number (and sometimes, vaguely, in quality and ambition) as the years passed, and a reasonably talented roster of stars. Yet everything they did had the look of corner-cutting, haste, and economy. Actors were under-rehearsed; sets were shoddy; camerawork was frequently slap-dash and often deliberately dark and murky, to conceal the lack of anything worth photographing. Above all, there was a constant sense of cramped space, of players acting against simple flats, obvious back-projection, or being pushed into corners. Monogram Pictures, with their similar line of product, at least had slightly roomier studios; their sets were modest but serviceable. And Republic, with their slick production trimmings and sharp, crystal-clear photography, turned out near masterpieces, in comparison with the PRC output.

Once, in their earlier days, PRC (through producer Seymour Nebenzal and director Douglas Sirk) accidentally turned out a film *(Hitler's Madman)* that was so good that they didn't know what to do with it. It was *too* good to get the attention it deserved with a PRC trademark introducing it; also slightly too expensive to be sure of recouping its cost through PRC's distribution. Accordingly, PRC sold their super-production to MGM—who marketed it as a useful "B." Conversely, when Universal made a grade "B" horror film (*The Brute Man*) which they decided was too bad and too tasteless to meet their none-too-exacting standards, they sold it to PRC—who were delighted!

The one advantage of such cheapness as PRC's (to the film scholar, if not to the hapless paying customer) is that when a director of real talent was trapped in the PRC net, one really had a chance to see that talent and initiative working, undisguised by production camouflage. Not that PRC ever had many major directors working for them, but at various (either very early or very late) phases of their careers, such directors as Joseph H. Lewis, William K. Howard, Edgar Ulmer, and Frank Wisbar worked for them, and Wisbar's contribution—*Strangler of the Swamp*—despite being a bare 60 minutes, and economical even by PRC standards—was about the most interesting of their limited contribution to the horror film *genre.*

Horror films, to be effective, don't necessarily need big budgets—but they do need time, care and a certain sophistication, qualities that at PRC were usually in short supply. Their *The Devil Bat* had been standard Mad Doctor stuff, salvaged to a large degree by the relish which Bela Lugosi brought to his villainy. It was later remade, even more cheaply, under the title *The Flying Serpent,* with the salvage responsibility this time in the capable hands of George Zucco. Somewhat inconsistently, PRC also made a sequel called *The Devil Bat's Daughter,* in which the villainy was now shifted to a psychiatrist, trying, for his own ends, to drive the daughter of the former Mad Doctor to madness herself. In a somewhat unconvincing finale (especially to those who saw the original), the Lugosi character was reinstated as a kindly and misunderstood benefactor of mankind, who actually didn't commit any of the crimes that we saw Bela performing with such glee! *Dead Men Walk* was standard, cheap, sensational Vampire material, and *The Mad Monster* was no better. *The Monster Maker,* with a slightly more credible script than usual, and two solid actors (J. Carroll Naish and Ralph Morgan) in the leads, was several notches above the average, however. Which brings us to *Strangler of the Swamp.*

In the very early 30s, Frank Wisbar (a director always more associated with artistic experiment than with commercial success) made a remarkable German fantasy film entitled *Fahrman Maria (Ferryman Maria),* which starred that unique actress Sybille Schmitz, so effective as the Vampire's chief

A publicity pose from *The Devil Bat's Daughter* with Rosemary LaPlanche and John James; Frank Wisbar's second horror film for PRC.

victim in Carl Dreyer's *Vampyr*. Although not a horror film, it dealt partially with the supernatural, and like so many German films of its type, featured a personalized Death. While it perhaps owed its initial inspiration to Fritz Lang's *Destiny*, it was a unique and original film that has surprisingly been ignored by the standard histories of film, including Lotte Eisner's otherwise very thorough coverage of the German fantasy film, *The Haunted Screen*. Only in David Stewart Hull's *Film in the Third Reich*, published as late as 1969, does one find the film finally acknowledged—and, happily, praised.

Wisbar's Hollywood career was, unfortunately, quite unworthy of him, largely limited to the 1940s and "B" products at PRC and Republic—including the aforementioned *The Devil Bat's Daughter*. But the action-and-melodrama-oriented production executives at PRC for once were sold a bill of goods themselves, for Wisbar's *Strangler of the Swamp* is a simpler reworking of his old classic *Fahrman Maria*. The heroine—named Maria, and played by Rosemary La Planche—arrives to take over the operation of the lonely ferry when her grandfather, who runs it, is killed. The community is haunted by the spectre of a man hanged years before for

Charles Middleton confronts the real killer of the man for whose murder he was wrongly executed

a murder of which he is innocent; he returns periodically to cause the deaths (usually by accidental hanging—entrapment by undergrowth vines, or the rope of the ferry itself) of the men responsible for his death. His curse extends to their descendants too, and can only be ended when one of them voluntarily offers his or her life to him in final expiation. Ultimately, in order to save the man she loves (Blake Edwards, in his pre-director and pre-Julie Andrews days), Maria offers herself to the wraith. In the traditional, German romanticist-fantasies, like *Nosferatu,* the sacrifice would be accepted, and the woman would die—bringing peace and life to those she loved. However, such a denouement would have been unthinkable for PRC, already caught napping with this Gothic mood piece. They settled for the wraith's being satisfied by the gesture and returning to the grave, having first made his own peace with God, and leaving the way clear for a traditional happy ending.

Like most of the old German fantasies, the film is totally stylized, and virtually all studio made. There are at most three genuine exteriors; one of a country road leading to the village, two of a field bounded by trees, but both are so dark and under-lit that they seem almost less real than the rest of the film. The basic set of the deserted ferry, the river, and the beginning of a forest on the other side—the noose hanging from one of the trees—is cunningly constructed so that it can be used for master long shots, picked up from different angles enabling the camera to shoot its closeups, and then used again in lengthy travel shots, with the camera trucking along by the side of the ferry. The twisted trees, the lack of either sunlight or moonlight, the constant ground mist, all contrive to hide the boundaries of what must have been a very small set indeed, and to give it real style. The other sets are limited to a few interiors (a cabin, a living room, an office) and a graveyard, but most of the key action is wisely laid around the one set on which the money was spent—the river and the ferry.

The first third of the film is particularly effective: the (justified) fears and superstitions of the villagers, the matter-of-fact acceptance of the supernatural, the eerie clanging of the ferry signal at night, and the gradual manifestation of the wraith, coming to a first climax when he confronts the man who actually committed the murder and brings about his own strangulation by the ferry rope. The appearances of the ghost (played by Charles Middleton) are sparse and well-handled; no special effects or shimmering lights, merely a grim, barely definable shape that merges with the shadows and the night. Later on, it is admittedly a mistake to have the wraith speak—especially in that he only confirms what the audience already knows. Even though he is meant to be a partially sympathetic figure, he somehow becomes too human a figure when he speaks, less malevolent in that he can presumably be reached by reason and conversation. Too (and this is probably the responsibility of PRC, trying to turn what they must have considered at best, a misfire, and at worst, a disaster into a standard piece of horror merchandise), the musical score works very much against the film. Music, of course, can be tremendously effective in the horror film in the establishment of mood and the underlining of shocks; but silence has its place, too, especially in a story such as this, set in an atmosphere of silence and desolation. The lurid bogeyman music reminds us all too often that this is a "B" horror movie—and prevents us from straining to listen for sounds and voices from the night. Like so many horror films, this one never quite sustains the tension of its opening sections—but it is too brief for that tension ever to evaporate entirely, and the closing reels re-establish much of it. Make no mistake about it, *Strangler of the Swamp* is a grade "B" movie, and not an unsung masterpiece.

Its economies even extend (effectively) to the use of painted flats fronted by a few hanging vines and shrubs, and diffused by dry-ice or optically created mists, such "scenes" serving as master establishing shots, the camera moving in on them to give the illusion of depth and space. Nor does it try very hard to horrify, content to be an atmospheric mood piece. Since the spectre/strangler and his victims-to-be are all sympathetic to a degree, there isn't much conflict there either. The boy-girl romance and happy ending is satisfying enough—but one feels that audiences wouldn't have been too upset if the strangler had succeeded in dispatching all of his unwitting enemies and their descendants, before returning to the grave.

But lowest-rung grade "B" or not, it is a commendable attempt to do something different with a standardized *genre* (serious ghost stories were still rare on the screen in 1945, although that same year's *Dead of Night* gave them new impetus) and, most of all, it is an example of how genuine feeling and style can be extracted from even the cheapest film if the director cares. *Fahrman Maria* (a genuine if minor classic) has been ignored by historians and critics of the cinema; *Strangler of the Swamp* managed to escape the attention of even such thorough chroniclers of the horror film as Carlos Clarens and Dennis Gifford.

Wisbar, who returned to Germany and television work after the war, is now dead. Perhaps the inclusion of this film in a book entitled *Classics of the Horror Film*, with the awareness that it is *far* from a classic, is the kind of romantic gesture that Wisbar and his two Ferryman Marias would have appreciated.

31 The Body Snatcher

Boris Karloff, Bela Lugosi

(RKO Radio, 1945) Directed by Robest Wise. Produced by Val Lewton. Screenplay by Philip MacDonald and Carlos Keith, based on a short story by Robert Louis Stevenson. Camera, Robert de Grasse.

With Boris Karloff, Bela Lugosi, Henry Daniell, Edith Atwater, Russel Wade, Rita Corday, Sharyn Moffat, Donna Lee, Robert Clarke, Mary Gordon, Bill Williams.

Val Lewton produced nine horror films for RKO Radio, all of them aiming at horror by suggestion, rather than statement, and employing intelligent writers (DeWitt Bodeen in particular) and new, young directors, still fresh and full of enthusiasm. *Cat People* was the first, and probably the best, even though it has been so acclaimed in later years that those coming upon it now for the first time must inevitably be disappointed. One of the perennial problems of "B" pictures is that critics see so few of them; when they do stumble across a good one, they lose all sense of proportion, and extol the film for virtues and intentions which need the sense of surprise and discovery for those virtues to remain intact. A *Cat People* elevated to the level of *The Picture of Dorian Gray* no longer retains the same sense of initiative; but to encounter a *Cat People* on the budgetary and commercial level of a *Mad Ghoul* is stimulating and rewarding.

The great material of *Cat People* is all concentrated in its second half, and the literate but very slow first half makes one wonder (at first) what all the shouting was about. The Lewtons were always interesting, though their standards were somewhat uneven. *The Leopard Man* had a terrifying opening and brilliant individual moments, but a weak climax and sets too often revealed the paucity of budget. Despite its well conveyed atmosphere of claustrophobic evil, *The Seventh Victim* didn't quite come off, and *The Ghost Ship* seemed to be striving too hard to turn a psychological melodrama into a horror film, just *because* it was a Lewton production. *The Curse of the Cat People* is discussed elsewhere in this book, and the others —Tourneur's *I Walked With a Zombie* and Robson's *Isle of the Dead* and *Bedlam* (defeated by its own pretentions and enlarged budget, but still offering some beautifully bizarre moments and some fine low-key photography)—are all much better known. Sadly, theatrical exhibition of these films in recent years has been virtually non-existent, and a whole generation of moviegoers has grown up knowing them only from television—which, in many cases, is not knowing them as they were at all. Apart from the damage done to such carefully constructed films by breaking them up for commercials, they have been seriously hurt by cutting. The one sequence that is directly responsible for *Cat People's* being considered a classic—the beautiful and chilling episode in the swimming pool—is almost invariably cut from TV prints, not only because it is a dark sequence that does not register well on television, but also because, while it is a key sequence, it is a little unit in itself. It *can* be cut *in toto* without leaving a jagged edge. Since other (though less dynamic) sequences make the same plot point, continuity is not impaired—even though the overall power of the film is dealt a death blow.

The Body Snatcher, however, is quite certainly the equal of *Cat People*, and possibly its superior, but strangely enough, it is one of the least respected. Even now it is regarded mainly as an example of early Robert Wise, not as a significant film on its own. In England, though audiences at the time were not aware of it, it was carefully trimmed of some of its grimmer scenes. It was still a good film, since it depended more on dialogue and characterization than on visuals, yet it received a very lukewarm reception from the critics, with such phrases as "fair" and "misfire thriller" cropping up with regularity. Perhaps one of its problems was that it *sounded* like a horror film. For box office reasons, Boris Karloff and Bela Lugosi were given the best billing, another misleading suggestion that it was "blood and guts" of the old school, and regardless of the fact that it was Henry Daniell who really had the lead, with Karloff in the top supporting role.

Despite the fact that its very theme indicates more "physical" horror than many of the other more psychologically motivated Lewton films, *The Body Snatcher* is one of the most literate and restrained of all horror films. There are the odd shock effects, to be sure (and so well edited that they remain effective and achieve their attention-grabbing ends even on repeat viewings), and a climax of pure nightmare quality, but the film's finest achivement is the image of latent malevolence created by Karloff as the cabman/grave-robber, acquiring bodies (initially from graves, later more directly) for medical school usage. As a sort of outside-the-law Uriah Heep, kind to children and his horse, yet persecuting a basically decent man above his own station purely for the sense of power and

Russell Wade, Henry Daniell, Boris Karloff

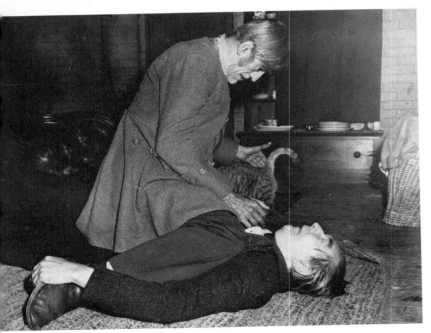

Boris Karloff, Bela Lugosi

perverted self respect it gives him, Karloff is superb. How sadly he was wasted in routine horror roles. His dialogue here is beautifully written to begin with, and equally well delivered. That excellent actor Henry Daniell is somewhat overshadowed by Karloff, yet his performance, too, is first-rate, and it is good to see him in a leading role for once.

The whole film reflects all the care, photographic excellence and production ingenuity (not least, in the utilization of sets from bigger pictures) that distinguished the best of the Lewtons. Just how good a film *The Body Snatcher* really was is emphasized by a comparison with one of the Hammer blood baths from the early 60s—*The Flesh and the Fiends*—likewise dealing with the days (and profession) of Burke and Hare, but with far less taste and subtlety.

For all of its restraint, *The Body Snatcher* still came up with one of the grimmest climaxes of any horror film. Having stolen the body of a woman from a fresh grave, Dr. MacFarlane (Henry Daniell) is driven to madness by his conscience. Careening along in his coach at the height of a thunderstorm, he becomes convinced that the corpse has changed into that of Gray, the cabman (Karloff), whom he had killed earlier. As he stops to examine the body and make sure, a lightning flash (and a sudden tracking shot into a closeup) reveals the chalky-white face of Karloff. In a panic, Daniell whips up the horses, and the emaciated corpse of Karloff, still half encased in its shroud, slumps over him in an unholy embrace, the sound track repeating an earlier threat of Karloff's ("You'll never get rid of me!") as the coach plummets off a cliff. Subsequent examination of the two bodies reveals that the stolen corpse was, of course, still that of the woman. Yet that one classic image of terror that has invaded all our nightmares at one time or another, to be in the embrace of a dead person, is such an overpowering one that the "rational" explanation of hallucination doesn't altogether settle all doubts.

Apart from being a good horror film, *The Body Snatcher* is a disturbing one, since the "villains" are both fascinating and even likeable, and the villainy itself is perpetrated for a worthwhile end. The ambiguous, semi-mystical literary quote, with which Lewton liked to end his films, provides a last minute note of upbeat optimism, but certainly doesn't dispel the effectiveness of what has gone before.

32 Cat People
Night of the Demon
Curse of the Cat People

Night of the Demon

CAT PEOPLE

(RKO Radio, 1942) Directed by Jacques Tourneur. Produced by Val Lewton. Scenario, DeWitt Bodeen. Camera, Nicholas Musuraca.

With Simone Simon, Kent Smith, Jane Randolph, Alan Napier, Tom Conway, Jack Holt, Alec Craig, Elizabeth Russell.

NIGHT OF THE DEMON

(U.S. title Curse of the Demon) *(Columbia, 1958) Directed by Jacques Tourneur. Produced by Hal E. Chester. Screenplay by Charles Bennett from* Casting the Runes *by Montague R. James. Camera, Ted Scaife. Music, Clifton Parker.*

With Dana Andrews, Peggy Cummins, Niall Mac-Ginnis, Maurice Denham, Athene Seyler, Liam Redmond, Reginald Beckwith, Ewan Roberts, John Salew.

THE CURSE OF THE CAT PEOPLE

(RKO Radio, 1944) Directed by Robert Wise and Gunther Fritsch. Produced by Val Lewton. Original screenplay by DeWitt Bodeen. Camera, Nicholas Musuraca.

With Simone Simon, Kent Smith, Jane Randolph, Ann Carter, Elizabeth Russell, Eve March, Julia Dean, Erford Gage, Sir Lancelot, Joel Davis, Juanita Alvarez.

Jacques Tourneur, son of Maurice Tourneur—perhaps the greatest pictorialist director of the silent screen—started as an editor, and established himself as a director of note with *Cat People* and *I Walked with a Zombie*, the first two of the nine intelligent horror films that Val Lewton produced for RKO Radio in the early 40s. Other subsequent directors included Mark Robson (who edited *Cat People*) and Robert Wise (an editor on *Citizen Kane*).

Tourneur's importance to the Lewton unit has often been underrated by critics, although his skill was quickly recognized by Hollywood and he was soon promoted to commercially more important properties. His initial, bigger films reflected some of the pictorial eloquence of his father, and the

quality of understatement that was a characteristic of the Lewton films. His big 1946 Western, *Canyon Passage*, contained only short, spasmodic moments of violence and action, and much of its savagery was merely suggested, while a good deal of traditional action took place off-screen. When, years later, Val Lewton was to produce a Western himself (*Apache Drums* for Universal), it was fairly obvious that he had seen, remembered and emulated Tourneur's stylized approach. By the early 1950s however, Tourneur, still commercially reli-

Cat People: Simone Simon, Tom Conway

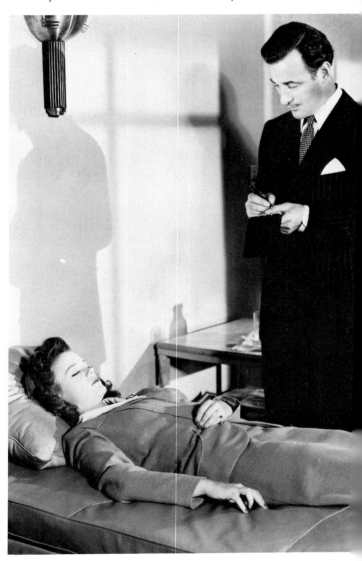

Cat People: Kent Smith, Jack Holt, Alan Napier, Jane Randolph

able, seemed somewhat *passé* in terms of an original and recognizable directorial style. Then, along came *The Night of the Demon,* which he made in England, to show that in the intervening sixteen years he had lost none of his old cunning.

Considered together, the two films provide an interesting contrast in styles. Both films are related in that they spin tales of the supernatural, and both have a methodical skeptic as the hero. When he is convinced—and scared—despite all the logic he can muster, so is the audience. The utilization of the whole arsenal of film grammar is basically the same in both films: some of the most telling effects are achieved by shock cuts of sound, or picture, or both; or by the delaying or accelerating of *anticipated* scenes, so that the audience is caught off guard.

But in terms of overall design, the two films are quite different. *Cat People,* with its totally manufactured variation on the Werewolf theme, eschews all of the standard effects of fog, creaking doors, trick photography, and monstrous changeovers. Working on Lang's old premise that nothing that the camera can show can possibly be as horrible as what the mind can imagine, it shows nothing—and suggests all. (Only once is an actual leopard shown in a supernatural context; Lewton fought against it, but was overruled. However, it does

little damage, as the scene can still be interpreted as a subjective imagining on the part of the trapped hero and heroine.) The backgrounds are modern, normal, and unspectacular, unglossy studio reconstructions of New York's offices, museums, Central Park Zoo, and environs. The people are ordinary, even dull and pompous. While the moments of horror are ambiguous and fragmented, the film leaves one with the deliberately uneasy feeling that the only explanation must be an acceptance of the supernatural. The episode in which the heroine, swimming in a darkened hotel swimming pool, is menaced by the unseen presence of the Cat Woman—or by a real leopard—is not only a classic episode of economical screen terror, it works on a second level too, since its symbolic imagery is essentially Freudian. With its basically realistic setting, and its logical use of light, shadow, and distorted sound, it is a perfect example of the Fritz Lang *modus operandi,* of turning the everyday into a black, nightmare world of unseen menace.

The Night of the Demon, likewise intelligently scripted, goes to the other extreme of *showing* its Monster. Luckily, its Demon is such a lulu that it lives up to the fearsome descriptions of it (something that most movie Monsters do not). Tourneur, in later interviews, claims that it was never his intention to show the Demon, that he had wanted to follow the pattern of his Lewton films and merely suggest it, and that its graphic physical depiction was included at the insistence of the producer, who wanted real meat in his film. Tourneur made no such protests at the time of release, however, and one wonders whether these latter-day protestations are entirely genuine. Certainly the construction of the film, and the scenes in which the Demon's presence is undeniably felt, even when not visible, leave no doubt at all as to the creature's existence. The whole point of the film, in fact, is not that horrors can be created within the mind, but that some horrors are so unthinkable that the mind must deny them in order to retain its sanity. The final line of the film—the time-honored, "There are some things it is better not to know!"—comes after a materialization of the Demon, which is ambiguous only to those who want it to be ambiguous.

Tourneur, like Lang, takes his thrillers seriously. There is some humor in *Night of the Demon* in the person of the villain's slightly dotty mother, dabbling in the charades of seances, while her son (another screen incarnation of Aleister Crowley,

183

Night of the Demon: Niall MacGinnis, Dana Andrews

and extremely well played by one-time rugged, outdoor hero Niall MacGinnis) is the evil central force in a malestrom of witchcraft, conjuring up demons, giant cats, and sudden storms, to demonstrate his powers. But she is there primarily to illustrate the impotency of normalcy against such total evil, just as Hitchcock's master criminals in *Saboteur* and *The 39 Steps* were surrounded by loving wives and families. There is a kind of mordant humor in *Cat People*, too, but it is mainly in the writing of Bodeen. The psychiatrist who thinks to effect a cure by simply telling his patient to go home and lead a normal life is a little hard to take seriously! And the vivacious Negro waitress, who seems to serve her customers according to their personalities—Bavarian Cream for one, and, somewhat contemptuously, "The apple pie for *you*" to the cloddish hero—underlines in a very lighthearted way that everyone is, in a sense, a captive of his own destiny, type-cast by life. But there is no constant undercurrent of humor, as there always is with Hitchcock. He, for example, would doubtless have extracted some visual humor from the disturbing scene in which the Cat Woman enters a pet store, only to have the normally docile cats and birds screech in terror until the whole store

is in an uproar. Tourneur means you to believe in and take seriously all that he is showing you. When he borrows, significantly it is more from Lang than from Hitchcock.

Much of *Night of the Demon* takes place at night, and two sequences in a deserted forest are very reminiscent of the climactic chase from Lang's *The Testament of Dr. Mabuse*. Even drab old Clapham Junction Station—one of the most unpromising of locations—seems almost to take on the fatalistic characteristics of one of Lang's unreal way-stations between life and death. Tourneur's inability to spoof (or more likely, his lack of interest in so doing) was shown by his much later Karloff-Rathbone-Lorre horror satire *Comedy of Terrors,* which, in Tourneur's hands, emerged as leaden burlesque.

Night of the Demon, which borrowed many touches and individual moments of cutting from the earlier *Cat People,* increased and sustained its pattern of chase and suspense. It is undoubtedly a better (and more genuinely frightening) film than *Cat People,* and, more importantly, it is the last genuine horror "classic" that we have had. In the 16 years that have elapsed since it was made, one or two films have come close to it—most particularly, *Burn Witch Burn* (its similarity stressed by its British release title, *The Night of the Eagle*)—but none have quite equaled, let alone surpassed it. In time, it may well prove to be not only the apex, but the climax to the *genre* of "thinking" horror films introduced by Val Lewton over a decade earlier.

The Curse of the Cat People was handicapped by the double misfortune of a title that tried to pass off a fairy story as a horror yarn, and by being touted as a sequel to the original *Cat People.* As such, it could hardly fail to disappoint the traditional horror fanciers, nor could it reach those who would most appreciate it, and its distribution was slight. Apart from reemploying some of the same characters, it is really only the vaguest kind of sequel to the original. Indeed, to explain how a malevolent supernatural Werecat could become, after death, a kindly and protective spirit friend to the child of her former husband, the original writer (Bodeen) had to insert several explanatory lines of dialogue which falsified and distorted the events of the original. In only one sense was there real continuity: the father (Kent Smith in both films), originally an unimaginative dullard, proved to be even less successful as a father than he had been as a husband. His attitude throughout is one of stupid condescension, and even at the film's

Curse of the Cat People: Simone Simon

fadeout, he is still lying to his much more imaginative daughter.

The menace in *The Curse of the Cat People* (which contains neither curses nor Cat People) is nebulous and deliberately vague. Nothing more horrifying occurs than the hair-raising telling of the "Headless Horseman" legend to a frightened child by a half insane, old actress—and the disturbed child's later belief (when lost on a country road at night) that she is about to encounter the ghost. Yet the moments of terror, built by imagination out of nothing—as the majority of a child's fears are—reach heights equal to those of the scratching from within the coffin in *Isle of the Dead*, the sealing up alive of Karloff in the asylum walls in *Bedlam*, the sudden stopping of the bus with the catlike hiss, in *Cat People*, or the sobbing in the deserted village and the terrifying journey to the Voodoo village in *I Walked with a Zombie*. And, as in all good fairy tales, poignancy and beauty walk hand in hand with fear. It would be exaggerating to say that *Curse of the Cat People* approaches the beauty of Cocteau's *Le Belle et la Bête,* or Autant-Lara's *Sylvie et le Fantome,* but it does have the same kind of beauty.

One suspects that no one was quite sure whether this film should have been complete fantasy or complete horror film. The film was also not helped by a split directorial credit; Gunther Fritsch started the film, and relinquished to Robert Wise when he was called to service with the Army. The effects of compromise and indecision show. Certain scenes were shot a number of ways. In one version of the climax, for example, the ghost of the former Cat

Woman played a far more positive and melodramatic role, including the unlocking of a jammed closet door to enable the child to hide from the crazed woman who seeks to kill her. In the final release version, this element was eliminated and fairy tale magic won out over prolonged suspense, a preferable solution. Despite the occasionally uneven quality throughout, one feels that this is one of those rare cases where the fussing was justified, and where the final version was not a "butchery" of what might have been.

SS A Last Furtive Look Around

One of the major problems in compiling a survey book of this kind is that, since 1960, the horror film has become a mass-produced stardardized *genre*, almost literally replacing the "B" Western, which breathed its last in the mid-50s. There have been welters of *Frankenstein* and *Dracula* movies and wholesale so-called adaptations of Poe, Monsters, Mutants, and Mad Scientists, on an assembly line basis, more and more frequently in color. Few of these recent horror films have been really good; many of them have been remakes of specific earlier films, and patently inferior to them, despite being, in some cases, more elaborate. But the sheer number of them, and their generally low quality, have by an automatic process of percentages and comparisons, forced even the routine horror films of yesteryear into a much higher qualitative bracket. Thus, while a film such as *Dracula's Daughter* (1936) would, in the mid-1940s, have been dismissed as a minor effort, today it automatically finds itself up among the higher echelons. In view of the admittedly arbitrary standards by which many films have been selected for appraisal in this volume, many others certainly rate an approving nod in passing.

Dracula (1931): Bela Lugosi, Helen Chandler, Dwight Frye

Nosferatu (1922): Max Schreck

The Vampire legend has probably provided more fodder for the contemporary horror film than any other specific *genre*, not only because of the legal, public domain status of the Dracula figure, but also because Vampirism has far more erotic possibilities than most brands of chiller, and in the recent years of relaxed censorship, producers have been quick to explore the possibilities of sex and nudity in the Vampire's domain. Actually, such ingredients were there from the beginning, though seldom exploited. F. W. Murnau's 1922 German classic, *Nosferatu,* the first version of *Dracula,* contained a decidedly erotic (and typically romanticist) element in that the heroine welcomes the Vampire to her bedroom and keeps him by her side until after the sun has risen, thereby destroying him, and saving her husband and friends, at the cost of her own life. These scenes had a decidedly sensual quality, despite the physical repugnance of the Vampire, and the typically Germanic use of stylized shadows.

Nosferatu, once aptly described by a critic as "a chilly blast of doomsday," is quite possibly the screen's first *real* horror film, if one passes over the John Barrymore *Dr. Jekyll and Mr. Hyde,* made two years earlier. Influenced by the cutting patterns of D. W. Griffith, *Nosferatu* was a much faster film than the average German fantasy of the period. Too, Murnau shot most of the film outdoors, in genuine villages or in an authentic castle, giving the film a great deal more realism than most other totally studio-bound German films. It retained the expressionism of the period, but it was an expressionism drawn from naturalistic rather than artificial devices.

Max Schreck, who played Dracula, underwent subtle changes of makeup throughout the film so that, while one wasn't aware of it, his looks got progressively more repellent; one never took him for granted as a standard bogeyman. He was totally without the redeeming social graces of Bela Lugosi, in the later Hollywood version, and literally looked like a sallow, living corpse. In many scenes of attack and depradation, his grotesque, elongated shadow preceded him like an evil omen, and he was constantly surrounded by indirect as well as immediate victims, the trappings of death—funerals, disease, pestilence, rats—following in his wake. The imagery is both terrifying and richly romantic by turn, and the film—a remarkable achievement, especially given the prevailing standards in Germany at that time—is still one of the very best Vampire essays, let down only by the extroverted and heavily over-

Dracula: Bela Lugosi, Helen Chandler

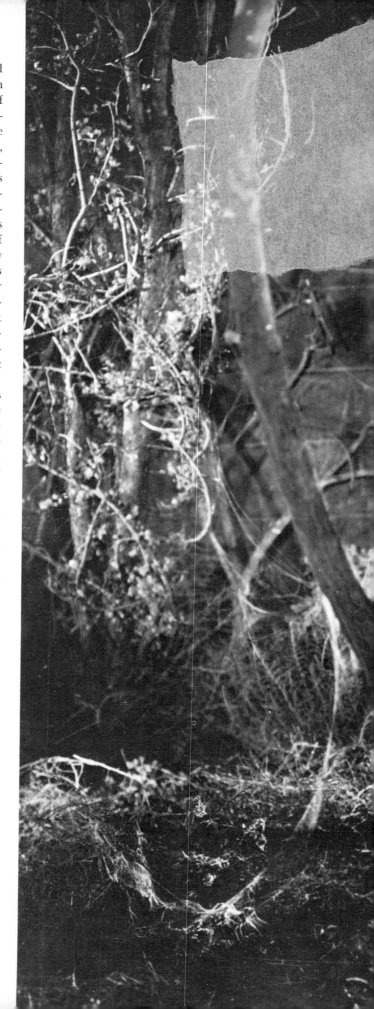

The initial pre-production trade advertisement for *Dracula;* Lugosi's name is not as yet mentioned, but that of prominent author Louis Bromfield, slated to do the screen adaptation, is.

Say "DRACULA" to them and their hair stands on end in delightful anticipation of the mystery and thrills to come. Say "DRACULA" and you're talking of a stage play that broke records for attendance in New York and every road-show city on the map. Louis Bromfield author of "The Green Bay Tree" and other best sellers is adapting it for the screen . . . The director is Tod Browning who gave you THE UNHOLY THREE and OUTSIDE THE LAW (now breaking records in first run houses everywhere).

played acting of Alexander Granach (in a parallel of the Renfield role), and just about every member of the cast other than Schreck.

Tod Browning's 1930 version of *Dracula* was never quite the definitive Vampire film that it deserved to be, or that its opening two reels indicated it could have been. Those opening reels, sparse in dialogue and rich in visuals, are obviously dominated far more by the pictorial style of cameraman Karl Freund (who later proved that he knew all about directing as well) than by the static and stage-bound style of Browning. The camera, almost like a phantom itself, floats through the crypt of *Dracula's* castle in stately, unhurried fashion. The atmospheric sets, the mobility of the camera, the skill of the glass-shots (particularly one of the coach entering Borgo Pass), and the composition of individual frames (*Dracula's* three white-gowned wives gliding in to claim a victim) are all far more characteristic of Freund's work than of Browning's.

There is an indefinable and magical quality to the photography here: something about it makes the rigid and unfriendly passengers in the coach look as though they are holding back awful secrets. And when the coach itself leaves the inn and heads up the little hill into the twilight, one feels that this *is* Transylvania, and that phantoms are waiting just over the hill. Yet this was the same familiar little hill on the Universal back lot that Western stars and sheriff's posses had galloped up and down for years—and would continue to use into the 60s, when the area was built up and the hill reserved for the tourist trams. Whatever quality Freund instilled into the film was dissipated when the plot abandoned Transylvania and settled in London. From there on in, it followed the play rather than Bram Stoker's difficult but rewardingly chilling novel. All the marvelous visual highlights of the book were merely *talked* about in the film, in some cases maddeningly described as they were occurring—just outside camera range. The still colorful plot, the fine playing of Edward Van Sloan as Van Helsing, and the rich dialogue in his encounters with Lugosi, make it an enjoyable film still, but it is stilted, pedestrian, and sadly in need of a musical score to bring some vitality to its many lifeless passages.

So successful was *Dracula,* however, that it is surprising that a sequel was not planned immediately, both to cash in on the subject itself, and also to exploit Lugosi, as Karloff was to be exploited following the success of *Frankenstein*. But it was almost six years before a followup film was made.

Dracula: Bela Lugosi

Dracula: Bela Lugosi, Dwight
   Frye

Dracula: Dracula's wives

Dracula: Dwight Frye (left) as Renfield, and Edward van Sloan as Professor Van Helsing

In 1936, despite the presence in the studio of James Whale, Louis Friedlander, and other directors who had earlier made successful horror films, Universal, curiously, handed their two main horror properties of the year to Lambert Hillyer—a major director of grade "A" action films and William S. Hart Westerns in the silent years, and in the 30s concentrating on quality (but relatively unimportant) "B" Westerns.

Neither of the two films, *Dracula's Daughter* or *The Invisible Ray,* can be considered major horror films, and indeed *The Invisible Ray,* by far the more elaborate of the two, can more accurately be classified as science fiction. But they are remarkably smoothly done and succeed in establishing mood so well that it is worth noting that they represent Hillyer's only work in the *genre.* On other occasions, too, the use of a Western director on horror films has had happy results. Used to working quickly and improvising frequently, the Western director, if he is worth his salt, is often able

to extract far more in terms of production value from his modest budget than the regular director, since it is practically in the "luxury" class when compared with the money he is normally allocated. As producer, director and/or writer, another Universal Western and serial veteran, Ford Beebe, brought real class to such films as *Son of Dracula* and *The Invisible Man's Revenge,* while over at Republic, Lesley Selander did likewise on films like *Catman of Paris.*

For many years, *Dracula's Daughter* was always pushed aside casually, perhaps because it lacked a key personality, like Karloff or Lugosi, on which to focus attention. Also, in 1936, the initial sound horror cycle was fading away, and a film like this—all plot and mood, little in the way of action or spectacular thrills—seemed tame compared with such recent contemporaries as *The Bride of Frankenstein* or *The Raven.* Today, however, its values look more substantial. It's a thoughtful, well constructed little film with some excellent camerawork,

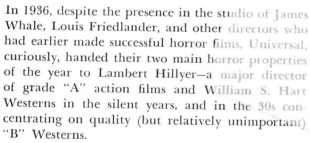

Dracula: Bela Lugosi, Helen Chandler

199

Dracula: Carlos Villarias as Dracula in the Spanish-language version made simultaneously by Universal, and directed by George Melford

a first class score, and some really well written passages of dialogue. The performances are uniformly good, with Edward Van Sloan repeating as Van Helsing, Otto Kruger making an interesting and off-beat hero, and Gloria Holden and Irving Pichel doing rather well as Vampire and loyal slave. The opening reel is especially satisfying, picking up exactly where *Dracula* left off, dropping a couple of characters and, admittedly assuming that everyone saw *Dracula,* not bothering with a résumé.

With a well controlled undercurrent of humor (taking a bizarre turn right away, when comic-relief policeman Billy Bevan is killed off unexpectedly), this first section of the film is extremely well done. The middle portions have occasional lags, the pace slackens, and there is too much bantering byplay between hero and heroine. But well before the end, the loose strings are tautened and the pacing of the final reel leaves nothing to be desired. Even in the slower middle area, there are rewarding sequences, specifically, the Vampire's utilization of a young girl (well played by Nan Grey) to test her own powers of resistance to the Vampire taint—a sequence that has the hint of a Vampiric-Lesbian relationship that was carried to a more erotic extreme in Vadim's later *Blood and Roses.*

Most of our favorite lines and situations are trotted out. Edward Van Sloan has his inevitable "We must destroy it!" line, a product of the brand of singlemindedness that he brought to his earlier encounters with Dracula, the Frankenstein Monster, and the Mummy. The doctors muse again about the significance of those two little punctures over the jugular vein, and the Vampire, in addition to tossing off that old standby about eternal life, repeats *verbatim* one of her father's best-remembered remarks, "I never drink—*wine.*" Her entrances to and exists from the coffins of native earth are photographed (by George Robinson) in exactly the same way as Lugosi's similar scenes in the original—a hand raising the coffin lid, a cutaway, and then a pullback—presumably on the theory that getting in and out of coffins is both cumbersome and graceless, and the illusion of undead elegance is better served by not showing the actual mechanics.

All told, *Dracula's Daughter* holds up rather well. The few big sets look expensive, and standing sets (e.g., Ming's laboratory from *Flash Gordon*) are cunningly disguised. In its own way, it is almost a model of how care and style can make a fairly

Dracula's Daughter: Gloria Holden

201

Dracula's Daughter: Irving Pichel, Gloria Holden

Dracula's Daughter: Nan Grey, Gloria Holden

202

Dracula's Daughter: Nan Grey, Otto Kruger

inexpensive picture look like a much bigger one. The mystery remains as to why Universal didn't produce a much more elaborate sequel to *Dracula,* just as it is such a mystery why a quickie like *Son of Kong* followed the original *King Kong.* But while *Son of Kong* was a most unworthy sequel, even playing it all for laughs as though to kill it off once and for all, *Dracula's Daughter* is a followup that one can both enjoy and respect.*

*In recent years, definitive historical studies of Vampiric folklore and of the original (non-Vampiric but decidedly bloodthirsty) Count Dracula have proliferated. One hopes that the scholarship concerning folklore and legend is more reliable than the incidental film "history" that has crept into these volumes. A 1973 British book entitled *The Vampire In Legend, Fact and Art* and claiming to be "the most exhaustive popular study of the Vampire ever published" rhapsodizes over scenes in Lugosi's *Dracula* that were *never* filmed and exist only in the novel—such as the marvelous scene that should have been filmed of Dracula climbing head down, batlike, down the sheer wall of his castle. Compounding his errors, the author goes on to the first of many more filmic mistakes by referring to Lugosi's re-creating the Dracula role in *Dracula's Daughter*—in which Dracula appears for but a brief moment, when his body (a dummy figure) is consumed by fire!

Subsequently, the Vampire reappeared on the screen periodically, but with no regularity, until the 1960s. 1943's *Son of Dracula,* directed by Robert Siodmak, was a restrained, intelligent thriller, somewhat shy of the sustained horror set-pieces that the *afficionados* expected, but with good dialogue, plot construction, and one or two exceptionally well devised pictorial special effects to compensate. A novelty of the species was that the heroine (Louise Allbritton), far from resisting the advances of the Vampire (Lon Chaney, Jr.), was morbidly attracted to him, and willingly stepped over the threshold into Vampirism herself. The following year's *Return of the Vampire* was far more traditional stuff. Made for Columbia, and directed by Lew Landers, an old hand at fast-moving if not particularly inventive chillers, it brought Vampirism up to date by giving it a London Blitz background in World War II, and threw in a Werewolf (Matt Willis) for good measure.

The sets (dominated, of course, by graveyard and crypt) were goodlooking, if somewhat over-generously endowed with dry-ice mist, and the acting was definitely a cut above the average. Nina Foch,

Son of Dracula: Louise Allbritton, Lon Chaney Jr., Robert Paige

The Vampire's Ghost (1945): One of the less successful entries; with John Abbott

always an interesting actress, and incidentally a Werewolf in *Cry of the Werewolf,* gave the part of the potential Vampire victim far more poignancy than the script really required, and Frieda Inescourt was a refreshing change-of-pace as the businesslike British doctor, a feminine parallel to Professor van Helsing. But, of course, the film's primary *raison-d'être* was the opportunity to see Lugosi playing a bonafide Vampire again, for the first time since *Dracula,* and he made the most of his rich dialogue and colorful fog-accompanied entrances and exits. His Vampire this time was singularly ill-humored, and devoid of the smooth social graces of Dracula. The film moved briskly and talked far less than *Dracula,* yet it obviously lacked its stature; what a tragedy that Lugosi, the definitive Vampire, never made a definitive Vampire film.

The success of *Return of the Vampire* caused the *genre* to be adopted by "B" film specialists, and the first—and one; of the worst—of these was 1945's redundantly titled *The Vampire's Ghost.* Typical of Republic, its excitement highlight was a lively barroom fistic brawl! Vampires have never fared too well in "B" pictures, since that kind of film just doesn't have the running time or the budget for a carefully evoked atmosphere, and usually settles for cheap, quickly arrived at thrills. A notable exception was 1935's *Condemned to Live,* perhaps the only really interesting film that the poverty-row independent company Invincible ever made. Well written, well acted, especially by Ralph Morgan, and exceptionally well photographed, it didn't have the money for even limited special effects, and became one of the most subdued of all Vampire films .

In 1958, Hammer Films, in England, launched their long-running resurrection of Count Dracula with *The Horror of Dracula,* a remake of the

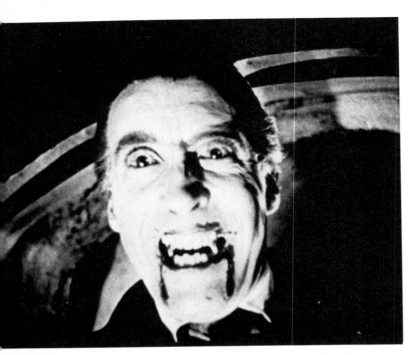

The Horror of Dracula (1958): Christopher Lee

original. Color, unless really creatively used, has never been a major asset of the horror film, and creativity and stubtlety were not Hammer characteristics. Apart from the shock effect—soon nullified through over-use—of blood dripping from Dracula's fangs, or spurting from a stake-impaled corpse, color added nothing to, and detracted much from the bulk of the Hammer horror films. Too, most of them were set in European locales, and were betrayed by the odd combinations of rural and Cockney accents that marked the coach drivers, inkeepers, gravediggers, and assorted peasants as being unmistakably 20th Century Britons, and of a pay scale and talent substantially lower than the Laurence Olivier-Clive Brook-Ralph Richardson breed of English actor, who could certainly have made those roles come convincingly to life had they been so inclined. Early on, the Hammer Films opted for shock, sensation, and speed, rather than atmosphere and conviction. Nevertheless, of all their *Dracula* films, the first *was* the best. Christopher Lee's Dracula was somewhat one-dimensional, and as the series progressed, Dracula's personal involvements in the plots became minimal. On the other hand, Peter Cushing, an excellent actor, somewhat wasted in his nearly twenty years of film work prior to *The Horror of Dracula,* was a first-rate Van Helsing, and has since lent real style, presence, and even believability to the many absurd horror films that he has been associated with.

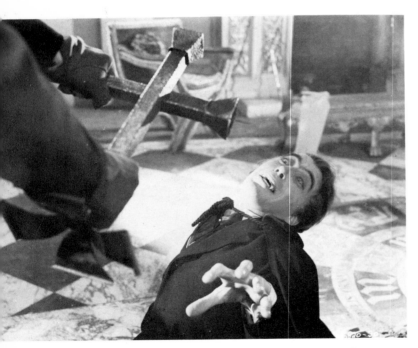

The Horror of Dracula (1958): Christopher Lee

Brides of Dracula (1960): Peter Cushing, by now a veteran at Edward van Sloan's old Van Helsing role, and a regular nemesis for Dracula

206

Hammer's best Vampire film was one that, by their standards, was comparatively unimportant: 1963's *Kiss of the Vampire*, directed by Don Sharp. For once, it was a simple tale, concentrating on mystery and on atmosphere, until its tastefully savage finale. It exploited the sensual aspects of Vampirism far more than the same studio's Dracula films had done, and a macabre ball sequence, in which the Vampires dance in bizarre masks, seemed to have been inspired by the semisurrealist fantasies and mysteries of Feuillade, Cocteau, and Franju in France. *Kiss of the Vampire* disappeared from theatres quickly, doubtless considered too mild in the face of far more savage, contemporary horror films, but it will probably stand the test of time far more than most of its companion films. Though filmed in color, its use of color was subdued and often muted, with prominent greys and browns giving an appropriately cheerless look to interiors and exteriors.

In the midst of so much Eastman color attention being paid to Vampires, Italy came up with a welcome and ultra-stylish return to black and white in 1960's *Black Sunday*, directed by Mario Bava, Italy's own somewhat more flamboyant answer to James Whale. Italy's horror films—which have proliferated in the past decade—have always had a rather unhealthy tendency towards the excesses of *Grand Guignol*, to dwelling on the detailed unpleasantries of death or torture. There has been an especial obsession with facial disfigure-

Kiss of the Vampire (1962): The simplest and best of Hammer's vampire films. Vampire Noel Willman and victim Jennifer Daniel

Kiss of the Vampire: Noel Willman (right) and vampire cult

Kiss of the Vampire: Clifford Evans in equivalent of Van Helsing role, and Jacqueline Wallis

207

Kiss of the Vampire: The ball sequence, reminiscent of the old Feuillade films

Black Sunday (1961): One of the best of Mario Bava's ornate Italian Gothics

ment, and an almost clinical attention to the methods by which it was achieved (a girl's head enclosed in a cage of live rats being quite typical). *Black Sunday* is not entirely free of this morbidity, and the detail of its opening execution sequence, unpleasant in the extreme, and the later facial mutilation of the revived Vampires, perhaps exploit sadism and pain unduly. But for the rest, the film is a (pictorially) marvelous exercise in baroque horror—black and nightmarish throughout, and despite the excess of decor, effective in creating a land in which phantoms are accepted as commonplace. It is perhaps the best of the (too) many Bava horror films, and excess, not only of design but also of technique and content, is its only major flaw.

Too much happens, and too quickly; there is too much to look at in the handsomely designed sets; there is too much technique, and the over-use of shock cuts and zoom lenses reminds one too often that this is just a horror *movie*. Furthermore, it is inconsistent: the baleful Vampire comes back in response to a centuries-old curse, spreads death and destruction, as much by the strength of his will as by personal attack, and yet, in a simple fist fight with a mere mortal (and not a particularly muscular one, at that) is at the same automatic disadvantage as the villain in a Western fight sequence. However, if one accepts the lack of logic that provides some of the film's best surprises, so one must accept the same lack of logic elsewhere, and *Black Sunday* is one of the few recent horror films which, while dwelling on physically repellent ingredients, is still an atmospherically gripping film.

Blood and Roses (1961) is arguably the best film of that interesting but erratic French director, Roger Vadim—and if nothing else is notable, his was the only serious attempt to film Sheridan LeFanu's classic horror tale, *Carmilla*.*

*Although Dreyer's outstanding *Vampyr* was allegedly based on it, it really used nothing save the idea of a female Vampire. In the early 1970s, Hammer Films made a brace of Vampire films, officially based on *Carmilla—The Vampire Lovers*, and *Lust of a Vampire*—but both merely used the premise of the original for films in which sex, Lesbianism, and nudity were so exploited that thrills and atmospherics took a decided second place. Increasingly, after these two films, nudity and sex proliferated in Hammer horror films. Commercially, if not aesthetically, this was understandable, since in Britain these films would automatically be classified by the censors "for adults only," and the two ingredients meant tapping two markets. However, for U.S. release where the juvenile market was a key one for horror films, severe editing removed much of the sex element, and not a great deal was left.

Black Sunday: Barbara Steele, a minor but interesting cult figure (heroine and villainess) of horror films of the sixties.

Blood and Roses (1961): Roger Vadim's stylish adaptation of LeFanu's "Carmilla"

Blood and Roses was a slow, elegant film, much of it shot on location in picturesque rural France, where chateaus and castles are still fairly commonplace. Again, the influence of Cocteau and Feuillade was quite strong, and the sensuous handling of the Lesbian sub-plot was tastefully erotic. The overall effect was that of uneasiness rather than fright, and the film was, in essence, a grotesque fairy tale. However, color was used intelligently, and it was color that was responsible for the film's most chilling highlight: a dream-delirium, experienced by the Vampire's victim, in which her loss of blood—and her weakening condition—is reflected in the single, pale red in which the dream is either photographed or printed.

Another European-made Vampire film, Roman Polanski's *Dance of the Vampires* (1967), was almost an indisputed classic, but marred in its U.S. release version by heavy re-editing (presumably in an attempt to lessen its bizarre sense of humor and strengthen its appeal as a straight horror tale). One of the most carefully made of all Vampire films, it re-creates the period, costumes and backgrounds of Transylvania with skill and realism, and adds to the suspense values by utilizing "heroes" who are particularly vulnerable and possessed of only the most basic information in dealing with the Vampire scourge.

Although there are one or two "inside" jokes, these mainly pay subtle homage to previous Vampire

films, the most obvious of them being Polanski's decision to play the young hero himself—perhaps because he looks so much like the hero of Murnau's 1922 *Nosferatu*. Other jokes are rather barbed thrusts at what have now become familiar Vampiric traditions. One especially remembers the Jewish Vampire chortling with glee when his victim-to-be ineffectually thrusts a Christian crucifix in his face!

Comedy and horror weld uncomfortably well in this film, and "uncomfortable" is perhaps the right word. It is disconcerting to find comic (or at least likeable) characters reappearing as deadly Vampires, to find oneself liking the graceful Vampire Count (extremely well played by Ferdy Mayne, who, like Peter Cushing, had been long wasted in minor character parts) and accepting him at first as a rather sympathic individual; to find the hero more afraid of a young Vampire's homosexual advances than of his blood-sucking tendencies. The comedy in *Dance of the Vampires* also lulls one into the false belief that it is to be a spoof, and thus one is much more vulnerable to the total seriousness of the final sequences. Comedy is a much more personal thing than horror; it is relatively easy to scare people, not so easy—since less universal themes and emotions are involved—to amuse them.

Thus, the effectiveness of *Dance of the Vampires* is unpredictable, and depends a great deal on one's reaction to its comedy content. Yet it is a much more original horror film than Polanski's subsequent *Rosemary's Baby,* where the source novel and intelligent casting and acting had a great deal more to do with its success than Polanski's merely efficient direction. Next to Carl Dreyer's *Vampyr,* it may well be the best of all Vampire movies.

Quite incidentally, it was the first of the Vampire movies to permit evil to triumph over good. Science fiction films of the 50s gradually demolished the tradition of the automatic happy ending and the notion that man's innate goodness will somehow find a way to destroy invasion, disease, or other scourges from outer space. Several science fiction films casually, and often shockingly, came to their climaxes with the acceptance either of our doom or of our being "taken over" by beings or forces from another planet. Since the "villains" were rarely individuals, there was no question of censorship's requirement of good triumphant, with "moral compensation" for the evil-doer being broached. Moreover, censorship was in a state of flux and change. Thus, it was not long before the horror film began to follow suit, and in films like *The Haunting, The Haunted Palace,* and *Dance of the*

Blood and Roses: Elsa Martinelli, Annette Vadim

Blood and Roses: Elsa Martinelli, Annette Vadim, Mel Ferrer

Vampires, evil—and in many cases evil *individuals* —did come out on top at the end. Usually, however (*The Haunting* was an exception), the climactic revelation was done in semi-gag form, a last-second wink at the audience, designed not to send them home worried and scared, as with the science fiction films, but merely to remind them that the whole thing was a romp not to be taken seriously. Fortunately, the last-moment gag in *Dance of the Vampires* has the same puckish and ghoulish sense of humor as the rest of it: after the initial quick laugh comes the realization of the horror that still lies ahead.

Sadly, yet another European Vampire film, Germany's *Jonathan* of 1970, had all the earmarks of a potential classic, and was flawed in this case, not by cutting but by additions. When first offered for sale outside of Germany, it was received with great enthusiasm by critics who were invited to screenings for their reactions and opinions—but with apathy by potential distributors who found it too slow and lacking in action for contemporary audiences. After a year or more of no takers, the producers decided to make their property more marketable via the usual route of inserting additional violence and sex, most especially violence. The result: a film of now uneven mood in which the carefully wrought and stately atmosphere of the original (rather like Dreyer's *Vampyr* crossed with the inexplicable plot turns of Hitchcock's *Vertigo*) was minimized by sudden switches to scenes of almost hysterical ferocity and sickening brutality.

Some of the violence was their originally, and intentionally. Although the film does not belabor the point, it was at least partially intended as an allegory, contrasting the tyranny of Vampirism (a whole community is preyed upon and kept in subjugation by a colony of Vampires) with that of Nazism, or any other Fascist occupation and enslavement. The point ultimately made (hardly an original one, since Kevin Brownlow's *It Happened Here* offered the same argument several years earlier) was that Fascism and terror (or Vampirism and terror) can only be destroyed by the same means. Thus, when the farmers and peasants are finally roused to retaliation, their own barbarism is fully as bloodthirsty and repugnant to human dignity as that of the Vampires. The increase in violence throughout the film nullifies this climactic point, however. The best elements of the much altered film remain the essentially placid ones. The muted color photography, and the slow pacing of the camerawork, do much to achieve as absorbing an atmosphere of a phantom-ridden land as Dreyer's earlier film.

One notable innovation was the use of classical music during the Vampiric attacks on women; the willingness of the victims, and the ritualized reverence of the Vampire, literally transform these episodes into genuinely erotic and even moving love scenes. Another noteworthy aspect of the film was its obvious desire to be a kind of homage to Bram Stoker's original *Dracula* novel. While far less clear-cut in its story line, and certainly not based on *Dracula,* it does draw incidents from the book that previous films had bypassed, among them the grisly suggestion of the Vampire's kidnapping a peasant woman's babies as a source of blood for his wives and the woman's destruction by wolves when she tries to reclaim them. (As in the book, the horror of the situation is left entirely to the imagination; no babies are actually shown, nor is their fate spelled out.) Most critics seemed totally unaware of the film's relationship to *Dracula*— so unaware, in fact, that many of them reviewed it under the impression that Jonathan was the Vampire, instead of being a derivation from the novel's original hero, Jonathan Harker. The re-editing of the film, ironically enough, did not serve the commercial purposes intended. The reviews were generally serious and appreciative, but exactly the kind of reviews to *discourage* attendance by run-of-the-mill horror devotees. In the United States at least, the film disappeared quickly, and chances of its ever being restored to its original, less stomach-turning, version seem extremely slim.

35 Werewolves

The Wolf Man: (1941): Lon Chaney Jr.

Werewolf of London (1935): Henry Hull

Werewolves have been given far less generous screen time than Vampires, perhaps because (if well done) the makeup and special effects involved in changeover scenes are costly and time consuming, and, too, because the Werewolf is a semi-sympathetic creature of fairly limited range. Although Vampires and sundry Monsters had been rampaging across the screen during the silent era, it wasn't until 1935 that the first Werewolf proper came to the screen in Universal's *Werewolf of London*. Even then, the necessity for the Monster to be both menacing and sympathetic created problems, and the mannered and basically unsympathetic playing of Henry Hull didn't help. Nor did the curiously rambling plot, which had definite elements of *Dr. Jekyll and Mr. Hyde* woven into it. Like all Universal horror films of the period, it was slick and good to look at, but it was well below their normal standard.

They didn't try again until 1941, with *The Wolf Man*, one of the best of the new brand of Universal thrillers, star-laden, glossy, streamlined. Its horror content was not strong, perhaps because this time the stress was more on characterization than on plot, and in order to keep the Werewolf (played by Lon Chaney, Jr.) a sympathetic lead character throughout, his forays into nocturnal prowlings were short and relatively restrained. In terms of production mounting, however, the film was wholly successful: music, sets, camerawork, makeup, and cast were all out of the top drawer. Warren William's participation was almost totally limited to the periodic exclamation, "The jugular vein has been severed!" but Claude Rains, Bela Lugosi, Evelyn Ankers, Maria Ouspenskaya, Ralph Bellamy, and Patric Knowles were better served and certainly comprised a cast of better than average strength for a film of this type.

Well above the "B" level of such Universal thrillers as *The Night Monster*, yet by no means an un-

Werewolf of London: Warner Oland, Henry Hull

The Wolf Man: Claude Rains, Lon Chaney Jr., Evelyn Ankers

qualified "A," *The Wolf Man* was literate, restrained, hardly the horror film it could have been, yet withal the "definitive" Werewolf movie. The following year, Fox, obviously seeking to cash in on it, produced a remarkable little film called *The Undying Monster*, virtually a model of how to give a "B" picture real class. Perhaps not even wanting to make a full-blown horror film, hoping to strike a balance so that the film could serve both on a horror double bill (with *Dr. Renault's Secret*), and also as a standard mystery support to other Fox pictures, Fox aimed at mystery and suspense, rather than horror.

As in *The Wolf Man*, the setting was one of the lonelier areas of the British Isles, and a neat little Werewolf jingle was recited on occasion, to remind one of family curses and the fairy tale nature of the adventure. However, the werewolf was seen but sparsely, even in his tragic downfall, and the stress throughout was on atmosphere and on unseen horror. Directed by John Brahm (who did so beautifully with the Ripper thriller *The Lodger*), the film has some of the best art direction, interior and exterior, and most beautifully lit photography of "B" films, but it is some kind of classic among "B" film. It may not be a classic in making small budget production seem to have all the mounting and care of a superdeluxe opus.

Lon Chaney repeated his Wolf Man characterization in a number of followup Universal films, and the Werewolf figure was absorbed into the standard rogues' gallery of cheapies at Universal, Columbia and PRC.

No films dealt with the Werewolf as effectively or as handsomely as these two straightforward, intelligent films from the early 40s, *The Wolf Man* and *The Undying Monster*. Columbia's 1956 *Werewolf* was a commendable attempt to deal with lycanthropy in a restrained, even human fashion, spending as much time with the plight of the Werewolf's family as with the Wolf Man himself. However, since the tragic ending was pre-ordained, and in order to increase sympathy for the Werewolf, his prowlings and attacks were kept to a minimum; the film had precious little suspense or action, and seemed to be merely marking time, going over well trodden ground in a less sensational fashion than usual.

Not surprisingly perhaps, it is television that appears to be taking up the supernatural horror thriller with a freshness and on a scale that Hollywood has long since abandoned. *The Night Stalker* (1973), a first rate chiller about a contemporary

John Howard, Dudley Digges

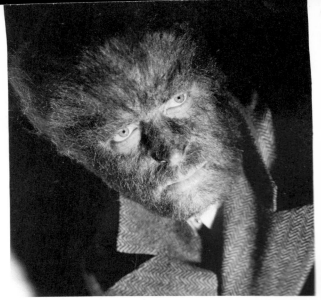

The Undying Monster (1942): The werewolf in the film is never seen in such extreme closeup and is actually one of the stars of the film, not the unbilled player who wears the makeup for the publicity stills, and who probably also played all the long shot scenes in the film itself.

Examples of the fine lighting and atmospheric sets of this admirable little "B":

John Howard

The Undying Monster:
Heather Thatcher, Dudley Digges

Vampire in Las Vegas, was such a smash success on TV that there was talk of instantly diverting it to theatrical release. That never happened, and it is always difficult to judge the genuine merits of a thriller without being able to observe audience reaction at the same time. Regardless, it was certainly one of the best of the comparatively few serious Vampire movies. Television appeared to be trying to give the Werewolf equal time early in 1974, with *Scream of the Wolf*, but as so often happens, the ad and the early atmosphere were merely camouflage for a bizarre but very non-supernatural murder.

Werewolf in a Girl's Dormitory (1963): Degeneration of the genre into cheap imported European quickies mixing violence and sex.

Curse of the Werewolf (1961): Oliver Reed

qualified "A," *The Wolf Man* was literate, restrained, hardly the horror film it could have been, yet withal the "definitive" Werewolf movie. The following year, Fox, obviously seeking to cash in on it, produced a remarkable little film called *The Undying Monster,* virtually a model of how to give a "B" picture real class. Perhaps not even wanting to make a full-blown horror film, hoping to strike a balance so that the film could serve both on a horror double bill (with *Dr. Renault's Secret*), and also as a standard mystery support to other Fox pictures, Fox aimed at mystery and suspense, rather than horror.

As in *The Wolf Man,* the setting was one of the lonelier areas of the British Isles, and a neat little Werewolf jingle was recited on occasion, to remind one of family curses and the fairy tale nature of the adventure. However, the Werewolf was seen but sparsely, even in his climactic downfall, and the stress throughout was on atmosphere and on unseen horror. Directed by John Brahm (who did so beautifully with the Jack the Ripper thriller *The Lodger*), the film has some of the best art direction, interior and exterior sets, and most beautifully lit photography of any "B" film. It may not be a classic among horror films, but it is some kind of classic in making a small budget production seem to have all the lavish mounting and care of a super-deluxe opus.

Lon Chaney, Jr., repeated his Wolf Man characterization in a number of followup Universal films, and the Werewolf figure was absorbed into the standard rogues' gallery of cheapies at Universal, Columbia and PRC.

No later films dealt with the Werewolf as effectively or as handsomely as these two straightforward, intelligent films from the early 40s, *The Wolf Man* and *The Undying Monster.* Columbia's 1956 *The Werewolf* was a commendable attempt to deal with lycanthropy in a restrained, even human fashion, spending as much time with the plight of the Werewolf's family as with the Wolf Man himself. However, since the tragic ending was pre-ordained, and in order to increase sympathy for the Werewolf, his prowlings and attacks were kept to a minimum; the film had precious little suspense or action, and seemed to be merely marking time, going over well trodden ground in a less sensational fashion than usual.

Not surprisingly perhaps, it is television that appears to be taking up the supernatural horror thriller with a freshness and on a scale that Hollywood has long since abandoned. *The Night Stalker* (1973), a first rate chiller about a contemporary

John Howard, Dudley Digges

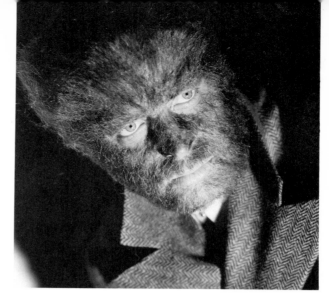

The Undying Monster (1942): The werewolf in the film is never seen in such extreme closeup and is actually one of the stars of the film, not the unbilled player who wears the makeup for the publicity stills, and who probably also played all the long shot scenes in the film itself.

Examples of the fine lighting and atmospheric sets of this admirable little "B":

John Howard

The Undying Monster:
Heather Thatcher, Dudley Digges

Vampire in Las Vegas, was such a smash success on TV that there was talk of instantly diverting it to theatrical release. That never happened, and it is always difficult to judge the genuine merits of a thriller without being able to observe audience reaction at the same time. Regardless, it was certainly one of the best of the comparatively few serious Vampire movies. Television appeared to be trying to give the Werewolf equal time early in 1974, with *Scream of the Wolf,* but as so often happens, the ads and the early atmosphere were merely camouflage for a bizarre but very non-supernatural murderer.

Werewolf in a Girl's Dormitory (1963): Degeneration of the genre into cheap imported European quickies mixing violence and sex.

Curse of the Werewolf (1961): Oliver Reed

216

℔ Edgar Allan Poe

The Black Cat (1941): Of all the "adaptations" of the Poe classic, this one had the least resemblance to its inspiration.

The number of horror films claiming to be based on stories by Edgar Allan Poe is prodigious; but those that can claim real kinship to his original stories are few, while those that may be considered to have done them justice are rarer still. Poe has been a godsend to horror film producers, since his stories are in the public domain and thus legally available to all without payment of fee or royalty. Further, his name is so strongly associated with horror and the macabre, that its use in advertising is often as potent a factor as a star's name. Alas, too often, his name—and a single idea from one of his stories—is all that has emerged on screen in films officially adapted from or "inspired by" his classic tales.

In fairness to Hollywood (and to Britain, France, and Germany, other countries that have made films from his works), Poe is not easy to adapt to film. Although his writing is full of marvelous visual images, it is less strong on the clear-cut narrative style required by the average movie. One reads them not for their stories, but for their mood—and one should read them with a lively imagination that can pick up where his pen leaves off. His extremely unpleasant little tale "The Strange Case of M. Valdemar," about a man whose brain lives on after his body dies, makes grisly reading because its concept is horrifying, and allows the reader to create his own image of a living yet decomposing corpse. One reads it with the stench of death in one's nostrils. Yet, when adapted into a properly tight short story format, as one of three stories in the compendium *Tales of Terror,* the emphasis was on the purely visual—and Vincent Price, with rivulets of a chocolate syrup substance rolling down his face, was merely another artificial, studio-created bogeyman.

An ideal outlet for Poe on the screen would have been through the Val Lewton unit at RKO Radio —had studio economics of the time permitted the production of two- or three-reel versions of Poe. As it is, some of the best films from Poe are to be found, not unexpectedly, in the silent era, where the lack of sound automatically created that world of unreality and imagination that was so essential to Poe. Jean Epstein's 1928 *The Fall of the House of Usher*—fairly short, semi-surrealistic, unburdened by much plot or the need to reshape material or characters to fit star images—was, and is, by far the best screen evocation of Poe to date. Much earlier, D. W. Griffith's *The Avenging Conscience* (1914) took a number of Poe themes and wove them into an original, but still faithful-to-Poe story

of madness, murder, and conscience; a remarkably subtle and sophisticated film for that early period. (*Murders in the Rue Morgue* was also done the same year, though sadly, no prints appear to have survived.)

It was not until the coming of sound, however, and the advent of the horror film cycle, that Poe came into his own as a box office commodity—although some of the most worthwhile Poe adaptations were those made as semi-experiments by newcomers to film: Brian Desmond Hursts's interesting and expressionistic British version of *The Tell-Tale*

Murders in the Rue Morgue (1932): Bela Lugosi, Noble Johnson

Murders in the Rue Morgue (1932): Bela Lugosi

Murders in the Rue Morgue: Bela Lugosi, Noble Johnson

Murders in the Rue Morgue: Leon Ames, Sidney Fox,
and Caligariesque rooftops

Heart (unsubtly released in the U.S. as *Bucket of
Blood!*) or Jules Dassin's one-reel version of the
same story for MGM in the early 40s. For the most
part, however, Poe's name was cavalierly attached
to films which borrowed the *titles* of his work, and
perhaps a single incident to justify the pillaging
of that title. 1932's *Murders in the Rue Morgue*
owed far more to *The Cabinet of Dr. Caligari* than
to Poe. The Karloff-Lugosi *The Raven* and *The
Black Cat* were perhaps *homages* to Poe, but certainly not adaptations, while the much later "versions" were so played for comedy that Poe's association with them was virtually an insult.

The long-running series of Roger Corman "adaptations" were more seriously intended—but they
were horror films first, Vincent Price vehicles second, showcases for Corman's tired and repetitive

The Raven (1935): Boris Karloff, Bela Lugosi

The Raven: Boris Karloff, *before* operation by Lugosi

The Raven: Boris Karloff *after* operation by Lugosi

The Masque of the Red Death (1964): Hazel Court in one of the devil worshipping sequences with which Roger Corman embellished his version of Poe.

The Raven: Karloff

The Haunted Palace (1963): Officially billed as Edgar Allan Poe, but actually far more Lovecraft, this was one of the better Roger Corman horror films of the 60's. With Debra Paget, Vincent, Price.

techniques third, and of only negligible interest as adaptations of Poe. With the scores of Poe films that have been produced—his themes made threadbare through use and re-use even though the basic qualities have remained untouched, his name (for movie audiences, at least) now merely a convenient *genre*-label, like Zane Grey's for Westerns—it is sad to realize that *only* Epstein's *The Fall of the House of Usher* really came close to putting the real Poe on the screen. But much the same could be said for Bram Stoker, whose difficult (but brilliantly effective) writing style has likewise been largely untouched by Hollywood. *Dracula,* of course, has been pillaged for characters and incidents, but its real style has escaped the adaptors, while the many other Stoker writings have been ignored. Lovecraft and Ambrose Bierce have only been very lightly touched upon by the movies as yet; perhaps they—and a serious, respectful, sophisticated approach to Poe and Stoker—may help to form the nucleus for some future cycle of stylistic horror films by a James Whale, Jacques Tourneur, or Val Lewton as yet undiscovered or possibly not yet born.

The Haunted Palace: The economy of the studio-bound graveyard set (used also in *Comedy of Terrors* and other films) is particularly obvious in a still, though concealed to some degree by color and lighting in the film itself. Lon Chaney Jr. at left, Vincent Price centre.

The Dunwich Horror (1970): Although it didn't come off, Lovecraft received far more serious attention than Poe in this quite stylish film made to cash in on the new Devil Worshipping cycle made so fashionable by *Rosemary's Baby*. With Dean Stockwell, Sandra Dee.

The Dunwich Horror: Sam Jaffe, High Lama of Shangri La made a rather spectacular leap up (or down?) as a High Priest of a New England Satanist cult.

37 Madness

The Beast with Five Fingers: Victor Francen, Robert Alda, J. Carrol Naish

Madness as a plot ingredient for horror films has been little exploited outside of the traditional Mad Doctor, and for perfectly understandable reasons. For one, the world of the madman is not a particularly entertaining or even visual one. An intelligent and honest study of madness could not only be harrowing (and lacking in showmanship), but could also be extremely painful to some (as *The Snake Pit* proved to be). The few horror films built even remotely around madness have usually tended to use it as a convenient last-reel explanation, justifying much of the preceding illogic and visual fireworks as hallucinations in the mind of a madman. Robert Wiene's 1919 German classic, *The Cabinet of Dr. Caligari,* used such a solution, as did *The Beast with Five Fingers* (1946), directed by Robert Florey, whose few horror films contained obvious echoes of *Caligari*. In fact, his *Murders in the Rue Morgue* (1932) was so careful a re-working of the *Caligari* plot, and so meticulous an attempt to re-create the sets and photographic style of silent German films (it was photographed by Karl Freund), that it seemed quite out of place among the much slicker horror films surrounding it, and even today seems a creaky and oldfashioned film, although this is not necessarily a liability.

The Beast with Five Fingers, in any event, is one of the best Hollywood horror films dealing with madness in a non-serious and hokey way. The fine sets, the score by Steiner, the outstanding camerawork, full of subjective shots of the disembodied hand of a dead musician playing the piano and scuttling across the floor, and not least, the interesting cast of non-stereotypes, combined to make it one of the most interesting horror films of the 40s, marred to a degree by unnecessary comedy. This latter tends to destroy (though only at the very end of the film) the genuine atmosphere of horror that has been created, and that is only partially explained away by the hallucination theory. According to Florey, it was one of many elements that distorted the film from his original intention, and over which he had no control, but flawed or not, *The Beast With Five Fingers* is still one of the last elegant echoes of Hollywood's stylish old horror films.

One can hardly call Luis Buñuel's Mexican *El* (1952) a "horror film," yet it has moments of virtually unbearable horror (where one almost refuses to believe what is merely being suggested on screen), and is certainly the most clinical dissection yet of a paranoiac's descent into total madness. There are moments of typical Buñuel surrealism and hallucination images, and some of his most refined (yet savage) attacks on the church. Yet the film is most compelling, not in its bravura cinematic sequences, but in its steadily built up collection of details through which, only gradually and even reluctantly, the audience becomes aware of the charming and personable hero's mania.

Arturo de Cordova makes of this man a totally believable, and ultimately tragic figure. In the final scene, pretending to have found peace in a monastery, he is separated from his wife (who has since remarried) and his child, is denied even the help of the church (which can offer him only platitudes and no real salvation) and, convinced he is still sane, walks a zigzag path away from the camera (a motif used earlier to establish his madness) towards the black, tomb-like monastery, the strident, discordant music emphasizing that he is not at peace, and never will be. Although *El* is an entertaining film on the superficial level of a suspense thriller (and seems at least in part to have influenced Hitchcock's *Vertigo*), it is a genuinely *horrifying* one in its merciless commentary on the patterns of madness. In that respect, it is a far superior film to Roman Polanski's *Repulsion*, which has some impressively visual manifestions of madness, but begins with its psychopathic heroine already totally round the bend, and with none of Buñuel's documentation as to how she got there.

The Beast with Five Fingers (1946): Victor Francen, Peter Lorre

The Maze (1953): Veronica Hurst, Katherine Emery

The silent (1927) *The Cat and the Canary* and the sound (1932) *The Old Dark House* so completely wrapped up the "Old House" *genre* that no subsequent films have been nearly so successful. Many of them aimed directly at comedy rather than thrills, although the increasing attention paid to the serious ghost story lately has seen the renewed use of the "Old House" as a background. Surprisingly, none of the "Old House" comedy-thriller standards (*The Cat and the Canary* and *The Gorilla* had each been filmed three times, last in 1939) were trotted out again to see service as stunt attractions in the short-lived period of 3-D, a framework in which they might have worked well. A third and inferior version of *The Bat* was made, but not until well after the 3-D excitement had died down. The last versions of *The Cat and the Canary* and *The Gorilla,* both made in 1939, when the horror film was in the process of being revitalized, were slick and interesting, but disappointingly commonplace.

The Gorilla, smartly directed by Allan Dwan for Fox, could have been a first-rate, light horror film if allowed to keep to its basic plot line. Very good lighting, camerawork, and sets, and amusing, if obviously red-herring performances from Bela Lugosi and Lionel Atwill, established the right mood immediately, and the admittedly sparse scenes involving the Gorilla had quite a grim flavor. However, the film starred the Ritz Brothers, zany comics whose acceptance was always a matter of individual taste, but who could be very funny if they had good material. Unfortunately, *The Gorilla* was one of their final films for Fox, and as often happens with the last contractual obligations of a star (or stars) nobody felt like building them up for their next studio (Universal) to reap the benefit. The comic material they had to work with was absolutely zero, and being good troupers, they worked twice as hard in their own particular vacuum, and merely accentuated the paucity of comedy by bringing the film to periodic halts for sustained mugging or back-chat.

More successful was the same year's *The Cat and the Canary,* made this time by Paramount, a much simplified version of the old classic, devoid of the imaginative, pictorial style of the Universal originals, but at least keeping to its basic format and not trying to enlarge upon an already sufficient comedic content. With the whole film set in the atmospheric old mansion (transferred from upstate New York to a Louisiana swamp), the concentration was on mystery and suspense. Bob Hope's quips enlivened the film, but actually slowed it down

far less than some of Creighton Hale's more long-drawn-out comedy in the 1927 version. Those old reliables George Zucco (as the lawyer) and Gale Sondergaard (as the housekeeper) played straight, and were rewarded with some of the best lines. Unfortunately, the use of the Cat figure was limited, and in the closing reel the film rushed over its potentially best material to a very sudden and none-too-exciting climax. Incidentally, bland as they seem today, both *The Cat and the Canary* and *The Gorilla* were considered frightening enough by the British censors to be awarded the adults-only "H" certificate, although it's also possible that the censors handed out that rating rather promiscuously, hoping to discourage Hollywood from turning out too many such films. They even gave the "H" rating to an admittedly tasteless but not very horrifying two-reel Columbia comedy called *Sweet Spirits of Nighter!*

The Cat and the Canary clicked far beyond expectations, and Paramount hurriedly pushed its felicitous co-stars—Bob Hope and Paulette Goddard—into another "Old House" barnstormer, *The Ghost Breakers,* which had last been filmed in the early 20s (and was to see service a third time as a Martin and Lewis vehicle). This time the results were wholly successful, and even in 1974 the film holds up well as one of Hope's best vehicles, and as one of the best examples of the theatrical comedy-thriller *genre* smoothly transferred to film. Even though, unlike *The Cat and the Canary,* it doesn't get to its "Old House" until the last half of the film, it maintains a crackling pace throughout.

The film opens with an outsize (special effects-created) electrical storm in New York, and within minutes is into a murder and a parade of gaunt and sinister figures. Despite the presence of the inevitable scared Negro manservant (Willie Best), there are virtually none of the long comedy set-pieces that became so tiresome in such films as Abbott and Costello's *Hold That Ghost,* and the humor is limited to the lightning-paced cracks of Hope, which serve as punctuation, and keep the already fast film even more on the move. When it gets to Cuba and its off-shore island and haunted mansion, the film shifts into yet higher gear. The sets and glistening photography would do credit to a major horror film of the earlier 30s, the encounters with a Zombie and a real ghost, genuinely frightening, and exploited for their horror content, not merely thrown in quickly as obligatory "Old House" ingredients and then dispensed with rapidly, as happened too often in *The Cat and the Canary.* Directed by the veteran George Marshall, *The*

Ghost Breakers is both funny and thrilling, and is one of the few films of its species that has not dated at all.

In recent years, the better "Old House" thrillers have transferred themselves to the more serious *genre* of the ghost story. Possibly the last interesting example of the traditional "Old House" film was William Cameron Menzies' *The Maze,* which, though made quickly and economically to cash in on the early 50s 3-D craze, featured some interesting production design and depth-illusion sets. Even the final revelation of the awful hidden secret—that the Lord of the Manor was actually a giant (if benign) frog—wasn't quite as embarrassing as it might seem in print, due to the quite remarkably sober quality of the writing and the acting.

The Gorilla (1927): With Alice Day

The Cat and the Canary (1927): Martha Mattox and one of the movie's many fine sets

The Cat and the Canary: Lawyer Crosby (Tully Marshall) is prevented from giving away the secret of the will.

The Cat and the Canary: Lawyer Crosby's body discovered in a hidden panel

The Cat Creeps (1930): A sound remake of *The Cat and the Canary,* with Lawyer Crosby (Lawrence Grant) again about to be effectively prevented from passing on vital information to heiress Helen Twelvetrees.

The Cat Creeps: Neil Hamilton, Montague Love

The Cat and the Canary (1939): Paulette Goddard at the mercy of "The Cat"

The Cat and the Canary: Bob Hope and Paulette Goddard flanked by key "Cat" suspects Douglas Montgomery and John Beal (right)

The Gorilla (1939): The Ritz Brothers and title star

The Ghost Breakers (1940): Bob Hope and Paulette Goddard menaced by zombie Noble Johnson

The Gorilla: Edward Norris, Bela Lugosi, Anita Louise

The Monster and the Girl (1940): More simian mayhem: Ellen Drew protects herself from gorilla with a human brain. Oddly enough this typical horror pot-boiler had a plot-line (well-disguised!) revolving around a white slavery ring.

The Terror (1928): Presumably lost, this was the first sound horror film; with May McAvoy

Horror Island (1941): A minor but enjoyable old-house romp; with Peggy Moran

39 Hauntings and Possession

Burn Witch Burn: Margaret Johnston

Through linking themes, films of witchcraft, possession, and ghosts have somehow merged into one *genre* throughout the late 60s and early 70s. One of the best, *Burn Witch Burn,* was made in Britain in 1962, under the direction of Sidney Hayers. The title has given rise to some confusion, and has no connection with the novel, by A. Merritt, which saw earlier screen service via Tod Browning as *The Devil Doll.* Actually, *Burn Witch Burn,* though an appropriate title, was merely an American retitling from the British *Night of the Eagle* which,

in turn, was based on the Fritz Leiber novel *Conjure Wife.* This had also seen earlier Hollywood usage in the interesting but short and simplistic *Weird Woman,* in Universal's *Inner Sanctum* series of the early 40s, with Lon Chaney Jr. *Burn Witch Burn* suffered from too close a juxtaposition to *The Curse of the Demon,* by Tourneur; in fact, the British titles of both films (*Night of the Demon, Night of the Eagle*) stressed how one had probably inspired the other.

It followed the useful, if increasingly familiar

Burn Witch Burn (1962): Peter Wyngarde

pattern of making the hero a rigid scientist who does not believe in the supernatural, but is forced to accept it. Atmospherically, the film had several really chilling sequences, but it was too long for its own good. Moreover, the identity of the human mystery villain was all too obvious from the beginning, and while the supernatural element was genuine enough, and not "explained" away at the end, at the same time the concentration on menace and evil was split between the human and the supernatural agencies. Finally, the special effects were far less convincing than in *Curse of the Demon*. However, it was an extremely well written film, and excellently acted by Janet Blair, as the Voodoo-obsessed wife. The occasionally somewhat erratic editing was at least partially attributable to the hero's insistence on wearing indelicately tight trousers, forcing the director to shoot him in extreme long shot or extreme closeup much of the time! (This trivia information is recorded only to prevent future auteurists from discovering a definite pattern to the photographic style, and determining that medium shots for the wife and none for the hero are metaphors symbolizing a lack of communication between the two!)

No ghost story has ever had quite the chilling conviction of *The Uninvited*, discussed earlier, although a number have come close, and some have been far more ambitious.

Unquestionably, the least known of all ghost movies (especially in the U.S., where it was never released) is a little (literally) British film called *The Fatal Night*, made in 1948, and directed by—of all people—Mario Zampi, a specialist in comedy. Based on the Michael Arlen short story "The Gentleman from America," about a man spending a night in a haunted room, it works because it maintains the format of the short story, and has no need to add extraneous characters, subplots, or other padding. It ran for a mere 50 minutes (one of the reasons it had dubious commercial value), and like all good ghost stories, plants suggestions, and then leaves the viewer's (or reader's) imagination to do the rest. Even though it showed no visual horrors, it was quite frightening enough for the British censors to award it an "H" certificate.

Far less subtle, because it showed *everything*, repetitiously, and with underlining, via shock cuts and screaming music, was Bert Gordon's *Tormented* (1960). Yet it, too, created highlights of cold terror when it chose to hint, rather than state. Its plot concerned the haunting of a husband-to-be (Richard Carlson) by the ghost of his former mistress. She had been killed in a fall from a lighthouse (not engineered, but helped along by Carlson, whose future happiness she threatens), and her particular talent was the dumping of dank, wet seaweed on the wedding dress of his bride-to-be! One memorable highlight was the genuinely terrifying interruption of the wedding ceremony by the wraith who, though unseen, is accompanied by a gale that forces open the church doors, systematically blows out all the candles, and leaves a trail of seaweed to the altar. In view of the terrified reaction of the entire congregation, their nonchalant avoidance of the subject in conversation thereafter is a little hard to accept! With the subtlety of a Val Lewton, *Tormented* could have been one of the scariest of all ghost stories; even as it is, its shock value, though heavy-handed, does hit home occasionally.

The most elaborate and ambitious of all movie ghost stories—more so than Jack Clayton's *The Innocents,* though ultimately it is less successful—was Robert Wise's *The Haunting*, for MGM (1960). Unique in that the spirit world does finally win out and claims the film's heroine (Julie Harris), it somehow works less effectively than Wise's earlier horror films, particularly *The Body Snatcher* for Val Lewton. Its sets and camerawork (involving a cunning use of distorting lenses) are superb, the special effects (particularly a "breathing" door) uncomfortably convincing; yet so assured are all the technical devices, that again—as in *Black Sunday*—one is too aware of movie technique to be wholly absorbed by the film. One is never really afraid because one is always, if only subliminally, conscious of being on a movie set. To a degree, the same applies to 1973's *The Legend of Hell House,* a similar account of investigators deliberately spending time in a haunted house to get to the bottom of the phenomenon.

However, the investigators are so self-assured that if they are never afraid, there is little cause for us, the audience, to be scared either. Too, the film builds too methodically to its climax, the mysteries deepening and expanding, the pyrotechnic expertise of the special effects increasing in sound and fury, so that we are prepared for a ghostly equivalent of the last-reel laboratory holocaust in the horror films of old. When it comes—not before the now obligatory sex scene—it is a neatly satisfying wrap-up, but for all of its noise and determination to scare the wits out of its audience, it has not one moment to match the underplayed scene in *The Uninvited* where the young married couple first

The Innocents (1961): Pamela Franklin and Martin Stephens as the possessed children, Deborah Kerr as their Governess.

The Haunting (1963): Claire Bloom, Russ Tamblyn, Julie Harris, Richard Johnson

The Legend of Hell House (1973): Roddy McDowall,
Gayle Hunnicutt, Clive Revill

The Legend of Hell House: Pamela Franklin, the
possessed child of The Innocents, had grown up sufficiently in the 12-year interim to be physically seduced
by the ghost in this film.

sense the cold dampness in the little room upstairs!

Ghost stories have now been rendered outdated by the far nastier and unhealthier concentration on films of *possession*. Even standard pseudo-Hitchcock thrillers such as *Don't Look Now* have taken on this metaphysical quality, and they are often the poorer for it. *Don't Look Now* is certainly a fascinating pictorial exercise, and it would be unfair to criticize it for not having the light touch of Hitchcock. After all, it is not that kind of film. But it is so doom-laden from the very beginning, that one automatically senses the ultimate solution, even if one is unaware of the route that must be followed to get there. All of its "surprises" are predictable. In the area of straightforward possession, however, the films of the past decade have had a distressing tendency to be increasingly unpleasant and unhealthy, and worst of all, un-entertaining. *The Other* certainly had its merits, not least in that the more the audience was prepared to work with it, the more frightening it became in its implications. On the other hand, *The Possession of Joel Delaney* was so nauseating and downbeat, its climax so pointlessly revolting, that it was not worth the *effort* of working with it.

As this book goes to press, in the summer of 1974, we are very fortuitously confronted by a film which not only brings the horror film full cycle, but is also being touted as the most horrifying film ever made! The film is, of course, William Friedkin's *The Exorcist* which, in addition to other claims being made for it, will quite certainly go on to become the biggest box office grosser of *any* horror film. The lines (right around the block and beyond) at four New York theatres, day in and day out, in the most inclement of weather, guarantee it a gross which may ultimately put it among the top ten moneymakers of all time. Since its villains are devils—or *the* Devil, if you wish—it returns the horror film to its beginnings when, in the earliest Méliès trick films, well before Monsters, Vampires, and straightforward murderers, it was Demons and Devils—and Satan himself—that were selected as the most elemental of villains, guaranteed to scare and shock movie audiences.

Audiences for *The Exorcist* (dealing with the possession of a young girl by the Devil) have been warned that it is repellent and sickening, and yet are lining up masochistically to have it proven to them. There have been reports, many of them quite authentic, of mass audience walkouts, of vomiting and fainting in the theatre, and of audi-

The Other: Chris Udvarnoky, Uta Hagen

The Legend of Hell House: Clive Revill, Pamela Franklin

The Other (1972): Martin and Chris Udvarnoky were identical twins who starred in a chiller that didn't even let audiences in on what *kind* of a thriller it was (ghosts? possession?) until virtually the end.

A Christmas Carol (1938): Reginald Owen as Scrooge, with traditional manifestation of ghost.

The Exorcist (1974): A reversal of a traditional horror film image: In this case the black silhouetted stranger is a priest bringing aid.

244

The Exorcist: Linda Blair (on bed) is placated by friend and priest.

ences screaming, virtually on cue, at every perform-ance. There have also been reports of many of the walkouts steeling themselves to return at a later date to sit through it. The film certainly has its moments. The special effects, though wisely limited, and often obvious in design, are sometimes terri-fying. Color is used creatively, as is sound. Sound, in fact, is a major contribution to the film's suc-cess, since virtually all of the horror comes in the form of dialogue from the Devil, well handled, and spoken by Mercedes McCambridge, whose brilliant vocal acting actually **saves** the inept performance of the child star who is supposedly speaking. But again, *The Exorcist* does take the easy way out. It's not hard to manipulate an audi-ence that you've reduced to jelly by suddenly, and without warning, giving them closeup clinical de-tails of a spinal tap operation with blood surging into the camera, or again, creating with trickery but conviction the spectacle of the child vomiting green bile. It would have been much harder to manipulate the audience had the film been made in black and white and without its special effects. Not that a film maker shouldn't use all the tools at his command, but very often those tools are merely a substitute for talent. There's no denying that *The Exorcist*

does work with an audience; yet withal it's a cheap and shoddy picture, often amazingly crude in its in-ability even to link scenes smoothly, and totally devoid of the professionalism that marked that earlier if more conventional essay in possession *The Lady and the Monster*. With all its fire and fury, *The Exorcist* still manages to make one fear Devils less than Carl Dreyer's *Vampyr* made one fear Vampires! It is perhaps a symptom of our unhealthy times that audiences flocked to *The Exorcist*, want-ing to be scared, *intending* to scream, coming away haunted and sickened by it, yet somehow proud of having forced themselves to endure it. (As a foot-note, one might add that the faces on display in the lines outside the theatre were often as scary as any-thing on the screen inside!)

The Exorcist preceded into release a new German "thriller" entitled *Autopsy,* in which, needless to say, a detailed autopsy on a real body is performed in closeup and in color. If this is to be the new trend in horror films, we may be in for grim times indeed. Fortunately it takes time and perspective for any film to be elevated to a classic status; de-cisions as to whether *The Exorcist* and *Autopsy* are "Classics of the Horror Film" can thus, fortunately, be shelved for sterner times and stronger stomachs.